STOKES
BACKYARD BIRD BOOK

Printed in the United States of America on acid-free ∞, recycled ♻ paper

Edited by Anita Small
Cover and interior designed by Tara Long
Illustrations by Sandy Freedman (range maps) and Phil Guzy

Photo credits appear on page 295.

We're always happy to hear from you. For questions or comments concerning the editorial content of this book, please write to:
          Rodale Book Readers' Service
          33 East Minor Street
          Emmaus, PA 18098
Look for other Rodale books wherever books are sold. Or call us at (800) 848-4735.

For more information about Rodale magazines and books, visit us at
          www.organicgardening.com

Library of Congress Cataloging-in-Publication Data

Stokes, Donald W.
     Stokes backyard bird book : the complete guide to attracting,
identifying, and understanding the birds in your backyard / Donald and
Lillian Stokes.
          p.   cm.
     "A compilation of the bird feeder book . . . Stokes hummingbird book . . .
Stokes birdhouse book . . . and Stokes bird gardening book . . ."—T.p.
verso.
     Includes bibliographical references and index.
     ISBN-13 978–1–57954–864–3   hardcover
     ISBN-10 1–57954–864–4   hardcover
     1. Bird attracting.   2. Birdhouses—Design and construction.
3. Birds—United States.   I. Stokes, Lillian Q.   II. Title.
QL676.2.S754   2003
598—dc21   2003012744

This book is a compilation of *Stokes Bird Feeder Book* (copyright 1987 by Donald W. Stokes and Lillian Q. Stokes), *Stokes Hummingbird Book* (copyright 1989 by Donald W. Stokes and Lillian Q. Stokes), *Stokes Complete Birdhouse Book* (copyright 1990 by Donald W. Stokes and Lillian Q. Stokes), and *Stokes Bird Gardening Book* (copyright 1998 by Donald W. Stokes and Lillian Q. Stokes).

Reprinted with permission from Little, Brown and Company (Inc.).

     8   10   9   hardcover

STOKES BACKYARD BIRD BOOK

THE COMPLETE GUIDE TO ATTRACTING, IDENTIFYING, AND UNDERSTANDING THE BIRDS IN YOUR BACKYARD

A TREASURY OF THE BEST FROM DONALD AND LILLIAN STOKES

RODALE

Contents

Welcome to the Exciting World of Birds!

Attracting birds is not only a rewarding activity, but it is also essential to healthy birds, our environment, and ultimately ourselves. Human development of the landscape often robs it of the very features birds need—food, shelter, and nesting places. Housing developments replace forests, and shopping malls erase fields. With each new development, there is less habitat for birds. One of the best ways you can help reverse this trend is by making your property a rich and varied environment that will meet the needs of birds and other wildlife. You will find that your activities will inspire your neighbors to do the same, helping to create interests in common and a bird-friendly community. In its largest sense, attracting birds is restoring the American landscape yard by yard.

For us, attracting birds is not just a hobby but a passion. We can never have enough birds around us. There is always the challenge that by expanding our plantings, managing our habitat, putting out food, or building structures, we can attract another new species to breed, feed, or nest on our property.

We have just moved to a small farm in southern New Hampshire which, because of the Bobolinks that nest in the fields, we call Bobolink Farm. In the first two years, we've already had 154 species of birds visit, and we are working hard to attract even more. Each species is a different story, like this one.

Last year we put up a large nesting box in the hope of attracting a Screech-owl, but this year a female Hooded Merganser chose it as a place to raise her broods. We had no sooner made a new break in our stone wall for a path than a female Mallard decided to build a nest and lay eight eggs right in the taller grasses next to the opening. We will walk around the wall until her young are safely hatched and dabbling about in the nearby water.

We have Tree Swallows nesting in boxes scattered about our fields, but we are still awaiting our first nesting Barn Swallow. To help make them feel welcome, we leave the barn door open permanently and have nailed boards as little nesting ledges on all of the roof beams. Our many crab apples attract Baltimore Orioles and Cape May Warblers to drink the nectar in spring from the colorful blossoms; the small apples are eaten by Cedar Waxwings in winter, and any remaining fruit is stripped from the trees by hungry migrating Robins in early spring. The birds are a constant source of entertainment and daily reminders of the beautiful natural world in which we all live.

We are thrilled to bring you the very best from our most popular books in the Stokes Backyard Nature Book series. Together, our four books on hummingbirds, bird feeding, birdhouses, and bird gardening have sold almost 2 million copies, and each is the best-selling book in its field. Now they are joined together in this new and creatively designed compilation. In this single volume you will find all of the essential information you will need to attract greater numbers of beautiful birds to your property.

We want to thank the editors at Rodale for putting together such a spectacular and attractive volume from the best of our books. *Stokes Backyard Bird Book* is divided into five main sections: attracting birds to your backyard, bird gardening, birdhouses, bird behavior, and profiles of birds you are likely to find in your backyard. Each section is filled with the very information you need to transform your yard into a bird-friendly property. We wish you all the best of luck with the birds.

Yours in Nature,
Don and Lillian Stokes

Part 1 Attracting Birds to Your Backyard

THE JOY OF ATTRACTING BIRDS IS OPEN TO
EVERYONE AND IS REMARKABLY EASY.

There are four main things that birds need from their environment: food, water, nesting spots, and shelter. To know if you have these basic four elements on your property, try looking at it from a bird's point of view. Can a bird see something to eat? Is water available? Where might birds nest? And where could a bird find shelter from predators? In this section, we offer you guidance on the essentials of food and water for birds and touch briefly on shelter and nesting sites, which are covered in more detail in later sections.

As we look at the four main needs of birds, remember the concept of diversity. Nature is built upon a multitude of complex interdependencies. The more your yard can begin to reflect the variety of the natural world within a small area, the better it will support birds and other wildlife.

1

Food and Feeders

One of the best ways to attract birds to your yard is to provide them with food they like. Many species of birds prefer specific types of food or a certain style of feeder because of their natural feeding style. For example, chickadees favor sunflower seeds in a hanging tube feeder, and sparrows like taking mixed seed from ground feeders. The types of feeders you choose and the food you provide will greatly influence what birds—and how many—visit your yard.

CHOOSING FEEDERS AND FOOD

A variety of bird feeders offering a variety of seeds is an essential part of any backyard bird station. Feeders attract a wide range of birds to your property, where the birds will then be able to take advantage of your yard's other features like water and garden plantings.

Consistent use of bird feeders throughout the year and over several years will attract increasingly more birds. Birds become familiar with your feeder setup and will fly longer distances to visit. Also, migrating birds will find it and stop each year on their way north or south.

Another benefit of feeders is that birds attract other birds. All birds watch other birds to see where they are feeding in the hopes that they will discover food for themselves. We are convinced that, on our property, we attract other species

Q: When should I start or stop feeding the birds?
A: The answer is easy—start now and keep going. Feeding birds is delightful to do throughout the year, and birds always need our help. We keep feeders going all year on our property. We have year-round residents that we see all the time; we have spring and fall migrants that come to fuel up on their journey; and we get summer-breeding birds who need extra help during the difficult time of breeding and who bring their young to the feeder from mid- to late summer.

Even though birds use feeders, they use them mostly as a supplemental food source. They get the majority of their food in the wild.

Still, if you must stop feeding, the best time to stop would be in summer when wild foods are plentiful.

What's That Bird?
EASTERN KINGBIRD

ID Clues: About 9 inches long with black
    back and white underparts;
    conspicuous white tip on the black
    tail; males and females look alike.
Habitat: Open areas with some trees
Food: Insects caught in air or picked off
    ground
Nests: Nest of bark strips, plant fibers in
    tree 10 to 20 feet high

that do not even use the feeders simply because of all of the activity around our feeders.

The most important factor for a successful feeding area is to offer a variety of foods in the proper settings. Feeders attract seed-eating birds, while most garden plantings attract fruit-eating birds. Thus, feeders along with plantings attract the greatest number and variety of birds. See the section on gardening for birds, beginning on page 35, for information on bird garden plantings.

THE BEST FEEDER SETUP

The feeder setup that will attract the most birds will offer four basic foods: sunflower seed, thistle seed, mixed seed, and suet. For information on hummingbird feeders see "Attracting Hummers" on page 14.

SUNFLOWER SEED

More birds are attracted to sunflower seed than to any other type of seed. Sunflower seed is available in two basic types: striped sunflower seed, which has gray and white stripes; and black oil sunflower seed, which is smaller and all black.

You can also buy black oil sunflower seed with the hulls removed (hulled). Buying hulled sunflower seed has many advantages. It is more concentrated, so you will not need to carry and store as many bags. It is also less messy around the feeder: The birds eat all of the seed and do not leave the hulls behind. While larger birds like the cardinal often eat the larger striped sunflower seed, all studies show that birds prefer black oil sunflower or hulled sunflower seeds over striped sunflower seeds.

Sunflower seed can be offered to birds in a variety of feeder styles, which essentially are variations of either the tubular feeder or the house hopper–type feeder. These feeders can be hung or mounted on trees, poles, or even your kitchen window.

Common Feeder Birds Attracted to Sunflower Seeds

Cardinal
Black-capped Chickadee
Carolina Chickadee
American Goldfinch
Purple Finch
House Finch
Northern Flicker
Evening Grosbeak
Blue Jay
Western Scrub-Jay
White-breasted Nuthatch
Red-breasted Nuthatch
Pine Siskin
House Sparrow
Starling
Tufted Titmouse
Downy Woodpecker
Hairy Woodpecker
Red-bellied Woodpecker
Red-headed Woodpecker

CHOOSING A GOOD SUNFLOWER FEEDER

Walk into any store with bird feeders and you will be greeted with a bewildering array of choices. We recommend that you invest your money in a well-made feeder in the beginning; it will last a long time and will reward you with years of enjoyment. Here are some overall features to consider for buying any feeder:

- Easy to fill
- Holds lots of seed so you don't have to fill it as often

- Easy to take apart and clean
- Clear parts made of heavy plastic (such as Lexan), which is unbreakable and cannot be chewed by squirrels
- Protects the seed from rain and snow
- Metal perches and reinforced openings (on a tube feeder) so squirrels cannot chew it
- Manufacturer's guarantee, if possible

THISTLE SEED

Thistle seed is a small black seed that is a favorite of American Goldfinches, Pine Siskins, and other finches. Thistle, now called niger seed, comes from Ethiopia and India and is not related to our common wildflower thistle. It is an expensive seed, but finches really enjoy it. A thistle feeder is a special tubular feeder that has tiny holes small enough to keep the seed from spilling out but large enough to let the birds peck at it. It can be hung or mounted on a pole. You can also offer thistle in a small mesh bag or "thistle sock," which is easily hung from a post or tree trunk.

MIXED SEED

Mixed seed can include a variety of seeds, such as cracked corn, white millet, peanuts, and safflower seeds. Mixed seed also has sunflower seed in varying proportions, which makes it even more attractive to a variety of birds. Some mixes, especially bargain mixes, can

Quick Tip

Since birds really love sunflower seed, it is best to get a feeder that holds 2 or more quarts of seed and is easy to fill.

Basic Feeder Styles

From left to right: A **house hopper–type feeder** has an attractive rustic look. Larger models hold large quantities of seed and allow several birds to perch at once. Many have easy-to-fill designs and can accommodate a baffle to keep squirrels away. A **tube feeder** is easy to fill, has metal-reinforced perches and holes that are squirrel-resistant, and displays seed clearly to birds. Large models hold lots of seed and allow the option of attaching a tray underneath to catch scattered seed and/or a domelike squirrel baffle above. A **seed bowl or bin with baffle feeder** holds lots of seed, protects seed from weather, and displays seed clearly to birds. It accommodates many birds at once and is easy to fill and clean. It comes with a squirrel baffle (often adjustable). A **window feeder** brings birds up close to your window for exciting views.

contain "undesirable" seeds, like milo, wheat, oats, or rye. "Undesirable," however, is in the eye of the beholder. For example, many eastern birds tend to shun milo, while some western birds love it.

Try different mixes and see which ones appeal to the birds living in your area. There are a wide variety of mixes available today. Some are even formulated to appeal to certain species. For example, a blend for cardinals would contain a higher percentage of sun-

flower seeds. A woodpecker blend would contain more nuts. Choose mixes that contain higher percentage of cracked corn for ground-feeding species such as sparrows and doves.

CHICKADEES TEND TO TAKE ONE SEED FROM A FEEDER, FLY AWAY TO A NEARBY PERCH, EAT IT, AND THEN FLY BACK FOR ANOTHER.

Common Feeder Birds Attracted to Mixed Seed

Red-winged Blackbird
Cardinal
Black-capped Chickadee
Brown-headed Cowbird
Crow
Mourning Dove
Common Grackle
Blue Jay
Western Scrub-Jay
Dark-eyed Junco
Ring-necked Pheasant
Pigeon
American Tree Sparrow
Fox Sparrow
Song Sparrow
White-crowned Sparrow
White-throated Sparrow
House Sparrow
Starling
Tufted Titmouse
Eastern and Spotted towhees

predator, such as a hawk, appears. Many birds also have a pecking order in their flocks, and nearby shrubs provide a place for subordinate birds to wait while more dominant birds feed.

SUET

The last element of a successful feeder setup is suet, a special fat found near the kidneys of cattle. Suet is a high-energy food source for birds and is a favorite food of woodpeckers. You can ask for suet at your local supermarket meat counter, or you can buy already-made suet cakes.

Suet cakes have many advantages over straight suet. First, they have been melted down and solidified two or more times, which makes them less likely to melt or go rancid, as raw suet might. Also, suet cakes are frequently made with many added ingredients, such as peanuts and berries. Another advantage to suet

Mixed seed can be offered in tube or house hopper–type feeders that are hung or pole mounted—or placed on an open, elevated tray near the ground.

Put out only the amount that the birds eat up quickly. Do not let seed sit around, spoil, or become moldy. If seed is not eaten within several days, clean it up by raking the area and disposing of leftovers.

Position your feeders about 15 feet from cover, such as a brush pile or evergreen shrubs. This allows birds to dive into cover if a

Common Feeder Birds Attracted to Suet

Black-capped Chickadee
Carolina Chickadee
Mockingbird
Red-breasted Nuthatch
White-breasted Nuthatch
Starling
Tufted Titmouse
Downy Woodpecker
Hairy Woodpecker
Red-bellied Woodpecker
Red-headed Woodpecker

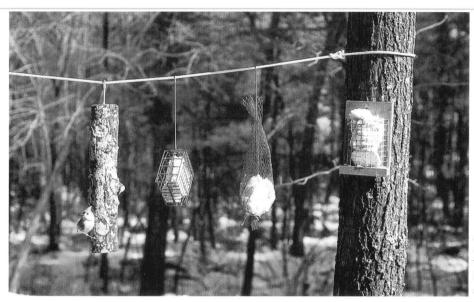

Left to right: Suet log (with Tufted Titmouse), suet basket, suet bag, and suet holder

cakes is that they come in blocks that fit neatly into suet holders.

You can offer suet in a suet holder—or even just an onion bag. A suet holder is a box or basket made of plastic-coated wire mesh. It lasts a long time, is attractive, and is easy to fill with all shapes of suet pieces. The plastic bags in which onions are often sold cost nothing and can easily be replaced when they wear out. Suet holders can be attached to tree trunks or hung on poles near or with your other feeders. Some house hopper–type feeders actually have places to put suet cakes at either end.

PLACING YOUR FEEDERS

It is best to have your feeder setup near some small trees or large shrubs where the birds can land and perch before going to the feeders, or where they can dive for cover in the case of

 Make It Yourself

Since suet-loving birds are used to feeding on tree trunks, a suet log stuffed with a homemade "suet" recipe mimics their natural environment and gives them a different tasty treat. Here's what to do:

Suet log: Use a branch or tree trunk that is about 2 inches in diameter and 1½ feet long. Drill several 1-inch-diameter holes along the length of the log and attach a hook in the middle of one end for hanging. Smear suet, peanut butter with seeds, or this special recipe in the holes.

"Suet" recipe: In a blender or food processor, combine 1 part peanut butter, 1 part vegetable shortening, 3 parts yellow cornmeal, 1 part white or whole wheat flour, and 1 part finely cracked corn. If it is too sticky, add more cornmeal or flour to make it manageable. Keep any extra in a plastic bag in the refrigerator.

In the winter, we also stuff this recipe into pinecones, roll them in mixed seed, and hang them on our outdoor Christmas tree for the birds. Dark-eyed Juncos and mockingbirds love them.

This is a nice feeder setup with thistle, suet, peanuts, and sunflower offered on aboveground feeders, and mixed seed scattered on the ground and on a tray. The rhododendrons behind the feeders are superb as shelter and cover for the visiting birds.

danger. We have one of our feeder setups near a stand of rhododendrons. The birds seem to like the year-round cover, and they often wait within the bushes before venturing out to feed on the ground. When something scares them, they dart back into the bushes until they decide it's safe to feed again.

If you are just starting, you may want to position your new feeder in an area that you can see from inside your house, but that is both close to shelter and far enough from your house to make the birds feel safe. Once birds are used to the feeder, you can try gradually moving it closer to your house for better viewing. (Keep it away from windows to prevent collisions.) This will give you maximum enjoyment from the birds that visit. You will be

FEEDERS ARE FOR THE BIRDS, BUT THEY ALSO ARE A WONDERFUL WAY TO BRING THE EXCITING LIVES OF BIRDS CLOSER TO YOUR HOME AND FAMILY.

amazed at how much is happening once you start looking.

We have our feeders outside our kitchen, and another set of feeders outside our office. One of our favorite activities is sitting at the kitchen table and watching the bird activity at the feeders. On an early-summer morning with the windows open, we delight in hearing bird

This feeder offers both safflower and sunflower seeds and has attracted a male Red-bellied Woodpecker (*left*) and a male cardinal (*right*). A White-breasted Nuthatch peeks down from the roof.

A male Rose-breasted Grosbeak feasts on sunflower seeds.

songs and seeing Rose-breasted Grosbeaks flying down to our sunflower feeder.

KEEPING YOUR FEEDERS CLEAN

Over the months, feeders and feeder areas can get messy with uneaten seeds, hulls from eaten seeds, and bird droppings. It is best to clean your feeders—even wooden ones—every few weeks. Dispose of any old or moldy food at *all* feeders, including ground feeders. Scrub feeders with a stiff brush or bottle brush inside and out with hot water and a mild bleach solution, rinsing thoroughly. Not only will your feeder area look better, it will be safer for the birds.

SOLVING PROBLEMS AROUND YOUR FEEDERS

The birds in your yard, like you, prefer to eat in peace. Providing them with feeders that keep out the competition—other animals, insects, and predators—will go a long way toward attracting more birds. If they feel threatened, they won't come back.

BAFFLING THE SQUIRRELS

Over the years we have become convinced that there are two types of people in the world of bird feeding: Those who want to keep squirrels off their feeders, and those who want to continually match wits with squirrels. Some people

---

Bird Feeder Journal

January 18, 8:30 A.M. *It snowed hard last night. There are 30 Evening Grosbeaks at the feeder; the numbers have been climbing since they arrived last November 23. Males and females crowd together on the ledge of the hanging house feeder, constantly competing for space.*

get so obsessed with keeping squirrels away that bird feeding becomes an unpleasant experience for them. Our philosophy about squirrels is to do the best we can to keep them from disturbing the birds as they feed, and then to enjoy them for their own equally fascinating behavior.

WHEN BURYING A NUT, GRAY SQUIRRELS USE THEIR NOSE TO PUSH IT INTO A HOLE, POSSIBLY LEAVING THEIR SCENT THERE; THEN, IN WINTER, THEY REMEMBER THE SPOT AND FIND THE MORSEL BY THE SMELL OF THE NUT OR THEIR SCENT.

There are two goals where squirrels and your feeders are concerned: keeping squirrels from getting to the feeder, and—if they do manage to reach it—keeping them from chewing the feeder apart as they go after the seed.

By far the best way to minimize squirrel damage at your sunflower feeder is to concentrate on the first goal and keep the squirrels from reaching the feeder. To do this, your best chance is to take the following steps, which we have found work 90 to 95 percent of the time:

1. Hang or mount your feeder at least 8 feet away from the nearest access, such as a tree trunk or limb, and 5 to 6 feet off the ground. Even this may require some adjustment if you encounter a squirrel with exceptional jumping ability. If your tube feeder has a seed-catching tray attachment that the squirrels are using as a landing platform, remove the tray.

2. Use a baffle—a round or umbrella-shaped physical barrier that squirrels are unable to crawl over—above any hanging feeder, or at least 4 feet up on thin metal posts just below a feeder. An even better approach is to put a stovepipe baffle, 2 feet long and 6 inches in diameter, over the supporting pole just under the feeder. You can buy some excellent clear plastic or metal baffles from many bird feeder suppliers. Or, you can make your own baffle out of sheet metal or other slippery material, but remember to make it wide enough so that the squirrel cannot crawl over it. Some people try placing empty spools of thread or other objects on wires that lead to a feeder to make footing difficult for the squirrels. We have found that baffles work best.

3. Offer cracked corn or "squirrel blend" mixed seed scattered on a tray placed on the ground away from the other feeders to divert squirrels (and chipmunks) from the aboveground feeders, where the more expensive seed is housed.

If they manage to get to your feeders, squirrels will be unable to chew it if it is made from tough plastic. They also can't chew through metal, so make sure your feeder has a metal

A Sharp-shinned Hawk will prey on small birds.

A silhouette of a hawk on your window may keep birds from flying into it.

by actually eating birds at your feeders. Sometimes, ordinary windowpanes can be just as dangerous to your backyard birds. Here are some things you can do to minimize deadly strikes in your yard.

For cats, eliminate any possible hiding places around feeders so that birds can easily see cats in the area. Keeping your feeders 15 feet from lifesaving shelter is a good idea. You may need to move tray feeders that are too near brush piles or shrubbery. Place birdbaths off the ground and away from shrubbery where cats could hide.

There are several species of hawks that prey on small birds. The most common species are the Sharp-shinned Hawk in the East, and Cooper's Hawk in the West. Because hawks are protected by law, the best solution to dealing with their presence is to provide your feeder birds with lots of places, like dense shrubbery and brush piles, to seek shelter if a hawk appears.

Birds sometimes see the reflections of sky and trees in windows and, mistaking them for open space, crash into them headfirst, often to

bottom and top, as well as metal-reinforced portals where birds get the seed.

In addition, some feeders actually prevent squirrels from eating out of them once they land on them. One type is an all-steel design with a platform on which the weight of a squirrel, but not lighter birds, closes the feeder door. Look in "Resources" on page 289 for bird feeder companies, which typically carry a variety of squirrel-stopping supplies.

DEALING WITH BIGGER THREATS

Squirrels are the biggest nuisances at feeding stations, but cats and hawks can create havoc

Q: Why aren't there any birds at my feeder?

A: If you have the right feeders, seeds, water, and plantings in your yard, be patient—the birds will come. In some areas, it takes the birds longer to find and use feeders than in other areas. Here are some factors to consider, however, if activity at your feeders seems particularly low.

It may be the wrong season. At certain times of year—especially late summer, fall, and early winter—there is often an abundance of weed seeds and berries for birds to eat, so they do not need to come to your feeders. Also, in spring and early summer, birds form pairs and are scattered over breeding territories.

It may be the wrong time of day. None of us watch feeders *all* day. Birds can come for very short periods, like just at daybreak, and then not come back at all; they may come at dusk, when it is hard to see them. Cardinals often show up only at dawn or dusk to feed.

Birds change their feeding behavior. Temperature, weather, time of day, time of year—all these factors influence a bird's feeding habits. In mild weather, when wild food is plentiful, birds will use your feeders less. When they are under more pressure to find food, such as during snowstorms, they will come more regularly to your feeders.

Some species come to feeders only in certain years. These include the Pine Siskin and Evening Grosbeak, which may be abundant one year and then absent the next, depending on how much food is available in the North. Many of the finches, such as American Goldfinches and Purple Finches, appear erratically at feeders and may wander widely in winter.

Your neighbors may have put up feeders. And, heaven forbid, they may be more attractive than yours! If you follow our guidelines, you will maximize the attractiveness of your own feeders and ensure a population in your yard.

You may live in a spot with very few birds. If there are not many trees, shrubs, or grasses in your area to offer shelter and nest sites, add them to your property—you'll be surprised at how many more birds you will attract.

their death. This especially occurs when they are frightened—maybe by a cat or hawk—and suddenly take wing, or when they are new to the area, as when they are migrating. The best solution is to keep feeders 30 feet away from windows. Another solution is to buy or make a black silhouette of a diving hawk or falcon and place it with the head pointing down on the outside of your window. Birds instinctively recognize that shape as meaning danger and may stay away from the window.

HANDLING OTHER ANNOYANCES

Some people feel that certain birds are more desirable than others. We do not feel this way. We try to attract all the birds we can, for each bird has its own fascinating behavior to observe and enjoy. Also, birds attract other birds, so a busy feeding station is highly desirable.

It is true that larger birds can eat great quantities of seed, and that can be expensive. Also, some larger birds, like jays, may beat out small birds for food. Our basic tactic is to offer some-

A Western Scrub-Jay grabs a nut.

Woodpeckers, like this female Red-bellied Woodpecker, may drum on houses to signal to each other.

thing for everyone. Offer the expensive sunflower seed to the smaller birds in the kinds of hanging feeders designed for them. Offer the larger birds the less expensive cracked corn and mixed seed in trays on the ground. If you really want to discourage certain birds, the best way is to temporarily remove the food they eat most often.

Many people have had cardinals, robins, and other species pecking at their windows or car mirrors, often at the same spot, day after day. This window pecking usually occurs during the breeding season in spring and summer. It happens because the bird sees the reflection of what it believes is another bird of the same species and sex in the glass and responds aggressively to defend its mate and territory. If you cover up the reflection, the birds will stop the pecking behavior.

Homeowners often complain about woodpeckers doing long, rapid drumming on the

side of their house, gutter, drainpipe, or even TV antenna. They are disturbed by the noise and concerned they may have bugs in the house that the bird is going after. You need to worry about insect activity only if the woodpeckers tap in an irregular rhythm that generally is not very loud.

If the taps are loud, rapid volleys, then the woodpecker is "drumming," the woodpecker's song to announce its territory or attract a mate. It is also a way for the male and female to keep in touch. The birds pick resonant spots to drum on and then continue to use them through the beginning of the breeding season. No wood will

These five hummingbirds are vying for the same feeder.

Example of an inverted bottle hummingbird feeder

be excavated and no damage done to your house, although you may be woken up early in the morning. The drumming will stop once the breeding season is underway. You can put a plastic drop cloth over the drumming spot to make it difficult for the woodpecker to land there.

ATTRACTING HUMMERS

One of the best ways to draw hummingbirds into your yard and have the enjoyment of watching them is to buy a hummingbird feeder, fill it with a sugar-water solution, and place it in your yard. Putting it near flowers or other plantings to which hummingbirds may be drawn will make it even more attractive.

STYLE IS A MATTER OF CHOICE

There are many fine commercial hummingbird feeders on the market and, depending on your personal tastes and fancy, any style will do the job. Flower patterns or red parts to attract hummers are common features on the two basic designs. One type consists of an inverted bottle that empties into a lower reservoir with feeding holes. The vacuum created at the top of the bottle is what keeps the liquid from draining out. The simplest form of this type of feeder is a small bottle with a rubber stopper and glass tube coming out the bottom. Water bottles sold in pet stores for guinea pigs or

More Hummingbird Feeder Styles

Both a window feeder (*left*) and a disk-style feeder (*right*) are easy to fill and clean, and there is little spillage of the sugar-water solution.

caged birds can also be used, usually with decorations like red ribbon streamers added to attract the hummers.

The other type of hummingbird feeder is a container with holes in its cover through which the hummingbirds reach to get the fluid. Many of these are thin disks with representations of flowers on the upper surface. Some models can be window-mounted with suction cups for

WHEN DRINKING NECTAR,

HUMMINGBIRDS OPEN THEIR LONG

BILL, EXTEND THEIR TONGUE, AND

LICK UP THE NECTAR—AT A RATE OF

13 LICKS PER SECOND.

close-up views of the hummers. You may want to experiment with different models of feeders to find which ones suit you best.

CHOOSING A GOOD FEEDER

You will be doing lots of filling and cleaning of the feeder, so make sure you can easily reach all areas to scrub them thoroughly. (Bottle brushes and pipe cleaners will make this job easier.)

Start with smaller feeders, and wait until your hummingbird customers are regularly emptying these before going for the larger sizes. You need to put in just enough solution for the hummingbirds to consume in a day or two so it won't sit too long in the feeder and spoil.

There are quality feeders made out of plastic, glass, or a combination of the two.

A female Broad-billed Hummingbird (*left*) perches for a drink, while a female Black-chinned Hummingbird (*right*) seemingly waits for a turn.

There are pros and cons to the use of each material. Plastic doesn't break, but some people feel that glass is easier to clean.

PERCHES ARE OPTIONAL

Perches are useful, although not essential, features on hummingbird feeders. If the feeder has perches, the hummers will use them. If it doesn't, the hummers will happily hover at the feeding holes, just as they do when drinking from flowers. When they want to perch they will go to a nearby shrub or tree. Hummingbirds do take frequent breaks from their energy-intensive hovering flight; one study found that they spend over 60 percent of their time perched.

PLACING YOUR HUMMER FEEDERS

The best place to put feeders initially is near flowers that are attractive to hummingbirds or where hummingbirds have been seen feeding. It is preferable to have already created a habitat where hummingbirds are likely to visit. To learn how to do this, see page 82.

Try to place the feeders where they will be protected from the wind and where there is some shade. Wind jostles the feeder and may make the sugar-water solution spill, a common problem. The hot sun shining all day on the feeder can cause the sugar-water solution to spoil more quickly.

MORE THAN ONE FEEDER WORKS

Hummingbirds can be very aggressive around sources of food and will try to keep other hummers away. A pecking order may form among the hummers at the feeder, with some birds or species being dominant over others. To reduce the competition and allow more hummers to feed, try putting up a

Quick Tip

Place hummingbird feeders out of the wind and in the shade.

What's That Bird?

BLUE-THROATED HUMMINGBIRD

ID Clues: About 5 inches long with large tail and wings; blue throat and white at the tip of the tail

Habitat: Tends to live along the edges of streams in mountains or canyons

U.S. Breeding Period: April to July

U.S. Breeding Range: Southeastern Arizona, southwestern New Mexico, and western Texas

Nonbreeding Range: Northern and central Mexico

Migration: *Northward,* March to May; *southward,* August to October

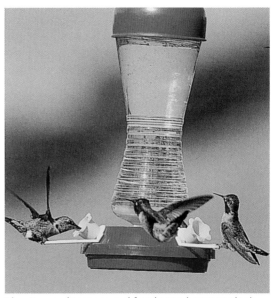

It's not unusual to see several female Anna's Hummingbirds competing for sugar-water.

second, third, or even more feeders, preferably out of view from each other.

THE SWEET STUFF

Hummingbird feeders are filled with a clear sugar-water solution that is easy to make in your own kitchen. Simply add 1 part sugar to 4 parts water; for example, 1 cup of sugar to 4 cups of water. Boil for several minutes and then cool to room temperature. Fill your feeders with the cooled liquid and store any extra in the refrigerator.

Why is this mixture attractive to hummingbirds? Table sugar is essentially a kind of sugar called sucrose, which is also the main sugar of flower nectar. The 1-to-4 ratio of sugar to water also approximates the roughly 20 percent sugar-water concentration found in the nectar of many hummingbird flowers. It is sweet enough to attract the hummers, without being too sweet. If you increase the concentration of sugar, it may be harder for the birds to digest; if you decrease the concentration, they may lose interest.

Boiling the solution helps retard fermentation since sugar-water solutions are subject to rapid spoiling, especially in hot weather.

ACCEPT NO SUBSTITUTES

Do not use honey, brown sugar, raw sugar, or artificial sweeteners in place of sugar. Honey and the other sugars ferment easily and can cause a fungus that affects hummingbirds' tongues, which can be fatal to the birds. Artificial sweeteners should also be avoided because they have no food value; they do not give the birds the calories that they need.

TOO MUCH RED CAN BE TOO MUCH

Because the color red is so attractive to hummingbirds, some people think adding red food dye to their sugar-water solution will help draw them into their yards. Using red food dye to color sugar-water solution has been a matter

This male Rufous hummer is sipping some tree sap.

HUMMINGBIRDS FEED 5 TO 8 TIMES EACH HOUR, BUT ONLY FOR ABOUT 30 TO 60 SECONDS AT A TIME.

of ongoing debate; some people suspect it may have a harmful effect on hummingbird health. In fact, red dye is not necessary since most feeders have enough red on them to attract hummers. We prefer not to add coloring.

IT'S NOT ALL SUGAR-SWEET

Hummingbirds get their nutrition by eating many other things besides the sugar-water from feeders and the nectar from flowers. Besides the tiny insects inside the flowers from which they sip nectar, hummers eat a substantial number of small insects and spiders, gleaning them from twigs and leaves like warblers or catching them in the air like flycatchers. They eat tree sap from holes drilled by sapsuckers, too. Just watch them sometime!

KEEPING YOUR FEEDERS CLEAN

Hummingbird sugar-water is highly susceptible to mold, harmful bacteria, and fermentation. If you don't regularly clean your feeders, you could be risking the health and possibly the lives of the hummers that use them.

Wash feeders out in very hot water every few days. In weather over 60°F, pathogens in the feeding solution can multiply rapidly, and the feeders should be cleaned **every 2 days.**

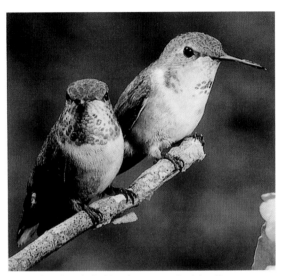

This Rufous female (*left*) and immature (*right*) will migrate several weeks after the male.

Male

What's That Bird?
MAGNIFICENT HUMMINGBIRD

ID Clues: A large, 5-inch bird with dark belly, green throat, and purple crown

Habitat: Likes areas rich in agaves, penstemons, honeysuckle, salvias, and thistles

U.S. Breeding Period: May to July

U.S. Breeding Range: Mountains of southeastern Arizona, southwestern New Mexico, western Texas

Nonbreeding Range: Central Mexico

Migration: *Northward,* March; *southward,* October to November

During cooler weather, it might be acceptable to wait slightly longer than 3 days.

You can add some vinegar to the hot water to remove mold or, for really tough cleaning jobs, use a tiny amount of bleach, making sure to rinse the feeder out thoroughly. If necessary, scrub hard-to-reach spots with bottle brushes and pipe cleaners.

PUTTING FEEDERS UP AND DOWN

Most species of hummingbirds are migrants, coming to North America only in the warmer seasons. Feeders should be up in time for their arrival, which will vary depending on where you live. In the South, it may be January or February; in the North, April or May.

Hummingbirds begin migrating south even when there are still flowers in bloom and in-sects available. In fact, males generally migrate several weeks ahead of females and immatures. The birds likely time their migrations according to changing day length or photoperiod. Thus, feeders that are left up may actually help mi-grating hummingbirds. As they begin their southward journey, the feeders give them the extra energy needed for their long flight.

Where hummingbirds are found year-round—on the West Coast, in the Southwest, and in a

A beautiful female Rufous Hummingbird drinks sugar-water at this hummingbird feeder through a bee guard, which helps keep bees away from the "nectar."

The long, down-curved bill of the Curve-billed Thrasher may help it feed from some hummingbird feeders.

few places in the Southeast—feeders left up all year may be life sustaining. In Ramsey Canyon, Arizona, for instance, there have been reports of Magnificent Hummingbirds coming to feeders every 20 minutes in a snowstorm.

SOLVING PROBLEMS AT YOUR HUMMER FEEDERS

The sweet taste of sugar-water "nectar" will draw other creatures besides hummers to your feeders. Some you may tolerate; others you won't want there. There are always options, however, to guard against unwanted guests.

BEES AND ANTS

A hummingbird feeder offers a free meal to nectar-loving bees, wasps, and ants, but there are several tactics to fight these tiny insects. To control bees and wasps, some people put mineral oil or salad oil around the feeder opening with a finger or a cotton swab; this makes it hard for the insects to get a foothold. If you try this, make sure not to get any inside the portal hole. Some feeders come with their own "bee guard," a little screenlike device that fits over the feeder holes and makes it hard for the insects to reach the fluid. Another type of "bee guard" is a flexible membrane that fits onto the portals; only hummingbirds can penetrate it.

In dealing with ants, the best tactic is to block their passage to the feeder. Some feeders come with a moat of water around the hanging wire, and ants cannot cross water. You can also buy an "ant cup," a plastic container filled with water that hangs above the feeder. Ants will not cross it to reach the nectar.

OTHER VISITORS

More than 58 species of birds, such as orioles, warblers, and thrashers—and even bats—have been reported feeding at hummingbird feeders. All sorts of other creatures have been reported coming to hummingbird feeders as well, including such wild animals as lizards, chipmunks, foxes, raccoons, and opossums.

You can welcome the other wildlife or discourage it. To protect your feeders from night-active mammals, you can take feeders in at night or hang them in places inaccessible to mammals. If other species of birds compete too much with hummingbirds for the feeders, add more feeders. Use oriole feeders to lure orioles away from hummingbird feeders.

Q: Why don't hummingbirds come to my feeders?

A: Many people put up hummingbird feeders and wait for the birds to arrive, only to have none appear. One's first inclination is to blame the feeders, but actually the situation is more complex. Here are some of the many reasons why you may not get hummingbirds at your feeders or, if you have had them, why they may have left.

You live in a poor habitat. Some areas do not have many flowers, shrubs, or trees that hummingbirds like, so few hummingbirds stop by.

You live in too good a habitat. If there are too many hummingbird flowers in your area, the birds may never bother with feeders. Likewise, when an abundance of wildflowers are available in the vicinity, hummers may temporarily desert feeders.

Some hummingbirds just may not be interested in feeders. Certain individual hummingbirds may develop their own particular patterns and be influenced by their prior experiences. Years ago, one hummer visited our garden and systematically ignored the feeder, no matter where we moved it or what we did to it. In subsequent years, other hummers used it.

It's the breeding season. Hummingbirds that used to cluster around your feeders may have moved elsewhere to breed.

Your feeding solution may have fermented or gone sour. Remember to keep your feeders filled with clean, fresh solution. If you leave them empty for too long, the hummingbirds may seek food elsewhere and not return.

You may not be looking when the hummingbirds arrive. Hummingbirds spend a lot of their time perched and much less of their time feeding. If there are not many hummers in your area, then it could be easy to miss seeing their visits.

The best advice we can give you is to think flowers first. In other words, create the kind of habitat with nectar-rich flowers, shrubs, and trees that will instinctively appeal to hummingbirds, then put up the feeders near the flowers that the hummingbirds are using. See "Create a Hummingbird Heaven in Your Backyard" on page 82 for more information. Be patient—it may take a while, but eventually the hummingbirds will arrive.

Water

All birds need water: It is essential for drinking and bathing. The birds that normally visit your feeders will appreciate the water you provide, and you'll get the added benefit of attracting other species—robins, thrushes, vireos, orioles, and warblers—that might not be attracted to your yard by feeders. Water is also a key feature in a beautiful garden, providing shimmering reflections of flowers and sky as well as the peaceful trickling sound of a fountain.

WATER EVERYWHERE

Water is easy to provide; all you need is a small pool, birdbath, or shallow dish. But water alone isn't really enough: You need to provide both safe access to it for drinking, and shallow areas in it where the birds can bathe. Create several different areas where you provide water; they will give the birds a choice.

CREATING A GOOD BIRDBATH

There are many ways to create a birdbath, from as simple as a trash can lid turned upside down to as complex as a flowing stream with waterfalls and pools. In all forms and styles, though, there are certain requirements you should meet to be sure that the bath will be useful for and attractive to birds.

THE RIGHT DEPTH

There are many attractive birdbaths sold in stores. Most smaller birds bathe in very shallow water, sometimes only about ½ inch

A small birdbath on your deck can bring birds in close. Here, a male robin is about to take a drink.

Birds need water every day. Here, two Common Ground-Doves and a Mourning Dove are drinking together. Doves can sip water up through their bill; most birds have to tilt their head back to drink the water they collect in their bill.

It is fun to watch birds bathe—each species does it a little differently. This male cardinal is really making the water fly.

deep. Often, they do not even get all the way into the water; they just stand at the edge and splash water onto their bodies with a rapid bill motion. Therefore, any birdbath that you create must have a gradual slope that is not slippery.

If your birdbath is about 1 to 2 inches deep, you can create shallow areas in it by submerging a few thin, flat rocks around the edge at varying depths. This gives the birds choices. If you have a larger pond or even a small

Water for Hummers

This male Costa's Hummingbird is taking a "drink" from a flower.

Hummingbirds do all or most of their drinking at flowers when they sip nectar, but they also need places to bathe. Hummingbirds are resourceful in this regard, using bits of water wherever they find them. These can include beads of water on a leaf, the shallow edges of a brook, or even the spray from a sprinkler.

If you want to make your birdbath hospitable to hummers, be sure it has areas of very shallow water where the birds can stand if they choose. We always put a few flat rocks in our birdbath to create different depths.

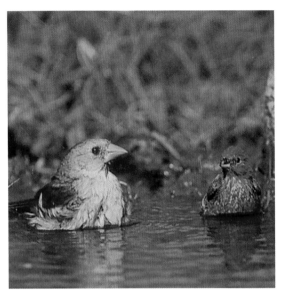

Here is a chance meeting between a male Painted Bunting (*right*) and a female cardinal (*left*) in a shallow, natural pool that is perfect for birds to bathe in.

artificial stream, be sure that smaller, safe, shallow areas exist where the birds can approach the water for bathing and drinking.

When larger birds such as grackles or robins come to bathe, they need deeper water. They seem to really like to get into it, splashing all about. Therefore, you will also want some deeper areas—2 to 3 inches—in your bird bathing areas.

THE WATER IN A BIRDBATH

SHOULD BE NO MORE THAN 3

INCHES DEEP—SMALL SONGBIRDS

DO NOT LIKE IT DEEPER.

 # Make It Yourself

Ponds and pools are wonderful additions to a backyard. They offer a natural setting for the birds to dip their beaks and provide room for water plantings in your bird garden. There are several ways you can add these giant birdbaths to your yard.

- Excavate a shallow pond area, place a smooth layer of sand over the bottom, then line it with thick black plastic, available at most lawn and garden stores. Place flat rocks around the edge of the pond to hide the plastic, and put a few water-loving plants among the rocks for a naturalistic effect.

- Excavate a deeper hole, smooth it out with sand, and buy a preformed black plastic pool to go into the hole. These come in all shapes and sizes, some rounded and some square. They are usually 1 to 3 feet deep and often have ledges around the sides to place pots of aquatic plants.

- If you cannot or do not want to excavate a hole, use a square preformed plastic pool above ground by building a small wooden frame to support the lip of the pool. Cover the outside of the frame with siding. This can be quite attractive, and the frame can be wide enough to provide a seating area around the edge of the pool.

If you make a pond or pool, the birds may be able to drink from it, but they will not be able to use it for bathing unless you create a shallow area where they can step in. This can be done by building up some large flat rocks at the edge or in the center of the pool.

KEEPING IT CLEAN

You will need a way to clean your birdbath; after a few visits by birds, there will be feathers and droppings in and around the bath. We use a scrub brush to clean out the birdbath each time we refill it. Water tends to evaporate quickly from birdbaths, and the birds also splash it out as they bathe, so plan to clean and refill your birdbaths every 2 or 3 days.

CHOOSING THE BEST SPOT

Place your birdbaths in areas that appeal to the birds and where they already come. Baths can be near feeders if the seed does not fall into them. They can also be in gardens.

It is best to put your baths near shrubs and/or small trees so the birds have a place to perch as they approach. This way, they can check for predators before bathing and perch to preen and dry off after bathing. We often put our birdbaths in the lawn, at the edge of our deck, and near our bird feeders. We always cut off a branch of a shrub or tree and either stick

Female

What's That Bird?
YELLOW WARBLER

ID Clues: A small, 5-inch, brightly colored yellow bird with reddish streaks on breast and yellow tail spots; female (shown here) is a duller yellow with fainter (or no) streaks compared to male; in Southwest birds are paler, in Florida Keys birds are brighter

Habitat: Shrubby areas, especially near water; willows and alders

Food: Caterpillars of moths, beetles, aphids, and other insects

Nests: Nest of milkweed stem fibers and other plant fibers in the fork of a shrub

Bird Feeder Journal

June 3, 8:30 A.M. We are camping in a high mountain canyon in the Southwest. On our morning walk today, we came across a pipe that had been attached to a spring and was dripping water onto rocks. There was a Painted Redstart that could not resist the sound and stayed in the area of the dripping throughout the hour that we stayed near the spring.

it in the ground or attach it to a stake so that it forms a good perching site right next to the water. We even tied a large branch near the birdbath on our second-floor deck.

If you have cats in the area, you may want to have the birdbath more out in the open with no shrubbery immediately nearby. This will make

What's That Bird?

CEDAR WAXWING

ID Clues: A sleek, crested bird about 7 inches long with a wide black eye stripe, brownish body, yellow belly (not visible here), and white under the tail; wings tipped in red, tail tipped in yellow; males and females look alike
Habitat: Open rural or suburban areas
Food: Insects and all types of berries
Nests: Nest of grasses and mosses placed in tree 5 feet high

it hard for a cat to hide and catch the birds by surprise.

We place our birdbaths at different heights. We have one in a hollowed-out rock that is sunk into the ground, and the birds seem to like this one the most. We have others that are 6 inches off the ground and others that are 2 to 3 feet high.

It is important to note that the tops of many tradi-

tional stone birdbaths are heavy and unsteady. Small children may be curious and pull on the birdbath, and it could tip over and fall. If small children will be frequenting your yard, either have the birdbath out of reach or use one with a top that is sturdily attached.

OFFERING WATER IN WINTER

Birds need water in winter as much as in summer. In some cases, they may need it even more: Many of their natural sources of water may be frozen and unavailable to them. In cold climates, some birds do eat snow and break off pieces of icicles for water, but even they will appreciate a source of fresh water. Some birds even bathe in winter.

Once we saw a whole flock of Cedar Waxwings flying out and back from their perches on a willow during a snowstorm. They looked like they were catching insects, but when we looked through our binoculars, we saw that they were catching snowflakes.

If you live in a warmer climate, keep water out all year. If you live in a colder climate, you will need a way to keep the water from freezing. The best way to do this is to use a small heating element, available commercially in several styles. (See "Resources" on page 289 for a list of suppliers.) They do not use much electricity, do not harm the birds, and keep the water just above freezing.

Quick Tip

To create a slow drip sound, poke a tiny hole through the bottom of a plastic milk jug, and suspend it over the birdbath.

Bathing in a Dust Bowl

Male Northern Bobwhite

The notion of bathing in dust may seem a little contradictory to us, but it works just fine for birds. Birds go to dusty spots, nestle down in the dust, fluff out their feathers, and rapidly flutter. This action infiltrates their feathers with dust, which they then shake out. After this, the birds often preen.

The function of dust bathing is not exactly known, but it most likely helps birds rid their feathers of mites or other small feather parasites.

To create a dust bath, choose a sunny area about 3 feet square near a feeder. Clear it of vegetation and make a hollow in the ground about 2 to 3 inches deep. Fill the hollow with fine dust, such as that found along the side of a dirt road. You can edge the area with small stones to keep vegetation from growing back in.

We have a naturally dusty site under the side of our garden shed, and one year we had a group of nine Northern Bobwhites who, almost daily, walked single file over to the dusting area to use it. House Sparrows in city areas often dust-bathe near home plate on baseball diamonds.

SOUND EFFECTS

Few things will attract birds more readily than the sound of dripping or trickling water. Birds seem to be irresistibly drawn to it. If there is a way to add this sound to your birdbath, then by all means do so.

This is particularly true in spring and fall, when migrating birds must locate water to help them on their journey. Many birds may rely on the sound of water to locate it more quickly in unfamiliar areas. The sound of water is particularly effective in attracting birds in desert areas, where water may be an even greater attraction than food. For decades, bird photographers have used the magical draw of water and always set up good drip fountains to attract birds to spots where a camera is all set to snap a picture.

There are several ways to create sound in your birdbath. A small recirculating pump connected to a fountain or bubbler in the center of your birdbath can create a babbling stream. Position the pump to carry the water to the top of a rock, where it can flow over the rock and drip into another pool. (Remember: Keep the water depth under 3 inches deep for the small birds.) Some companies sell drip pipes or misters already attached to a birdbath; you can also purchase these separately.

Shelter and Nests

The grass, flowers, shrubs, and trees in your yard help birds survive by providing insects, berries, and seeds to eat. They are equally important because they act as sheltering havens from weather and predators, and they offer a place to build a nest and raise young. For details on creating wonderful landscapes and houses for attracting, protecting, and keeping birds in your yard, see "Bird Gardening" on page 35 and "Birdhouses" on page 93.

SHELTER IN A STORM . . . AND OTHER TIMES

Birds need shelter from rain, snow, sun, wind, and predators. By providing a variety of shelter on your property, you will attract more birds. It's as simple as that.

Although birds may fly around in the rain as if it they were unaware of the downpour, they usually seek some kind of cover. We once watched a Downy Woodpecker cling to the trunk of a tree just under a larger limb throughout a heavy rainstorm. Many times during heavy rain we have seen birds pause under the eaves of our house hopper–type feeders. Dense evergreens and large, broad-leaved shrubs and trees provide birds with some protection from rain.

Dense evergreens provide good cover for birds during heavy snowfalls, and many species will fly into them and stay there until the storm has passed. Evergreen shrubs and trees also keep snow from accumulating on the ground

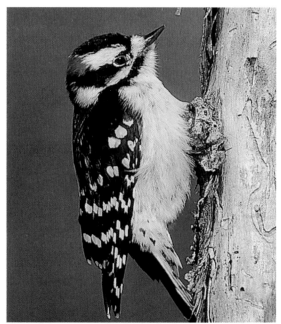

This male Downy Woodpecker has hunkered down and is grasping the tree as a shield against heavy winds.

A male Bullock's Oriole finds shelter in a cottonwood tree.

Female and male

What's That Bird?
BUSHTIT

ID Clues: Tiny, $3^{1}/_{2}$-inch gray bird with a tiny beak and long tail; coastal birds have brown cap, while inland birds show a brownish cheek; males have dark eyes and females have light yellow

Habitat: Open woods, chaparral, suburbs, parks, gardens

Food: Insects gleaned from leaves; seeds and fruits; feeders

Nests: Gourd-shaped nest of mosses, rootlets, lichens, spider silk suspended from twigs or branches 4 to 25 feet high

underneath them, enabling birds to look for seeds among the leaf litter. We have large rhododendrons right near our feeders. The birds use the shrubs continually for staying out of the snow.

Birds also need shelter from the sun, especially in very hot climates. We find that hummingbirds particularly like to sit in cool shade between their visits to our hummingbird feeders and nectar plants. Tall, broad-leaved trees are ideal; they provide dappled shade and let breezes through as the birds perch within them.

Strong winds can buffet birds around and cost them valuable energy. A windbreak or hedgerow that is planted perpendicular to the prevailing wind will attract birds, especially if feeders are placed on the downwind side. Birds roosting at night also need protection from chilling winds in winter. Large stands of dense evergreens provide this protection and may be used by species that roost in flocks, such as Mourning Doves and crows.

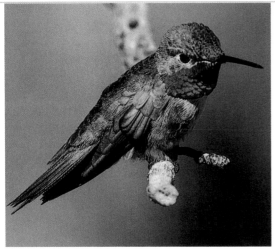

A male Broad-tailed Hummingbird rests on a perch in his territory.

Crows roost together at night.

Birds especially need protection from predators. They can usually fly away from ground predators, but aerial predators such as Sharp-shinned or Cooper's hawks attack in flight. Dense shrubs or evergreens near feeders will give the birds a way to escape the attacks of these birds of prey.

HOUSE AND HOME

Birds need places to build a nest and raise their young. We often say, "If you don't have breeding birds, you won't have feeding birds." In other words, don't just put out feeders; provide places for your birds to breed as well.

Different species nest in different habitats— and in various locations within those habitats. Some birds nest in cavities, like tree holes or birdhouses; others build their nest on the ground or on the branches of shrubs and trees. For example, Savannah Sparrows and quails nest on the ground among tall grasses. Cardinals, catbirds, and mockingbirds nest in shrubs with appropriate branching structure. Robins nest on horizontal limbs of trees, and orioles suspend their nests from the tips of drooping branches over open areas. Titmice need birdhouses or holes in dead trees, Chipping Sparrows need dense evergreens, and Barn Swallows need access to old outbuildings or barns.

As you can see, many diverse nesting areas are needed to attract a large number of nesting species. All properties can use more birdhouses, and most can use more diverse plantings to encourage breeding birds. To discover what your yard needs, look around your property for nests in winter (when leaves have fallen) to see where birds are already nesting. In spring and summer, look for nesting birds.

Birdhouses provide additional nest sites to birds that nest in natural cavities. There are 86

The Gambel's Quail nests on the ground near the base of taller vegetation.

Barn Swallows build mud nests on the sides of bridges or inside barns or outbuildings.

species of North American birds that nest in tree cavities. Some, such as woodpeckers, can excavate their own holes in trees, but the majority cannot. Many of our best-loved garden birds—including chickadees, titmice, nuthatches, Tree Swallows, wrens, and bluebirds—nest in tree holes and, therefore, love birdhouses. By putting up good birdhouses, you can have these birds nesting on your property.

Of course, gaining an intimate glimpse into the family life of birds is the real reward for building nesting spots or putting up a birdhouse. Wondrous and special moments will occur as you watch the birds raise their young. When we add birdhouses, we add homes for birds.

THE HIGHER GOAL

Adding food, water, nesting spots, and shelter to the environment of your property is not something you do just to attract birds; it is

much more. As we humans have gradually taken over the natural landscape for farming, roads, development, and housing, we have taken away the features of the environment that birds need for their survival.

All living things on earth are ultimately dependent on the complex interdependencies

A male Mountain Bluebird attends his nest.

Donald and Lillian Stokes

A young Tree Swallow nestling in one of our birdhouses calls out for more food from its busy parents.

The Joy of Nesting Birds

We can still recall the excitement of our first try at attracting nesting birds. We had put up five birdhouses in late March in our meadow. A few days later, we saw our first tenant, a beautiful Tree Swallow, peering cautiously into the entrance of a birdhouse. When a second Tree Swallow arrived, this meant we had a mated pair, and we eagerly awaited the joy of watching them raise a family.

Each day brought a new surprise. First, we saw the female carrying in strands of dried grasses as she fashioned the nest. One day, we saw the female fly off to catch insects, and we cautiously opened the nest box and discovered five snow-white eggs nestled in soft feathers that lined the nest of dried grasses. When both parents began to bring food to the nest, we knew the babies had hatched.

Near the end of the nestling phase, the feeding trips by the parents became more frequent, and we could hear the babies call excitedly when a parent landed on the house. Soon we saw little heads peering out: The babies were now big enough to vie with each other for a look at the world. Exactly 21 days after the babies had hatched, we were fortunate enough to see the first one leave the birdhouse. Soon all of the young had fledged, and in a few days they all had left.

Now that we're addicted to sharing in the family life of the birds, we have, over the years, added greatly to the types and numbers of nesting boxes on our suburban property. We have been fortunate enough to attract 12 species of cavity nesters and more than 30 other species of nesting birds.

Given the rapidly increasing destruction of suitable nesting habitats in this day and age, providing nesting boxes not only is a joy for us but is becoming more and more critical to birds' survival.

of the natural world. If the birds are doing well, then we are doing well and will continue to do well. If the birds are not doing well, then in the long run, neither will we.

By improving and diversifying the habitats in your own backyard, you are helping to restore the American habitat, bring back the native birds and other animals, and add to the long-term health of the human race in its interdependence with all other living things. It is a positive action that each individual can do right away.

Part 2 Bird Gardening

OVER THE YEARS, WE HAVE CONTINUALLY IMPROVED OUR PROPERTY BY GARDENING FOR BIRDS, AND IT HAS BEEN ONE OF THE RICHEST EXPERIENCES OF OUR LIVES.

At its most basic, bird gardening is planting trees, shrubs, and flowers on your property to attract birds. In a larger sense, it is trying to restore a diversity of habitats to the American landscape for the health of all living things, including ourselves.

Bird gardening helps birds to survive by providing all kinds of food. It also helps birds breed by providing nesting spots. For us humans, there is a joy that comes from bird gardening: getting to see the birds. It also teaches you about the native plants on your own property and what benefit they are to the birds.

Bird gardening is active participation in conservation. By improving and diversifying the habitats in your own backyard, you are helping restore some of the natural environment.

Gardening Basics

Undoubtedly, you want to get started right away attracting more birds to your property. Whether you are an expert or a beginner at gardening, there are some bird-friendly features to consider before you begin. You will be happy to know that no matter what the season or the size of your property, there are things that you can do now to begin making your garden an attractive, appealing place for birds.

GETTING STARTED

The most important concept in attracting birds is variety. Birds live in different habitats, and the greater the variety of habitats you create in your yard, the more birds you will attract. An important goal in creating different habitats is offering food and nest sites at all levels. There are basically four levels you should try to create:

- **Grass or groundcover level:** 2 inches to 1 foot high
- **Flower level:** 2 to 5 feet high
- **Small tree and shrub level:** 5 to 15 feet high
- **Tall tree level:** 15 to 40 feet high

To get started right away, try to add to your property whatever levels of vegetation are missing. Our property originally had only tall trees, so we have added lawn, shrubs, and small trees.

For those of you who are beginners at bird gardening, this chapter will introduce you to the basics of planning and planting your bird garden. You'll start by doing a brief inventory of your property, learn some helpful features of garden design, and then acquire some basic gardening skills.

INVENTORY YOUR PROPERTY

Here are some questions to ask yourself about your property that will help you evaluate which areas are already good for birds and which you can improve.

"What plants do I own?" Before adding or subtracting plants from your property, it is a good idea to know what you already have. What kinds of trees, shrubs, and flowers are already growing on your property? If you cannot identify them, get a knowledgeable friend to

This patch of garden contains plantings of varying heights as well as a birdbath, which can be a beautiful structure in any garden plan.

walk around your yard with you and help you name them, or use a good identification guide from your library or bookstore. Doing an inventory is a way to begin learning more about the native plants around you and realizing what value they may have for birds.

In addition, an inventory can save you money. You may already own some very helpful plants. Large trees, shrubs, and vines are especially valuable; if they must be replaced, you'll have to purchase smaller plants, often at considerable cost. So before cutting down what you might now consider "old bushes" and later discovering that they were berry-producing shrubs, first find out what they are.

"What habitats do I have?" Look at your property in terms of habitats; even a small property can have tremendous variety. Do you have a wooded area, lawn, or shrubs? Look at the soil to see where it may be rich and moist, where it's dry and poor. Notice where the sun rises and sets and where it shines on your property at midday. Even the position of your house can create different habitats on the shady side and sunny side.

Note where birds seem to be on your property now, including the areas they use in different seasons. All of these things are important to be aware of as you go about placing feeders and birdhouses and adding plants to your garden.

"What is next to my property?" Birds don't know where your property starts and ends. When deciding whether to stay, they look

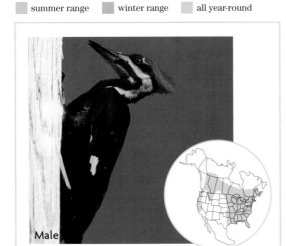

summer range   winter range   all year-round

Male

What's That Bird?

PILEATED WOODPECKER

ID Clues: Large, 18-inch crow-size bird; mostly black with a bright red crest and white stripes across the cheeks and down the neck

Habitat: Mature forests, suburbs with large trees

Food: Carpenter ants in large trees, insects, fruit; suet at feeders

Nests: Excavates in dead wood 15 to 70 feet high

may also influence what you decide to do on your property. For example, if you live next to a wooded park, then you may not need to add woods; you can add open space instead.

You may also want to cooperate with neighbors to make certain kinds of habitats larger. A patch of blackberries could extend across two properties and be bigger and more attractive. An oak tree on one property could be matched by an oak on the adjacent property, creating a greater mass of acorns and nesting habitat. On smaller properties, where many backyards meet, this is an excellent way to overcome the limitations of space and create a much larger bird garden that all the neighbors can enjoy.

GARDEN DESIGN

There is no reason why a bird garden cannot be beautiful as well as attract lots of birds. For those of you that are new to gardening and landscape design, here are a few ideas that may help make your garden and yard more pleasing.

Let the sun shine in. Plants need sun to grow and be productive. If you want plants that are healthy and produce a lot of food for the birds, give them the sunlight they need. If your property is completely wooded, take down some trees on the southern side to let in light. If you are planting tall trees, plant them on the north side where they will not reduce the sunlight on your property.

at a whole area and its resources. The size of the area depends on the species. A House Wren may look at only a small portion of an acre before deciding to stay, but a Downy Woodpecker will be looking at 20 to 40 acres, and a Pileated Woodpecker will need several square miles.

The land and habitats adjacent to your property and in your neighborhood will greatly affect the birds that come to your garden. They

Whether your property is large or small, create vistas so that you can see the birds and follow their activities in all seasons.

Create vistas. Try to create longer vistas from your house or from patios or seating areas that you frequent. When cutting down trees, create views; when planting trees, do not block views. These vistas can be good avenues for birds as they fly in and out of your property, and they also will enable you to see more birds and follow their activities.

Create varied heights of vegetation. In keeping with the idea of creating diversity on your property, remember the goal of having multiple layers of vegetation at roughly four different heights: tall trees; small trees and shrubs; flowers; and lawn or other groundcovers. Arrange these layers with the tallest features in the back and the lowest layers in the front. This will be attractive to look at and also allow you to see all of the different plants.

Get more than one of a plant. Many people, when starting out, buy just one of each flower or shrub, but it is often more attractive to birds—and people—if you group several of the same plant together. For example, one year we planted a single winterberry holly in a wet area of our property. It produced lots of beautiful red berries and attracted cardinals and Cedar Waxwings, which finished the berries off in a week. The next year, we found more hollies on sale and bought four smaller ones to make a much larger patch. It was more visible to

Quick Tip

Whether you're planting trees or cutting them down, keep the south side of your property open for better sunlight.

Create a natural effect on your property by imitating nature: Give flowerbeds natural, undulating borders and plant multiple layers of vegetation. This yard includes lawn, flowerbeds, shrubs, and trees all within a small area.

the birds, fed them for more than a month, and created a suitable nesting habitat the next spring.

Create a natural effect. When planting several of the same plant, place them together in odd numbers (threes, fives, and sevens) and in a naturalistic way, rather than in a straight line. When you create a woodland edge, make it an undulating border rather than just straight. In other words, make your yard and garden areas mirror the variety of nature.

Create plantings for year-round beauty. Most of us plant with only spring and summer in mind. When you're planning a garden for birds, also think about what your property will look like in fall and winter. Plant evergreen trees, shrubs, and groundcovers so there will be beauty, color, and shelter for birds in winter. Also look for shrubs and trees with colorful bark or interesting branching structure that will be pleasant to look at in winter.

BASIC GARDENING KNOW-HOW

Some of you may already be experienced gardeners. But for those of you who are just starting out, here are the basics skills of gardening.

THREE BASIC NEEDS OF PLANTS

Plants need sun, water, and nutrients to be healthy and productive. In the case of plants that provide food for birds, the more productive they are, the more birds they can feed.

Each plant has slightly different requirements for these three elements. Some plants need full sun, while others can survive well in partial shade. Some plants like to have their feet wet most of the time, and others prefer to live in porous soil and get watered every now and then. Some plants like rich soils; others are better adapted to lesser amounts of nutrients. When buying a plant, check with your nursery to find out its requirements.

PLANT ZONES

Each plant also has a certain climate to which it is adapted. The most important limiting factor in this regard is the minimum temperature in the coldest season. North America has been divided into plant zones based on this minimum temperature, and all plants are rated for the zones in which they do best. In the United States and Canada, Zone 1 is the coldest, and Zone 10 is the warmest. Zone 5 is typical of much of the Northeast, the Great Lakes states, and the mountain states. Average *minimum* winter temperatures in this zone are –10 to –20°F.

When choosing plants for your garden, check the map on page 42 to find out what zone you live in, and then pick plants that are hardy for your zone.

In the plant lists in subsequent chapters, we mention the region of the country in which each plant tends to be grown. If you pick plants from your region and your zone, they will be the easiest to buy and the easiest to grow successfully.

HOW TO PLANT A PLANT

When you buy a plant for your bird garden, you want to give it a good start. Much of this depends on planting it in a place where it will get the sun, water, and nutrients it needs—as well as how well you plant it.

Be sure that you have the correct tools on hand for gardening: a trowel, a shovel, and, if possible, a small wheelbarrow for lugging earth. Your plant, if it is fairly small, will come in a pot; if it is a shrub or small tree it may come with its roots in a ball of earth, wrapped in burlap or some other covering.

First, decide exactly where you want to put the plant by placing it in the spot and stepping back to check whether it looks good. Then, move the plant to the side and dig a hole a little deeper than the pot or rootball and about twice as wide.

Check the soil that you have taken out to see if it is the type of soil the plant needs. If the soil needs to be richer, mix it with some compost, which you can buy at a plant nursery. Put some of the soil back in the hole, take the plant out of the pot or unwrap its rootball, and place it in the hole.

Make sure that the plant sits at the right height in the hole; the level of the soil should come to the soil line on the plant (where the soil was in the pot, or the top of the rootball).

USDA Plant Hardiness Zones

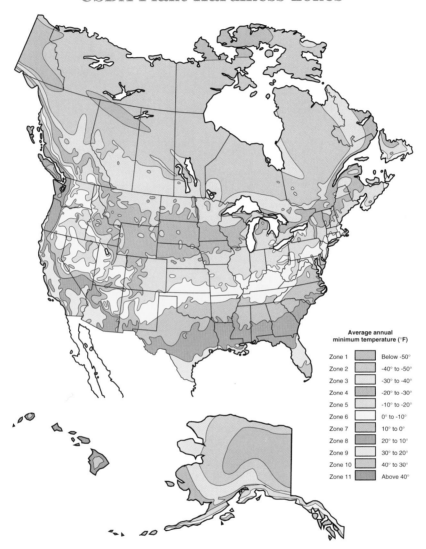

Average annual
minimum temperature (°F)

Zone 1	Below -50°
Zone 2	-40° to -50°
Zone 3	-30° to -40°
Zone 4	-20° to -30°
Zone 5	-10° to -20°
Zone 6	0° to -10°
Zone 7	10° to 0°
Zone 8	20° to 10°
Zone 9	30° to 20°
Zone 10	40° to 30°
Zone 11	Above 40°

Straighten the plant, and add soil to fill in the hole. Pack it down firmly enough to hold the plant in place, but not too hard, or water will have trouble getting to the roots. You can create a little well around the base of the plant to hold water and direct it to the roots.

Water the plant well. Continue to give the plant some water for the next few days; longer

Make sure that your plants get lots of sunlight, good soil, and adequate water, and they will produce more food, shelter, and nesting places for birds.

if the leaves show any wilting. If you want, add mulch—bark mulch, rotted leaves, or dried grass clippings—around the base of the plant to help conserve moisture in the soil and keep the plant from drying out.

CARING FOR PLANTS OVER TIME

If you do a good job gardening, your plants will grow vigorously. Amazingly, this is both a blessing and a curse. Healthy clumps of perennial flowers that were once well spaced may start to nudge one another's shoulders and compete. Successful shrubs and trees may create shade where there once was full sunlight.

For perennials, you can dig up the whole plant in fall or early spring and divide it into two or three parts with your shovel. Plant the divisions in a new area, or give them to a friend who wants to start a bird garden. In the case of shade trees and shrubs, either prune them back to let in sunlight, or move the plants in the newly shaded area to a spot that will be in the sun.

This is really one of our favorite features of bird gardening. Your property is always changing. You cannot hold a good and varied habitat at one stage of growth. It will mature, and you have to adjust with it and learn from it.

Flowers That Attract Birds

There are lots of common and uncommon flowers—asters, blazing stars, love-in-a-mist, marigolds, and zinnias—that look lovely in your yard and garden, but to birds, they're so much more than just another pretty feature. Flowers provide food, shelter, nesting materials, and more to birds—and not just when they're in bloom.

FLOWERS FOR FOOD AND MORE

The main attraction of flowers for birds is the seeds they produce. From late summer through winter, many flowers have dried stalks that remain standing to disperse their seeds. Most of the species that do this, such as goldenrod, aster, sunflower, and cosmos, are members of the Compositae family that produce many seeds on each flower head. This is why the birds love them—they can land at one spot and feast on the abundance of seeds.

Some flowers, like sedums and goldenrods, typically attract a lot of insects. These, in turn, attract insect-eating birds like warblers and flycatchers. A few flowering plants—baneberry, bunchberry, and jack-in-the-pulpit—produce berries, but their berry production is small compared to that of most shrubs and trees.

A natural bird feeder, a sunflower will attract jays, grosbeaks, cardinals, chickadees, goldfinches, and many other birds.

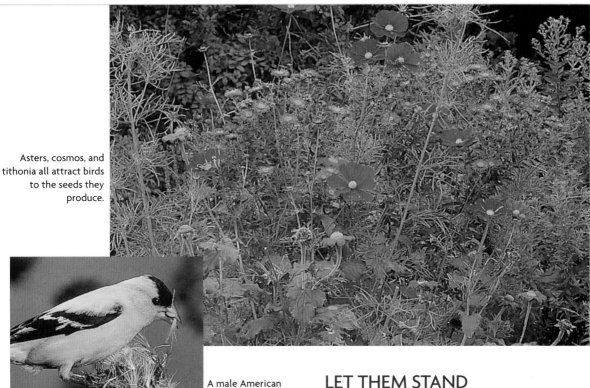

Asters, cosmos, and tithonia all attract birds to the seeds they produce.

A male American Goldfinch grabs some downy thistle filaments for a nest.

Wild strawberries are an exception: They produce a lot of fruit early and many birds do love them (of course, so do we).

A few flowers, like milkweeds, provide nesting material. We grow swamp milkweed in our perennial garden and let the stalks stand in the garden through winter until the following spring. The bark begins to peel off over winter, and in spring orioles pull off long strands to weave their suspended nests. We also have a wild stand of dogbane in our field; it is a relative of milkweed and birds also use it for nesting material.

LET THEM STAND

Many gardeners have the inclination to "tidy up" the garden in fall when blooming has stopped, cutting down all the stalks. But this is just when your bird garden is getting started. The standing stalks are full of seeds for the birds, and the birds will love it if you leave the stalks alone. In our garden, we leave our purple coneflower, black-eyed Susans, Joe-pye weed, ironweed, cosmos, and coreopsis standing all winter and, as a result, we can always find birds in our "winter garden."

In some cases, you never quite know which plants will be attractive to the birds. Last fall, we had up to 10 goldfinches all feeding at once on our Joe-pye weed. One fall during migration, we had Yellow-rumped Warblers on our many sedums—up to three at a time on the *Sedum* 'Autumn Joy,' apparently eating insects or insect eggs from the underside of its flower heads.

ANNUAL, BIENNIAL, PERENNIAL

Herbaceous flowers have three basic life cycles, and it is good to be familiar with them so that you can plan where and when your flowers will grow from year to year.

Annuals live only one year and must grow from seed each year. Biennials live two years, flower in the second year, and then die. Perennials continue to grow for many years but usually die back above ground each winter and remain alive as roots.

GO WILD OR NOT SO WILD

There are both wildflowers and cultivated flowers that attract birds with their numerous seeds.

What's That Bird?
SCISSOR-TAILED FLYCATCHER

ID Clues: A very long split tail gives this 14-inch bird away; pale gray body with pinkish flanks; males and females look alike

Habitat: Open areas with scattered trees

Food: Insects caught in air or picked off ground

Nests: Nest of soft plant materials placed in tree or on telephone pole crossbar

Great Bird Garden Flowers

Annuals
Bachelor's-buttons (*Centaurea cyanus*)
Cosmos (*Cosmos* spp.)
Sunflowers (*Helianthus* spp.)
Love-in-a-mist (*Nigella damascena*)
Marigolds (*Tagetes* spp.)
Mexican sunflower (*Tithonia rotundifolia*)
Zinnias (*Zinnia* spp.)

Biennials
Poppies (*Papaver* spp.)

Perennials
Asters (*Aster* spp.)
Coreopsis (*Coreopsis* spp.)
Purple coneflowers (*Echinacea* spp.)
Globe thistles (*Echinops* spp.)
Joe-pye weeds (*Eupatorium* spp.)
Wild strawberry (*Fragaria virginiana*)
Blazing stars (*Liatris* spp.)
Black-eyed Susans (*Rudbeckia* spp.)
Scabiosas (*Scabiosa* spp.)
Sedums (*Sedum* spp.)
Goldenrods (*Solidago* spp.)
Ironweed (*Vernonia novaeboracensis*)

A bird-friendly garden can be beautiful to us as well as great for the birds. This garden has butterflyweed, salvia, and verbena for hummingbirds and yarrow and Joe-pye weed to produce seeds for finches.

Some good wildflowers include goldenrod, yarrow, and aster. We have little patches of our property that we leave wild and let the plants grow. But even these areas need some management, or the shrubs will grow too tall and the wild grasses will take over. We keep our eye on them to be sure that the bird plants we want to grow there are healthy and productive.

There are some other good wildflowers that are so lovely we put them directly in our gardens. These include ironweed, coreopsis, and purple coneflower. We also put in many cultivars of these wild plants because they bloom longer and are more prolific. These include va-

Purple coneflower is not only beautiful all summer, its seedheads provide food for finches and other seed-eating birds all winter.

rieties of yarrow, aster, black-eyed Susans, and Joe-pye weeds.

There are also some strictly cultivated plants that we either grow from seed or buy from nurseries. Some of our favorites are cosmos, zinnias, and marigolds. These three are all annuals and need to be replaced each year.

Shrubs That Attract Birds

Shrubs are woody plants that usually grow between 3 and 15 feet tall. They are most often found growing naturally at the edge of woods, as the understory in woodlands, in open areas such as fields, and along roads, streams, and seacoasts. Shrubs are extremely important to birds and one of the keys to creating a bird-friendly habitat.

THE IMPORTANCE OF SHRUBS

Wherever there are lots of shrubs, there is a good chance there are lots of birds as well: Shrubs provide food, nest sites, and shelter for birds—in other words, just about everything they need. Most backyard habitats do not have enough shrubs for birds to use, but that can be easily remedied. Adding just a few shrubs will attract more birds quickly.

ADDING SHRUBS THAT PRODUCE BERRIES, PROVIDE GOOD NESTING STRUCTURE, AND SERVE AS PROTECTIVE COVER IS A QUICK WAY TO ATTRACT MORE BIRDS.

SHRUBS THAT PROVIDE FOOD

Shrubs produce a variety of food—berries, seeds, and nectar—and they also attract insects that birds eat. You can never have too many productive shrubs on your property.

Different species of shrubs produce berries at varying times of year. When planning your backyard habitat, try to make berries available to the birds in each season. Plants like honeysuckle, shadbush, and chokecherry produce berries early in summer. Good mid- to late-summer berry-producing shrubs are blackberry, blueberry, huckleberry, and elderberry. Shrubs that produce berries in fall include bayberry, viburnum, juniper, holly, and manzanita.

Fall berries can be extremely important to migrating birds. This is particularly true of bayberry, which produces a waxy fruit with a high fat content. This berry enables many species

Q: Why do plants grow berries?
A: Berries contain both a fruit portion and seeds. The fruit attracts birds, who eat it for its sugar or fat content. The seeds, which they eat along with the fruit, then pass through the gut of bird and are dispersed with a little fertilizer in the dropping of the bird. Thus, berries act as seed dispersal mechanisms for the shrub (with help from birds).

Most berries are produced on shrubs, although a few trees and wildflowers also grow them. Berries are small fruits, and they may have evolved just for birds. They are colorful, relatively odorless, and grow at the tips of thin branches. This is perfect for birds: They see color, have little sense of smell for the most part, and are light enough to get to the tips of branches. Larger fruits such as apples, in contrast, probably evolved primarily for mammals. They are large, fall to the ground, and usually ferment, giving off a strong odor that attracts mammals that have a well-developed sense of smell.

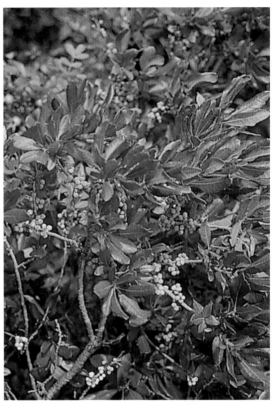

Shrubs produce fruit in different seasons. These bayberry fruits ripen in late summer, and many warblers and swallows take advantage of their high fat content to help fuel them on their fall migration.

that migrate along the coasts, such as warblers and swallows, to accumulate the fat reserves needed for their long journeys.

If you observe carefully, you will see that the berries produced by some shrubs—including sumac and rose—in fall are not eaten until winter. By also having these types of shrubs in your yard, you can offer birds berries all year.

In addition to producing berries, shrubs attract insects, which birds also eat. These include bees and flies that are attracted to pollen and nectar in the flowers, and caterpillars, beetles, and bugs that eat the leaves. These insects

are a major source of food and should not be exterminated. Birds especially need insects during breeding, when they feed them to their young as a source of protein.

A few shrubs produce seeds that birds eat. We have many alders growing in the wet areas of our property, and the goldfinches and Tree Sparrows feed on these seeds all winter.

There are also many shrubs that attract hummingbirds, which come to drink flower nectar; see "Create a Hummingbird Heaven in Your Backyard" on page 82.

SHRUBS AS NESTING SITES

Many backyard birds prefer to nest in shrubs. Shrubs offer sites that are off the ground but still protected from the winds and exposure associated with tall tree canopies. However, planting shrubs does not automatically provide nesting places for birds: The branching structure of the shrub has to be the right density to support the nest. If branching is too open or sparse, then there is no place to build the nest. This is true for many rhododendrons and some viburnums, which lack a three-way fork in the branches on which the bird can build the nest.

In other instances, the shrub may be so densely branched or full of thorns that the bird cannot get into the interior portion. We have had several barberry shrubs that were too dense, leaving no room for a nest, and we have had hawthorns that had many thorns too long for the birds to maneuver around.

Shrubs on our property that serve as nesting sites for birds include elderberry, rose, dog-

This male Eastern Bluebird is delivering an insect to either his mate while she incubates eggs or his young offspring.

Planting Berry-Bearing Bushes

When planting berry-producing shrubs, try to plant three to five of each variety. This will ensure a substantial quantity of berries that will outlast the first flock of birds.

Shrubs can produce many more berries if they get enough sunlight and are not overcrowded. Prune back competing plants, as well as any trees that may be shading your shrubs too much. These steps may double the berry production, resulting in a tremendous help to the birds. In other cases, when a shrub is too crowded or not growing vigorously, you may need to transplant it to a more suitable part of your property.

The placement of shrubs is also important for providing good nesting sites. Lone shrubs in the middle of an open area are not as attractive as groupings, or plantings with trees or tall wildflowers. These groupings of plants offer more protection from the elements and predators and a greater area in which birds can gather food.

A male cardinal plucks some fruit, one of the many riches birds glean from shrubbery.

Male

What's That Bird?

VARIED THRUSH

ID Clues: At 8 inches, similar in size and appearance to a robin, but with orange wing bars and eyebrow and a black (gray on female) breastband

Habitat: Moist coniferous woods

Food: Earthworms, insects on ground, spiders, snails, seeds, berries

Nests: Nest of twigs and moss placed on horizontal limb

wood, alder, and willow. Some birds, such as Yellow Warblers, also collect the fluffy seed dispersal filaments from willows and use them as the main material for their nest in spring.

SHRUBS AS SHELTER

Shrubs give welcome protection from wind, rain, cold, snow, and predators. Obviously, evergreen shrubs provide year-round shelter. We plant rhododendrons near our bird feeders, and the birds fly into them as a first stop before coming to the feeders. They dart for cover among them when they perceive danger in the area. Many ground-feeding species, such as towhees, thrushes, and native sparrows, also like to

Quick Tip

Select shrubs with dense, thornless branches that fork at least three ways. These features encourage nest building.

scratch around beneath them in the fallen leaves to look for seeds or insects.

Other evergreen shrubs that are good for shelter include juniper and holly (which also produce berries), laurel, and leucothoe. Deciduous shrubs are equally important as summer shelter for all of our nesting birds, providing protection from sun, relief from heat, and safe places for fledglings to perch while waiting for their parents to arrive with food.

The Best Shrubs for Attracting Birds

When shrub names are plural (for example, dogwoods), you can choose any species within that group. When names are singular (for example, American beautyberry), that is the only species in that genus that you should use. Region refers to the part of the continent where the plant grows best.

Shrub	Region
Early-Summer Berries	
Shadbushes, serviceberries (*Amelanchier* spp.)	All
Manzanitas (*Arctostaphylos* spp.)	NW, SW
Honeysuckles (*Lonicera* spp.)	All
Chokecherries (*Prunus* spp.)	All
Midsummer Berries	
Currants/gooseberries (*Ribes* spp.)	All
Blackberries, raspberries (*Rubus* spp.)	All
Elderberries (*Sambucus* spp.)	All
Buffaloberries (*Shepherdia* spp.)	NW, SW
Blueberries (*Vaccinium* spp.)	All
Fall Berries	
Madrone (*Arbutus menziesii*)	NW, SW
American beautyberry (*Callicarpa americana*)	SE
Dogwoods (*Cornus* spp.)	All
Euonymus (*Euonymus* spp.)	NE, SE
Mahonias (*Mahonia* spp.)	NW, SW
Wax myrtles, bayberries (*Myrica* spp.)	NE, SE
Redberry buckthorn (*Rhamnus crocea*)	SW
Viburnums (*Viburnum* spp.)	NE, SE, NW

Shrub	Region
Winter Berries	
Barberries (*Berberis* spp.)	All
Hollies (*Ilex* spp.)	NE, SE
Sumacs (*Rhus* spp.)	All
Roses (*Rosa* spp.)	NE, SE, NW
Shrubs for Nests	
Alders (*Alnus* spp.)	All
Saltbushes (*Atriplex* spp.)	SW
Redberry buckthorn (*Rhamnus crocea*)	SW
Roses (*Rosa* spp.)	All
Willows (*Salix* spp.)	All
Sages (*Salvia* spp.)	NW, SW
Elderberries (*Sambucus* spp.)	All
Spireas (*Spiraea* spp.)	NE, SE
Lilacs (*Syringa* spp.)	All
Yews (*Taxus* spp.)	NE, NW
Shrubs for Shelter	
Manzanitas (*Arctostaphylos* spp.)	NW, SW
Junipers (*Juniperus* spp.)	All
Leucothoes (*Leucothoe* spp.)	NE, SE, NW
Mahonias (*Mahonia* spp.)	NW, SW
Redberry buckthorn (*Rhamnus crocea*)	SW
Rhododendrons (*Rhododendron* spp.)	NE, SE, NW
Shrubs with Seeds	
Alders (*Alnus* spp.)	All

Vines That Attract Birds

There are many varieties of vines, including poison ivy, that help birds thrive. Vines, like shrubs, fulfill multiple needs of backyard birds. Even the smallest yard has room for a vine or two—and a single vine, trained up a corner of the house or a fencepost—can provide food, shelter, nesting material, and more for your feathered friends.

HOW VINES WORK

Woody vines are an interesting type of plant—they cannot support themselves adequately so they grow tall enough to compete for sunlight. Therefore, they use larger structures—including manmade ones as well as shrubs and trees—for support as they seek out the sunlight they need.

Thus, every vine needs a way to hold on to its supporting structure. Some vines, like honeysuckle and bittersweet, twine around their supports. Other vines, like catbrier and grape, have tendrils that wrap around smaller branches and supports. And a few vines, such as poison ivy and Virginia creeper, grow rootlike structures that actually attach to their supports with little roots or adhesive disks.

Quick Tip

Hammer in a few nails or place some fine netting on a fence that is too smooth for a vine to otherwise climb.

VINES THAT PROVIDE FOOD

Many of our vines produce berries that birds love. These include Virginia creeper, honeysuckle, catbrier, grape, and poison ivy. On our property we encourage catbrier, Virginia creeper, and grape, and we tolerate poison ivy in restricted areas where it will not harm anyone.

Interestingly, of these vines, the most popular among birds is poison ivy, which produces large quantities of small white berries in the fall. It seems strange that a plant so toxic to our skin when we touch it does not bother the birds at all. At least 55 species of North American birds are known to eat poison ivy fruits. The birds, of course, disperse the seeds in their droppings, and this is why poison ivy seems to grow everywhere we don't want it.

Virginia creeper is a good native vine that produces lots of blue berries in fall, when its leaves also turn brilliant red.

A female Ruby-throated Hummingbird looks into the gorgeous flowers of a trumpet creeper vine.

There are a few vines that are also favorites of hummingbirds because they offer nectar for the birds to eat. These include trumpet honeysuckle and trumpet vine. As their names suggest, both have long, tubular red flowers that are especially attractive to hummingbirds.

NEST SITES AND SHELTER

On our property we have a wonderful area filled with catbrier. The catbrier grows up the trees and has created a dense thicket that is impenetrable by us. To many, it might look like an overgrown and untended area, but we know it is a haven for birds. There are always birds in and among the stems, sunning, resting, and feeding on the berries or on the ground beneath. And when winter comes and all the leaves fall off the vines, we always see one or more nests that were built and used during the previous summer. It is a good, safe place for the birds.

Another important use of vines is as nest material. Grapevines have bark that peels off easily and is very flexible. The bark is also easy to split into finer strands. Many birds take advantage of these properties and use the bark as part of their nests. Catbirds, mockingbirds, and cardinals use it in the main structure of their nests, and smaller birds, such as goldfinches, vireos, and sparrows, use finer strands for their nest linings. It is worth having grapevines just for their attractiveness as a nesting material.

MANAGING VINES

Vines, by their very nature, are slightly unmanageable—they spread by climbing up other plants and, in some cases, shading them out. The best place to have vines is on some part of

The Best Vines for Attracting Birds

When vine names are plural (for example, honeysuckles), you can choose any species within that group. When names are singular (for example, bittersweet), that is the only species in that genus that you should use. Region refers to the part of the continent where the plant grows best.

Vine	Region
Best Vines with Berries	
Supplejack (*Berchemia scandens*)	SE
Bittersweet (*Celastrus scandens*)	NE, SE
Carolina snailseed (*Cocculus carolinus*)	NE, SE
Honeysuckles (*Lonicera* spp.)	All
Virginia creepers (*Parthenocissus* spp.)	All
Poison ivy (*Toxicodendron radicans*)	All
Greenbriers (*Smilax* spp.)	NE, SE, NW
Grapes (*Vitis* spp.)	All
Best Vines for Shelter, Nests, and Nesting	
Greenbriers (*Smilax* spp.)	NE, SE
Grapes (*Vitis* spp.)	All
Best Vines for Hummingbirds	
Coral vine (*Antigonon leptopus*)	SE
Cross vine (*Bignonia capreolata*)	SE
Trumpet vine (*Campsis radicans*)	NE, SE
Trumpet honeysuckle (*Lonicera sempervirens*)	All

your property where you do not mind if they take over, such as up a dying tree or as part of a hedgerow.

Another great way to use vines is along a fence, especially a chain-link or other less-than-attractive fence. The vines will use the support, hide the fence, and be a resource for the birds. Vines on a fence can also create a screen from another area, such as a compost pile, and hide that area in the summer months when you are most often outside.

We grow honeysuckle vines for hummingbirds along a split-rail fence and on teepees made of garden stakes. In the garden, prune them back frequently to keep them under control. We also have grapevines in our hedgerow and American bittersweet growing along a wire-mesh fence.

Trees That Attract Birds

Trees are the backbone of many yards, especially in older neighborhoods where trees have been growing for decades. Keep in mind that while trees provide all the basic needs of the birds in your yard, they also clean your air, shade your yard and home, act as windbreaks for your gardens, and serve as homes to many other types of wildlife—all part of a healthy, flourishing ecosystem, right in your yard.

TREES THAT SUPPLY FOOD

Trees supply a vast variety of foods for birds, not only because of the seeds, fruits, and nuts that they produce, but also because of the insects they attract.

Small seeds. Many trees, such as birches, have extremely small seeds that are produced in catkins at the tips of the branches. Small birds, like goldfinches, Pine Siskins, and redpolls, are light enough to hold onto (but not break off) the tips of the fine branches as they have their lunch.

Large seeds. Most trees produce larger seeds. These include elms, tulip poplars, ashes, and many of the coniferous evergreens such as hemlock, pine, spruce, and fir. Ash and tulip poplar seeds are fodder for birds with large conical beaks specially designed for shelling off the husk of these seeds. Cardinals and gros-

beaks, like the Evening Grosbeak, often can be found in the tops of these trees, seemingly glued to the branches as they pick off, shell, and eat the tree seeds one after another.

The seeds in some conifers present a real challenge to birds because they are inside a tough-scaled cone that protects the seeds. To get the seeds, the birds have to first pry apart the scales. Some birds, such as crossbills, have

Mountain ashes produce a lot of berries in northern latitudes, helping birds survive the cold.

Flowering dogwoods are not only one of our most beautiful native trees, they also produce red fruits that birds, like this Blue Jay, eat in late summer.

This male Eastern Bluebird is one of many birds that depend on berries, like those on this holly tree, to get through the winter.

bills with crossed tips that can pry apart the scales of cones; they then reach in with their tongues to get the seeds. Seeds in smaller cones, like those of hemlocks, can be eaten directly out of the cone by birds like chickadees, nuthatches, and titmice.

Berries. Many trees produce berries or larger fruits. Berry-producing trees include mountain ash, dogwood, cherry, mulberry, and manzanita, to name just a few. These trees often produce larger quantities of berries than shrubs do and can be a good source of food over a long period of time. Most trees produce berries that ripen in fall and are available to birds in fall and winter. A few, such as cherry and mulberry, develop berries earlier and are useful in attracting large flocks of birds in mid- to late summer.

Nuts. Some trees produce large nuts that birds eat. The most important and widespread of these are the oaks. Acorns are a main staple in the diet of Wood Ducks, jays, grackles, thrashers, and some woodpeckers. One problem with oaks is some years have a heavy production of nuts, while others are sparse. Many birds, such as Mexican Jays and Acorn Woodpeckers, take the acorns and store them

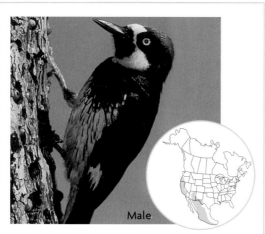

Male

What's That Bird?
ACORN WOODPECKER

ID Clues: About 8 inches long with black surrounding the beak and white on the forehead, chin, wings (just a patch), and rump
Habitat: Oak and pine woods, parks, suburbs
Food: Mostly acorns cached in drilled holes, insects, tree sap; suet at feeders
Nests: Excavates in dead or live trees

Catkins of some trees attract lots of flies and other small insects. This is particularly true of oaks, whose flowers bloom in spring, when warblers migrate through most of the lower 48 states. On our property we have made a point of saving lots of oaks and, as a result, we get to see many warbler species in spring.

Oak leaves also attract numerous species of flies and wasps that form galls—small deformations of the plant growth that insects live inside. These galls occur all summer and fall, and chickadees, woodpeckers, and other small birds peck them open to get at the insects. More galls form on oaks than on any other group of plants.

Many insects use bark crevices as a protected place to lay their eggs, develop, or overwinter. Birds like nuthatches, chickadees, warblers, woodpeckers, creepers, and wrens repeatedly search every inch of tree bark for these insects. Oak, hickory, cherry, cottonwood, and ash trees have furrowed bark that attracts insects and thus the birds. Trees with smooth or continuously peeling bark, like birch, beech, and cedar, may be less productive in this way.

Many trees also create a lot of debris, such as leaves, flower parts, and seeds, on the ground. This leaf litter provides a good place for beetles, ants, and other insects to live. Sparrows, towhees, grackles, thrushes, and quail like to scratch around underneath trees for seeds and insects.

in the ground or the crevices of trees. Acorn Woodpeckers make their living this way, actually excavating holes in trees or buildings and jamming the acorns into them.

Insects. Trees are also essential for birds because of the insects they attract. Many birds, such as warblers, vireos, and orioles, glean insects off the tree leaves and flowers. All trees have flowers, but many are inconspicuous and appear in the form of tassels called catkins.

These new Blue Jays are nestled securely among strong tree branches.

TREES FOR NESTING BIRDS

Trees help birds nest in a variety of ways. Their branches are sturdy nest supports. Crows and hawks nest in the crotches of large branches where they split off from the trunk. Robins, tanagers, grosbeaks, and other birds their size prefer to nest farther out, often where several smaller branches grow off a larger branch and provide a good platform. Vireos and orioles like to nest even farther out; they suspend their nests beneath the finer branch tips.

Trees are also the main home for cavity-nesting birds. Woodpeckers are the primary excavators of these holes. Downy Woodpeckers prefer to excavate in dead wood, while Hairy Woodpeckers usually excavate in live wood. It is important to keep a mix of both dead and live limbs on standing trees, as long as it is safe for humans.

After woodpeckers make the holes, other birds like bluebirds, wrens, Tree Swallows, and nuthatches use the abandoned holes for their own nests. Thus, any tree hole on your property is important to keep, for many birds may use it in successive years.

Some trees have a tendency to rot where branches have broken off; some suffer from decay in their heartwood. This provides softer wood where cavity-nesting birds like chickadees may be able to excavate their own nest

61

Evergreen trees, such as pines, produce cones with seeds that birds like this Black-capped Chickadee eat. Evergreen trees also provide shelter and seem to attract overwintering insects, which chickadees, nuthatches, kinglets, and creepers continually glean.

hole. Trees with this characteristic include birch, apple, ash, oak, poplar, aspen, and willow. Birch and cedar, as well as a few other species, have fine, peeling bark, and many birds gather this off the tree trunk to use in their nests.

TREES FOR SHELTER

Trees are also an important way of providing shelter for the birds on your property. Of course, evergreens provide year-round shelter for birds from cold, rain, and snow; hidden places for nests; hiding places from predators; and even daytime roosts, such as where an owl might hide for the day out of sight from harassing crows and jays.

Evergreens are also ideal when planted along the north side of your property. In winter, they protect feeders from the north winds and also absorb the low southern sun, creating a warmer, more appealing mini-habitat for the birds on the south side.

Trees can also be planted as a windbreak or snowbreak between two fields and become a place where the birds can take advantage of the food in the fields while still having the protection of the trees.

The Best Trees for Attracting Birds

Try to have trees from all five of these categories in your yard, and maximize diversity whenever possible. When tree names are plural (for example, pines) you can choose any species within that group. When names are singular (red mulberry, for example), that is the only species in that genus that you should use. Region refers to the general area in which the plant grows best. Check with your local nursery for more detailed growing conditions in your specific location.

Tree	Region
Best Fruit Trees	
Madrones (*Arbutus* spp.)	NW, SW
Hackberries (*Celtis* spp.)	All
Dogwoods (*Cornus* spp.)	NE, SE
Hawthorns (*Crataegus* spp.)	NE, SE, NW
Strangler fig (*Ficus aurea*)	SE
Hollies, possumhaws (*Ilex* spp.)	NE, SE
Junipers, red cedars (*Juniperus* spp.)	All
Crabapples (*Malus* spp.)	NE, SE, NW
Red mulberry (*Morus rubra*)	All
Cherries (*Prunus* spp.)	All
Cabbage palm (*Sabal palmetto*)	SE
Mountain ashes (*Sorbus* spp.)	NE, SE, NW
Best Seed Trees	
Firs (*Abies* spp.)	NE, NW, SW
Maples, box elders (*Acer* spp.)	All
Birches (*Betula* spp.)	NE, SE, NW
Ashes (*Fraxinus* spp.)	NE, SE
Larches (*Larix* spp.)	NE, NW
Tulip tree (*Liriodendron tulipifera*)	NE, SE
Spruces (*Picea* spp.)	All
Pines (*Pinus* spp.)	All
Hemlocks (*Tsuga* spp.)	NE, NW

Tree	Region
Best Shelter Trees	
Firs (*Abies* spp.)	NE, NW, SW
Junipers (*Juniperus* spp.)	All
Spruces (*Picea* spp.)	All
Pines (*Pinus* spp.)	All
Mesquites (*Prosopis* spp.)	SW
Hemlocks (*Tsuga* spp.)	NE, NW
Best Cavity Trees	
Birches (*Betula* spp.)	NE, SE, NW
Ashes (*Fraxinus* spp.)	NE, SE
Apples (*Malus* spp.)	NE, SE, NW
Sycamores (*Platanus* spp.)	All
Aspens, cottonwoods (*Populus* spp.)	All
Poplars (*Populus* spp.)	NE, NW
Oaks (*Quercus* spp.)	All
Willows (*Salix* spp.)	NE, SE
Best Nut Trees	
Oaks (*Quercus* spp.)	All

Healthy Lawns, Healthy Birds

Just like the trees, shrubs, and flowers around your yard, lawn areas are part of the multidimensional environment that birds need. Lawns provide open areas where birds can safely look for seeds, insects, and earthworms. But lawns are good for birds only if they are healthy, contain diverse plants, and are free of pesticides. In this chapter, we will give you many tips to make your lawn areas "bird-friendly."

HOW TO MAKE YOUR LAWN HEALTHIER

There are many ways to improve the health of your lawn and many reasons for doing so—you'll spend less time and money trying to keep it green and have more enjoyment from the birds that come to it. Plus, you'll feel good knowing you are helping, rather than harming, the environment.

CATBIRDS, CROWS, DOVES, SOME DUCKS, NORTHERN FLICKERS, GEESE, GRACKLES, MOCKINGBIRDS, ROBINS, SPARROWS, AND THRUSHES ALL LIKE TO VISIT LAWNS.

BETTER MOWING HABITS

First, set your mower to the highest setting that is right for your type of grass; this is 2½ to 3 inches for most grasses in the Northeast and upper Midwest. (Check a basic gardening book for mowing heights of other grasses.) Taller grass conserves moisture, encourages root growth and new grass shoots, produces more food for the plant, and creates a richer environment for insects and invertebrates that birds might like. We keep mowed areas around our bluebird houses, and this is one of the reasons they nest on our property: Bluebirds favor grass areas so they can sit on a perch, look for insects below, then dive down to get the insects and fly back to their perch.

Next, keep your mower blade sharp. You can tell if it is sharp by looking at the tops of your grass blades after mowing. If they are frayed, it is dull; if cleanly cut, then it is sharp. Cleanly

Robins often feed on lawns. Chemical fertilizers can change the acidity of your lawn so that earthworms no longer want to live there. Using organic fertilizer creates a good soil for earthworms and will make your lawn bird friendly.

cut grass reduces the loss of moisture in the grass and helps prevent the entrance of diseases into the plant.

Third, use a mower that automatically mulches the cut grass pieces by chopping them up. This will continually enrich the soil of your lawn as these tiny clippings decompose. Grass clippings do not create thatch; if they are short, they start to decompose within 1 week, and they feed nitrogen back to the grass by the second week.

Finally, mow your grass only when it needs it, rather than on a particular day of the week. Don't cut off more than one-third the length of the grass.

CREATING GOOD SOIL

Your lawn is only as good as the soil beneath it. Healthy soil will have the correct acidity (pH), contain organic nutrients and organisms that eat the grass clippings and thatch, and be airy, rather than compacted.

Check the acidity of your lawn soil with a little kit from your lawn and garden store. It should be have a pH between 6 and 7. If it is more acid or more alkaline than this, then the grass will not be able to absorb the nutrients in the soil, no matter how much fertilizer you add.

A pH of 6 to 7 is also important for encouraging a lawn full of microorganisms, such as bacteria and fungi, and larger invertebrates,

From spring through fall, bluebirds feed mainly on insects that they collect from short grass areas such as lawns. If you apply chemicals to kill weeds or insects in your lawn, it is very likely that you will harm the birds that feed there, such as this male Western Bluebird.

especially earthworms. These living creatures help break down thatch, grass clippings, and old roots into nutrients for the grass; they aerate the soil; and they enrich the soil with their own decomposition.

Add organic nutrients and beneficial microbes to the soil, either through the use of an organic fertilizer that may contain organisms or by spreading a thin layer (⅜ inch) of compost over the lawn. Chemical and synthetic fertilizers can actually harm the grass in the long run. While they give the grass a quick boost of green, they encourage surface root growth, which can lead to soil compaction, and they acidify the soil, making it inhospitable for earthworms and many other organisms. These

fertilizers have primarily soluble nitrogen, which quickly dissolves and leaches down through or runs off the soil, out of reach of the grass. Organic fertilizers have slower-acting nutrients that the grass uses gradually, and very little is lost into the water system.

The final way to help your soil is to keep it from getting compacted. Compacted soil does not let air or water penetrate and reach the grass roots. This creates stressed and unhealthy grass and also discourages the presence of microorganisms and earthworms. If you have regular routes that you use across your lawn that get compacted through walking, consider making them a path of pebbles or stone. The grass is beautiful, the path is easier to walk on, and you do not have an area of unhealthy lawn.

CHOOSING THE RIGHT GRASS FOR THE RIGHT LOCATION

There are two aspects of location to consider: your climate, and the specific area or microclimate on your property where you want lawn. There are many types of grass available, and each area of the country is best suited to certain types. The main types of grasses in northern climates include ryegrasses, fescues, and bluegrasses, which come in many varieties. In the South, the best grasses include Bermudagrass, bahai grass, blue gramagrass, buffalograss, carpetgrass, and zoysia grasses. (Check with a local nursery or garden store for picking the best grass for your area.)

Green-and-gold is a native wildflower that forms a beautiful groundcover and lawn alternative. In addition, the birds feed on the seeds that mature from the flowerheads.

In addition, there are special grasses available that are more resistant to insects. They have a fungus, called endophyte, which lives within them and makes them unpalatable to many lawn pests. Some grasses, such as ryegrasses and fescues, can be bred with the fungus already in the seeds. We use endophytically treated grasses on our property and they are wonderful.

NO PESTICIDES

If you want birds, avoid the use of all pesticides that contain chemicals harmful to birds. Even though many of these pesticides have been approved by government agencies, most experts agree that testing has not been thorough enough and many pesticide chemicals are strongly implicated as causing cancer and birth defects in humans, not to mention birds and smaller, more susceptible animals.

Before you or anyone else, like a lawn-care company, puts any chemical on your lawn, be sure that it is not dangerous to wildlife or you. This is one of the most important things that you can do to keep birds safe and protect the health of your local environment.

THE NO-GRASS LAWN

There are many ways to reduce the amount of lawn on your property and attract more birds at the same time. By doing this you are freed

This looks like ordinary grass, but it is actually full of a wide variety of plants, including clover, dandelions, sorrel, yarrow, and other wildflowers. It is low maintenance and creates a varied habitat for insect and animal life on which birds can feed.

What's That Bird?
WESTERN MEADOWLARK

ID Clues: A 9-inch bird with brownish back, bright yellow underparts, and a black V-shaped neck stripe; eastern species has slightly less yellow on cheek; males and females look alike

Habitat: Meadows, grasslands

Food: Insects and seeds on ground

Nests: Builds a domed nest of grasses on ground in tall-grass areas

from the extra time spent maintaining your lawn, and you will have more time to watch the birds you have attracted.

One of the best ways to accomplish this is by planting groundcovers that also produce berries. On our property, we use creeping junipers, bearberry, cotoneaster, and lowbush blueberries to fill in areas where lawn once was. You can also plant shrubs valuable to birds in some area of your yard where you have trouble growing grass, and then mulch under-neath them to keep weeds from growing. These areas can be very attractive at the edges of lawns and are a great resource for the birds.

THE PERFECT LAWN

What is the perfect lawn? It's a matter of opinion. Some may think that the perfect lawn is like an unblemished golf green. Others may say that the perfect lawn is artificial grass. Still others may say that the perfect lawn is one that you do not have to maintain.

We have many types of lawns on our property. We have one area of field that we mow for the bluebirds, and it has other plants besides grasses—dandelions, sorrel, plantain, daisies, wild carrot, and hawkweed, to mention a few. This is our idea of the perfect lawn for bluebirds and other field birds. It is rich in diversity, produces seeds of many kinds, contains many different plants that different insects utilize, and never needs fertilizer, water, or weeding.

We have another area of grass that connects our house to the field, and we grow some tough fescues in here. They are fine-bladed and feel good on bare feet in summer. We fertilize them with an organic fertilizer once a year in fall, but we never water them, for they are fairly drought-resistant.

We also have a small area of grass near our perennial flowerbeds that we like to look like a carpet of green. We have planted some good perennial ryegrasses there; we top-dress the area with compost once a year and weed it by hand. This is the perfect lawn for this small garden area.

So, be open to having different types of "perfect lawns" all over your property.

Good "Weeds"

"Weed" is not a botanical category; it's a relative term. Some people say a weed is any plant growing where you do not want it to grow. By this logic, even a rose might be called a weed if it were growing in the middle of your lawn. Indeed, many plants we call weeds in North America are valued in other parts of the world for food or as beautiful plants in the flower garden.

HOW CAN WEEDS BE GOOD?

While taking our bird gardening course, a participant once asked us, "I have a weedy area on my property and I do not know whether to get rid of it or leave it. How can I tell if the weeds are good for the birds?" The answer is that weeds can be good if they provide food or nesting areas for birds and they are not so aggressive that they crowd out native species of plants.

"GOOD" WEEDS PROVIDE FOOD OR NESTING AREAS FOR BIRDS *AND* DON'T CROWD OUT OTHER PLANTS.

Many plants that we often call weeds fit these requirements. And most of them are good for birds because they produce seeds. These include most of the upland weeds and all the

Encourage pokeweed on your property—the birds, like this catbird, love to eat the fruits that gradually mature throughout the last half of summer. It is a perennial and will continue to come up each year from the same spot.

Teasel (*left*) and mullein (*right*) are both "good" weeds. They provide lots of seeds for birds, and mullein attracts many overwintering insects, which this male Downy Woodpecker is probably looking for.

Good Weeds

Weed	Region
Annuals	
Pigweeds (*Amaranthus* spp.)	All
Ragweeds (*Ambrosia* spp.)	All
Goosefeet (*Chenopodium* spp.)	All
Filarees (*Erodium* spp.)	NW, SW
Sunflowers (*Helianthus* spp.)	All
Jewelweeds (*Impatiens* spp.)	NE, SE
Smartweeds (*Polygonum* spp.)	All
Biennials	
Thistles (*Cirsium* spp.)	All
Perennials	
Pokeweed (*Phytolacca americana*)	All
Dandelions (*Taraxacum* spp.)	All
Grasses	
Sedges (*Carex* spp.)	All
Crabgrasses (*Digitaria* spp.)	All
Panicgrasses (*Panicum* spp.)	All
Foxtails, bristlegrass (*Setaria* spp.)	All
Water Plants	
Smartweeds (*Polygonum* spp.)	All
Pondweeds (*Potamogeton* spp.)	All
Widgeongrass (*Ruppia maritima*)	All
Bulrushes (*Scirpus* spp.)	All
Cattails (*Typha* spp.)	All

grasses. A few common weeds also offer some other things for birds. Jewelweed provides nectar for the Ruby-throated Hummingbird in the East. Cattails provide roots and seeds for waterfowl, nesting supports for blackbirds, and sheltering cover for rails and other marsh birds. Thistles provide seeds and nesting material for goldfinches. Pondweed and widgeongrass provide food for ducks that feed on vegetation in ponds and lakes.

WEEDS ARE GOOD IN MANY PLACES

There are many places on your property where weeds can be kept for the benefit of the birds. Here are some spots where we encourage them—and you could, too.

Edges of property that are not mowed. We try to leave the grass tall so that the weeds have a chance to produce seeds.

Old garden bed that is not tended. The birds love it; all fall and winter it is a natural bird feeder that attracts lots of birds, including Dark-eyed Juncos and native sparrows. We often till the area each spring and let the weeds grow and go to seed.

Vegetable garden after harvesting. This area will produce weed seeds all winter for the birds. You can mulch over them in the spring to prevent them from sprouting anew early in the next season.

Bare spots around the property. These spots include compost and brush piles, as well as places where the snowplow, for example, has scraped away the grass.

Wet, marshy areas. We let the plants grow undisturbed and get many weeds, like smartweed and bulrush, growing there.

Areas that are mowed field grasses. They contain various "weeds" or wildflowers, such as foxtail and dandelion. We periodically let these grow long during summer, allow them to produce seeds, and then let the birds feed at will.

Invasive Exotics
and Natural Natives

Native species are plants (and animals) that have naturally grown and reproduced over a long period of time in a given habitat. Exotics are plants and animals that were taken from one geographical area and introduced into another as a result of human activity. To some extent, these terms are relative because they are based a certain time period and geographical area. While the history of life on earth has been one of continual movement of plants and animals into new areas, the movement of aggressive exotics is growing to a level some consider to be unacceptable.

GOOD PLANTS GONE BAD

Bioinvasion, the introduction of aggressive exotic species, can adversely affect the environment in several ways. For example, on our property, the shrub European buckthorn (*Rhamnus frangula*) has begun to invade the understory of our woods. It grows densely, crowds out other native woodland shrubs, shades out native woodland wildflowers—and produces berries that birds eat. The understory has become, in a few spots, a monoculture of European buckthorn.

Some might consider this a good thing; the plant produces berries that the birds eat, and hummingbirds drink nectar from its flowers. The problem is that it reduces the diversity of other plants in our forests and this, in turn, will eventually reduce the diversity of the animals that can live there.

Not all exotic species are a problem—some live in their new environment without taking over the entire surrounding area. But the exotic species that are wildly successful in their new habitat become dominant. In the Northeast and Upper Midwest of North America, the European buckthorn is crowding out many native species. The Southeast has many exotic plants; two of the most invasive (found only in Florida at the moment) are Brazilian pepper (*Schinus terebinthifolius*) and melaleuca (*Melaleuca quinquenervia*).

BIOINVASION IS A LEADING

DESTROYER OF NATURAL HABITATS,

SECOND ONLY TO DESTRUCTION

BY HUMANS.

Multiflora rose is imported from Asia, and in some areas of North America it is invasive and crowds out native species. At the same time, birds such as this cardinal love to eat the berries and nest among its dense branches.

Invasive Exotics

Wildflowers and Weeds
Garlic mustard (*Alliaria petiolata*)
Nodding thistle (*Carduus nutans*)
Spotted knapweed (*Centaurea maculosa*)
Canada thistle (*Cirsium arvense*)
Crown vetch (*Coronilla varia*)
Purple loosestrife (*Lythrum salicaria*)
Japanese knotweed (*Polygonum cuspidatum*)

Water Plants
Water hyacinth (*Eichhornia crassipes*)

Vines
Oriental bittersweet (*Celastrus orbiculatus*)
Japanese honeysuckle (*Lonicera japonica*)
Kudzu (*Pueraria lobata*)

Shrubs
Australian saltbush (*Atriplex semibaccata*)
Japanese barberry (*Berberis thunbergii*)
Russian olive (*Elaeagnus angustifolia*)
Winged euonymus (*Euonymus alatus*)
Common privet (*Ligustrum vulgare*)
Tartarian honeysuckle (*Lonicera tatarica*)
Common buckthorn (*Rhamnus cathartica*)
European buckthorn (*Rhamnus frangula*)
Multiflora rose (*Rosa multiflora*)
Brazilian pepper (*Schinus terebinthifolius*)

Trees
Norway maple (*Acer platanoides*)
Melaleuca (*Melaleuca quinquenervia*)
White mulberry (*Morus alba*)

WHAT CAN WE DO?

There are many things that each of us can do to help reduce the negative effects of plant bioinvasions. The first is to become aware of which plants are considered the most problematic. Many of the most aggressive species are shrubs that produce berries; they are so successful because the birds that eat the berries later disperse the seeds to new areas in their droppings.

In the past, government agencies actually recommended many of these species as plantings to at-tract birds. They were good—too good. Many are still sold by nurseries, compounding the problem.

Quick Tip
To remove invasive shrubs, dig them out or cut them to the ground and paint the stem tops with a safe herbicide.

Refer to the opposite page for a list of species that are considered by many to be the most invasive and aggressive, but that you might be tempted to use to attract birds. Try to avoid buying and planting these species on your property. If you already have them growing on your property, try to reduce their numbers gradually or eliminate them altogether.

Finally, use what you have learned, and educate other gardeners and bird lovers about the effects of invasive exotic plants on our native habitats.

7 Easy Ways to Attract Birds

If you are like us, you will want to do everything possible to get more birds to visit your property. In addition to bird gardening, we can recommend several other little tricks. They are as easy as 1-2-3; in fact, most of them require absolutely no work at all. Do any or all of them, and you will increase your chances of attracting birds.

CREATE A BRUSH PILE

There are many reasons birds love brush piles: They provide cover, attract insects that live among the decaying branches or on the ground beneath, and catch windblown seeds in their spaces. Some birds, like Carolina Wrens, may even nest in a brush pile.

A good way to make a brush pile is to gather fallen limbs and pruned branches from trees

Remember the Basics

Even little pools in your garden can be a strong draw for many birds.

Building a bird garden with special features like a brush pile is only part of the formula for attracting a variety of birds to your yard. Remember to include these special items for turning your yard into a bird magnet.

Bird feeders: Feeders that offer a variety of seeds are an essential part of any bird garden.

Birdbaths, pools, or ponds: Water attracts the birds and makes a garden beautiful. Its shimmering reflections can seem to double the number of flowers near it.

Birdhouses: Birdhouses provide important nesting sites for cavity-dwelling birds like chickadees. To some they are just collectors' items or antiques; to millions more, they are fun home and garden decorations.

and shrubs on your property, and then loosely stack them in an area about 10 feet by 6 feet (preferably where they will not be obtrusive to you or your neighbors). The pile should be airy and have lots of open spaces for small birds to flit in and out. Don't mix in soft vegetation, which will fill the spaces and rot.

Our brush piles are used most often during the winter; visitors include Black-capped Chickadees, Dark-eyed Juncos, American Tree Sparrows, Song Sparrows, White-throated Sparrows, Tufted Titmice, Carolina Wrens, House Wrens, and Winter Wrens.

STRING UP A BIRD PLANTING WIRE

A good way to add to your bird garden is to let the birds select and plant the plants themselves. To do this, string a clothesline or sturdy wire between two points—trees or posts work well—where you'd like a future garden. Make the line 10 to 20 feet long and at least 6 feet high (so no one will walk into it).

A GOOD WAY TO ADD TO YOUR BIRD GARDEN IS TO LET THE BIRDS CHOOSE AND PLANT THE PLANTS FOR YOU—JUST STRING A HIGH WIRE TO HELP THINGS FALL INTO PLACE.

Soon enough, birds will start to perch on the wire, and their droppings will fall below. Seeds (from plants they prefer, obviously) excreted in their droppings will be planted in the ground beneath. Over time, you will get a selection of the birds' favorite berry-producing plants. While this isn't the quickest method, it is relatively easy, and the birds get a say in what gets planted. The only caution is that some of the plants that arrive via the birds may be invasive exotics that should be weeded out. (See "Invasive Exotics and Natural Natives" on page 74 for more information.)

Birds that will help plant your garden include bluebirds, catbirds, mockingbirds, robins, and Cedar Waxwings.

LET DEAD TREES STAND

Dead trees and limbs are a wonderful source of food and homes for birds. As trees or limbs start to die, many insects use the loosened bark to find food, lay eggs, and overwinter. Some insects, such as beetles, will start to bore into the bark and the wood of the tree.

All woodpeckers will regularly visit sites with standing trees and branches. In addition, Bushtits, chickadees, Brown Creepers, nuthatches, titmice, certain warblers, and other small birds that eat insects will endlessly search over the limbs and trunks.

Dead trees also become valuable "condominium units" for bird species that excavate

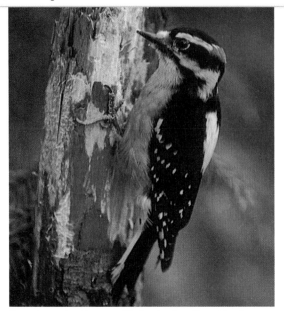

If you leave dead trees and limbs standing, they attract insects, which in turn attract birds that eat them, such as this male Downy Woodpecker.

nest holes in slightly softened wood. It is not unusual to see a dead tree with four or five nest holes in it, often quite near each other. Excavators include all of the woodpeckers and sapsuckers, as well as chickadees and some nuthatches.

Once these holes are made, there are many other species that will reuse them. These include bluebirds, flycatchers, American Kestrels, nuthatches, owls, swallows, titmice, wrens, and many others. These dead trees, with their excavated holes, are natural birdhouses.

Dead trees are also great places to see birds. Birds seem unable to resist stopping and perching in them in full, unobstructed view. Of course, you should have some consideration for safety and appearance. Leave dead limbs

and trees only where they will not endanger people or be a nuisance to neighbors.

REUSE YOUR CHRISTMAS TREE

After Christmas, you can make a present of your Christmas tree to the birds. After removing all ornaments, lights, and tinsel from the tree, stand it outside, a few feet from your bird feeders. The birds will use it as a perch before and after going to the feeder or for cover during rain or snow. You can also celebrate the season with your backyard birds by decorating a tree with food they will love.

LEAVE LEAVES ALONE

This idea will actually save you time and energy in your gardening chores: Don't rake up fallen leaves.

 ## Make It Yourself

Share the joy of Christmas with the birds by making some special food gifts to hang on an outside tree. Here are two bird-friendly ornaments:

- Use a needle to string popcorn and/or cranberries onto thread, and then drape the tasty strands over the tree.
- Securely tie some string to a pinecone, press suet or peanut butter between the scales, then roll it in bird seed and hang it from a branch.

Leave the leaves on the ground instead of raking them up, and birds like this Brown Thrasher will come and feed on the seeds and insects beneath them.

Obviously, you'll want to rake them from your lawn and driveway, but if fallen leaves gather under shrubs or in a wooded area where there is no grass, then you can attract more birds by leaving them there.

Fallen leaves provide nutrients to the soil as they decay and, as they accumulate, form an insulating layer over the soil that keeps it warmer and moister. Insects and other soil dwellers thrive under these conditions.

There are many garden birds that love to feed where there are fallen leaves, including thrushes, thrashers, towhees, and many sparrows. On our property we have many woodsy areas where we let leaves accumulate, especially under rhododendrons near our feeders.

Species that regularly feed there are cardinals, Brown Thrashers, Eastern Towhees, and, during migration, Fox and White-throated sparrows, and Hermit and Swainson's thrushes.

CREATE A HEDGEROW

A hedgerow is a long line of shrubs and small trees at the border of a field or lawn. It is a superb place for birds in all seasons, providing food, shelter, and nesting sites.

Plant a hedgerow along a sunny boundary between two properties, at the edge of a field, or in an open area you want to divide. Plant it with any of the berry-producing shrubs listed in "The Best Shrubs for Attracting Birds" on

Planting a hedgerow that contains a variety of shrubs is a wonderful way to provide food, shelter, and nesting habitats for many species of birds.

page 52. Include some small trees, such as hackberry, mulberry, or mountain ash. Over the years, you may need to cut back invasive trees or shrubs that do not produce food for birds.

The hedgerow at the edge of our field contains blackberry, highbush cranberry, gray-stemmed dogwood, eastern red cedar, mountain ash, and a mulberry tree. We also have invasive black locust and buckthorn trees that we periodically cut out.

Nesting, wintering, and migrant birds heavily use our hedgerow. Catbirds, Song Sparrows, Brown Thrashers, and Common Yellowthroats nest there. Cardinals, House Finches, Dark-eyed Juncos, and Cedar Waxwings feed there all winter, and during migration we have had Lincoln's Sparrows; Swainson's Thrushes; and Mourning, Black-and-white, and Yellow-rumped warblers.

PROVIDE NESTING MATERIAL IN SPRING

Birds need to find nesting material when they start building in spring. You can help them by providing materials for their use. These materials include short pieces of string (6 inches or less), human hair, dog fur, dry grass, pine

Quick Tip

Save the hairs from your brush, your next haircut, or the dog's grooming for a fast wad of nesting material.

A suet holder is a great way to offer nesting material to birds. This one is filled with fur combed from a golden retriever, and it attracts chickadees and titmice.

Female and male

What's That Bird?
RING-NECKED PHEASANT

ID Clues: Large, 33-inch bird with long pointed tail; male has green head, red wattles around eyes, and white neck ring; body is mixture of iridescent greens, browns, and golds with dark markings; female has rich brown color with dark markings on wings and back

Habitat: Farmlands with some woods or hedgerows

Food: Waste grain, seeds, acorns, berries, insects; mixed seed on ground

Nests: Nests on ground among tall grasses

needles, and strips of bark from grape, birch, or weed stalks. Place these materials in an open-mesh container, like a plastic fruit basket from the store, and hang the container somewhere in the open where birds frequent.

You can buy nesting material in bird specialty stores, or you can make your own. We hang a wire-mesh suet holder full of material from the lower limb of a tree, and we also provide a pile of pine needles for our bluebirds on the ground near their nest boxes. We leave chicken feathers for our Tree Swallows the same way—or just throw the feathers in the air if the birds are nearby for the swallows to gather in midair.

Create a Hummingbird Heaven in Your Backyard

We are always thrilled when hummingbirds return to our yard each year. We have found that the very best way to attract hummingbirds is to grow a profusion of flowers that they like, especially red, tubular flowers. Of course, there is more to creating a hummingbird habitat than simply planting red flowers. This chapter gives details for ways to turn your garden into a heaven on earth for hummers.

ALL THE NECESSARY ELEMENTS

A good hummingbird garden has more than just flowers: It's a whole habitat created to entice the hummingbirds to stay. The key word in creating habitats for hummingbirds, or for any kind of wildlife, is *variety*. Here are some of the elements of that habitat.

Both sun and shade. Be sure to have a mixture of sun and shade in your garden, which is easily created by a few trees and open areas. The flowers need the sun to grow, and the hummingbirds perch in the shade between feedings.

Lots of levels. Have different levels of vegetation, including tall trees, medium-height trees and shrubs, and flowers. Within planters or gardens, fill the front areas with shorter plants, backed up by medium-height plants, with the tallest plants in the rear. This tiering of plants gives you a good view of all the flowers and plants, and it provides the hummingbirds easy access to all the flowers. The different heights give the birds space around the blooms so they can hover and feed comfortably, and the taller plants provide a good choice of perches where they can rest, view the flowers, and protect their territory.

Lots of flowers. Plant flowers specifically adapted for hummingbirds—and other types as well. Try to choose species that bloom at different times, so that throughout the growing season you will always have something flowering. Flowers will provide nectar for the birds and will also attract insects, another hummer food. Plant large groups of each species so that they will offer more nectar and be visually attractive to the hummingbirds.

Add water. Like all birds, hummingbirds need water for drinking and bathing—this can

This is the hummingbird habitat that we have created in our yard.

be as simple as a birdbath. Place a mister in the middle of the bath, and you may see hummingbirds flying through it to bathe. They also will bathe in the spray from a sprinkler system. In the morning, they may even drink water from dewdrops on leaves.

Nesting material. Although it is quite easy to attract hummingbirds to your yard to feed, it is a little harder to know exactly what will make them want to nest there. Having a wide variety of plants gives the female, the architect, a choice of nesting sites and material.

To build their nests, most species need downy fibers, which form the bulk of the nest; spider silk, which holds the fibers together; and lichens, which they attach to the outside of the nest for camouflage. Plant willow shrubs, whose downy seed dispersal filaments are used for nesting, to help attract hummers and provide them with both nectar and insects at the willow flowers.

FLOWER POWER

Planting flowers is one of the most important aspects of creating a hummingbird heaven because hummers have a closer relationship to flowers than any other bird. The majority of these flowers should be so-called hummingbird flowers—red, tubular flowers to which hummingbirds are particularly attracted. These flowers can be one of two types: wildflowers, or cultivated flowers bought from nurseries, garden centers, and seed catalogs.

Two Ruby-throated Hummingbird nestlings are packed snugly inside a tiny nest of downy fibers and lichens.

THE EVOLUTION OF HUMMINGBIRD FLOWERS

Hummingbirds are opportunists and will feed at any flower with nectar. Then why does everybody make such a fuss about red, tubular flowers?

To answer these questions, we first need to consider some of the basics of flowers and understand that both the form and flight of hummingbirds have intricately coevolved with the species of flowers from which they drink nectar.

Flowers produce nectar to attract pollinators like birds and bees, which inadvertently carry their pollen to other flowers. This fertilizes the flowers, which then develop seeds.

Some flowers have become specially adapted to attracting hummingbirds and to

How Do Hummers Hover at Flowers?

Hummingbirds can fly forward, backward, and even upside down to escape quickly, as shown by this male Broad-billed Hummingbird.

Hummingbirds can hover better than any other bird because of the unusual structure of their wings. Other birds have wings with several movable joints, but the bones in a hummer's wings are permanently fixed and rigid, except at the shoulder joint, where the wing can move freely in all directions.

When hovering, a hummingbird's wings move forward, and then the leading edges rotate nearly 180 degrees, then back again. During this movement the tips of the wings trace a horizontal figure-eight in the air.

A hummingbird's wings make a figure-eight pattern while the bird hovers.

A Ruby-throated Hummingbird reaches into the tubes of columbine for nectar.

As you watch hummingbirds feed, look closely at their bills and faces for traces of yellow pollen. It may help you to determine which flowers they have visited. This male Anna's Hummingbird has its tongue partly out and pollen on its bill.

having their pollen carried from plant to plant by the birds. At the same time, they also exclude or discourage other flower visitors so that their nectar is reserved for the hummers.

You can recognize a flower specifically adapted to hummingbirds by several things. First, they are usually red, which hummers can easily see and distinguish from other colors (to bees and other insects, though, red appears just dark, and not as attractive). Second, they have evolved long tubes that only hummingbirds, with their long bills and tongues, can get into. Third, they orient their flowers horizontally or downward—hummingbirds can hover perfectly while they drink the nectar, but bees and butterflies cannot. And last, most of these flowers have no fragrance—making them less attractive to bees, which are often guided by

Fast Fact

A hummingbird's flight (pectoral) muscles account for 25 percent of its total weight, compared to 5 percent in humans.

scent, and no less attractive to the birds, who have very little sense of smell.

Hummingbirds visit flowers looking for a meal, while flowers want to have their pollen carried to another flower. To ensure this, hummingbird flowers have also evolved their stamens to get pollen on the hummingbird at just the right place. Most hummingbird flowers—including cardinal flowers, penstemons, and paintbrushes—drop pollen on the forehead of the bird. Arizona trumpets leave pollen on the hummingbird's chin, and flowers like columbine and currant get pollen all around the base of the bird's bill.

Wildflowers for Hummingbirds

When plant names are plural (for example, columbines), you can choose any species within that group. When names are singular (for example, cardinal flower), that is the only species in that genus that you should use.

Western Wildflowers

Columbines (*Aquilegia* spp.)
Red paintbrushes (*Castilleja* spp.)
Mountain centaury (*Centaurium beyrichii*)
Lady Bird's centaury (*C. texense*)
Grand collomia (*Collomia grandiflora*)
Tiny trumpet (*C. linearis*)
Scarlet delphinium (*Delphinium cardinale*)
Bleeding hearts (*Dicentra* spp.)
Red fireweeds (*Epilobium* spp.)
Coral bean (*Erythrina herbacea*)
Rock gilia (*Gilia scopulorum*)
Coral gilia (*G. subnuda*)
Scarlet creeper (*Ipomoea hederifolia*)
Desert trumpet (*Ipomopsis aggregata*)
Calico bush (*Lantana horrida*)
Desert lantana (*L. macropoda*)

Lilies (*Lilium* spp.)
Cardinal flower (*Lobelia cardinalis*)
Texas mallow (*Malvaviscus arboreus*)
Monkey flowers (*Mimulus* spp.)
Bee balms (*Monarda* spp.)
Devil's bouquet (*Nyctaginia capitata*)
Red penstemons (*Penstemon* spp.)
Red phlox (*Phlox* spp.)
Scarlet sages (*Salvia* spp.)
Snow plant (*Sarcodes sanguinea*)
California figwort (*Scrophularia californica*)
Red figwort (*S. coccinea*)
California Indian pink (*Silene californica*)
Mexican pink (*S. laciniata*)
Scarlet betony (*Stachys coccinea*)
Arizona trumpet (*Zauschneria latifolia*)

Eastern Wildflowers

Wild columbine (*Aquilegia canadensis*)
Cross vine (*Bignonia capreolata*)
Trumpet vine (*Campsis radicans*)
Indian paintbrush (*Castilleja coccinea*)
Red turtlehead (*Chelone obliqua*)
Fireweed (*Epilobium angustifolium*)
Spotted jewelweed (*Impatiens capensis*)
Pale jewelweed (*I. pallida*)
Red morning glory (*Ipomoea coccinea*)
Texas plume (*Ipomopsis rubra*)
Red iris (*Iris fulva*)

Canada lily (*Lilium canadense*)
Wood lily (*L. philadelphicum*)
Cardinal flower (*Lobelia cardinalis*)
Trumpet honeysuckle (*Lonicera sempervirens*)
Scarlet lychnis (*Lychnis chalcedonica*)
Bee balm (*Monarda didyma*)
Purple bergamot (*M. media*)
Smooth phlox (*Phlox laberrima*)
Wild sweet William (*P. maculata*)
Fire pink (*Silene virginica*)
Indian pink (*Spigelia marilandica*)

A Broad-billed Hummingbird enjoys some thistle.

This male Ruby-throated Hummingbird is taking nectar from Indian paintbrush, a native wildflower with many different species that are loved by hummingbirds.

WILD ABOUT WILDFLOWERS

It is interesting to note that as you move north from the equator, the number of native hummingbird species diminishes. There are as many as 163 species at the equator, but only 15 in the West—and just 1 in the East. The same is true of the numbers of species of native hummingbird flowers; there are fewer as you move north. It is also true there are far more wildflowers for hummers in the West than in eastern North America.

See the wildflower lists on the opposite page for flowers that are clearly adapted to hummingbirds. Purchase these from native wildflower societies; some nurseries also carry them. Check with local bird groups or specialty nurseries for other appropriate hummingbird wildflowers for your area.

Before buying a bunch of hummingbird wildflowers, look for what may already be growing

This male Broad-tailed Hummingbird is enjoying a meal at desert trumpet flowers.

in your garden area. If you find some, help them flourish where they are by cutting back the competition, creating more light for them, or giving them more water. You may be able to turn just a few wildflowers into a thriving patch of blooms.

Male

What's That Bird?

LUCIFER HUMMINGBIRD

ID Clues: 3½ inches long, with a purple
throat and long, down-curved bill, its
most distinguishing feature
Habitat: Open desert areas of the
Southwest, where one of its favorite
plants is the agave
U.S. Breeding Period: May to August
U.S. Breeding Range: Southeastern
Arizona and western Texas
Nonbreeding Range: Central Mexico
Migration: *Northward,* April and May;
southward, September

NURSERY FLOWERS

There are several things to consider when
choosing hummingbird flowers or other plants
from nurseries.

**Are they annual, biennial, or
perennial?** Annuals live just one
year, but they are often prolific
and bloom over a long period
of time; they are great for
container gardens. Biennials

This patch of cardinal flower, a native plant, will surely attract
hummingbirds—they love it.

live for two years but bloom only in their
second year; in their first year they usually yield
just a rosette of leaves. Perennials keep
blooming for years and are wonderful in garden
beds—they keep growing larger year after year.

How high are the plants? Plants of varying
heights create the tier of blossoms important
for seeing the hummers and for the hummers to
get to the plants.

**When and how long will each plant
bloom?** The goal is to have some hummingbird flowers in bloom at all
times. Try to get some early and
some late bloomers, and look
for others that will bloom
throughout the season.

Quick Tip

Put hummer flowers in each
area of the garden. This way
one hummer can't claim all the
flowers, and more may visit.

Photographing Hummingbirds

It is easier than you think to take quality photographs of nature's avian jewels, and your garden is the perfect hummer lure and backdrop for the camera. Here are some guidelines to help you begin. Just one friendly caution: Photographing hummingbirds can be addictive!

Equipment

Camera and lens. Any single-lens reflex (SLR) camera will work, but those with a $\frac{1}{250}$-second maximum flash sync speed and a motor drive will work better. You should have a 200 mm lens or zoom lens with a range of about 80 to 200 mm. A 300 or 400 mm lens with extension tubes is even more desirable.

Flashes. You will need two electronic flashes capable of being fired off the camera, as well as supports of some kind to hold each flash. Four flashes are even better because they provide total light coverage.

Feeder. To attract the hummingbirds, you need a feeder. It should have only one opening so it limits the bird's position relative to your field of view. If you attach a red flower to the hole, only the flower and the bird will show up in the picture.

Background. This can be a 16 × 20-inch board or mat that is hung behind the feeder.

Film. Your film should have an ISO of 64 to 100. Kodachrome 64 renders the finest detail in the feathers. Ektachrome 100 HC and 100+, as well as Fujichrome 100, are good choices for enhanced colors.

Setup

Hang the feeder with an invisible fishing line from a limb or suspended between two trees. The feeder should be level with the camera, and the camera should be at a height that allows you to look through it easily while you are seated.

Set the tripod-mounted camera at such a distance from the feeder that the hummingbird will fill at least two-thirds of the frame. When using forward-facing flashes for light, try placing the background 24, 36, and 48 inches behind the feeder.

Flashes and f-Stops

An electronic flash is essential for quality photographs. The speed of the electronic flash, not the speed of the camera shutter, controls the sharpness of the image of the hummingbird and its wings. Flash units with variable power control, such as Vivitar, work fine if they produce a flash duration of around $\frac{1}{5000}$ second in the manual mode. Flashes used through the lens flash metering may not give consistent results.

When using two flashes, place them on either side of the camera and aim them at a 30- to 45-degree angle toward the feeder. If you are using four flashes, aim three at the feeder and use the fourth as a highlight.

The distance flashes are placed from the feeder must be measured and consistent because it determines how much they light up the subject. Start with the flashes 24 inches from the feeder. To double the intensity of the light, move them to 17 inches from the feeder; to halve the intensity of the light, move the flashes to 34 inches away.

At each of these distances, try exposures of f/11, f/16, and f/22. One of these combinations of flash distance and exposure should be just right for your situation. An f-stop of f/16 or smaller is desirable for sufficient depth of field and for the bird's body and wings to be sharply defined.

Nursery Plants for Hummingbirds

When plant names are plural (for example, begonias), you can choose any species within that group. When names are singular (for example, carpet bugle), that is the only species in that genus that you should use. When you can select any species within a group, try to choose species that are red or orange; they will probably be more attractive to hummingbirds than other colors.

Shrubs

Abelia (*Abelia* × *grandiflora*)
Bearberries (*Arctostaphylos* spp.)
Beloperone (*Beloperone californica*)
Butterfly bush (*Buddleia davidii*)
Flowering quince (*Chaenomeles japonica*)
Hardy fuschia (*Fuschia magellanica*)
Scarlet bush (*Hamelia erecta*)
Hibiscus (*Hibiscus* spp.)
Jasmines (*Jasminum* spp.)
Beautybush (*Kolkwitzia amabilis*)
Honeysuckles (*Lonicera* spp.)
Azaleas (*Rhododendron* spp.)
Currants (*Ribes* spp.)
Gooseberries (*Ribes* spp.)
Cape honeysuckle (*Tecomaria capensis*)
Weigelas (*Weigela* spp.)

Trees

Red buckeye (*Aesculus* × *carnea*)
Horse chestnut (*A. hippocastanum*)
Silk tree (*Albizia julibrissin*)
Poincianas (*Caesalpinia* spp.)
Siberian pea tree (*Caragana arborescens*)
Palo verde (*Cercidium microphyllum*)
Orange trees (*Citrus* spp.)
Hawthorns (*Crataegus* spp.)
Royal poinciana (*Delonix regia*)
Cockspur coralbean (*Erythrina crist-galli*)
Eucalyptus (*Eucalyptus* spp.)
Silk oak (*Grevillea robusta*)
Tulip tree (*Liriodendron tulipifera*)
Flowering crabapples (*Malus* spp.)
Chinaberry (*Melia azedarach*)
Tree tobacco (*Nicotania glauca*)
Locusts (*Robinia* spp.)
Chaste-tree (*Vitex agnus-castus*)

Whether you use wildflowers or cultivated plants, you can add them to an existing garden to create hummer appeal. Remember to plant your flowers as early as possible to attract migrating birds—and convince them that your garden is a good place to stay for a while.

One of the simplest ways to create a garden of flowers is to buy several containers, like pots and barrels; group them together on a patio, path, or deck; and plant hummingbird flowers in them. We do this on a patio outside our kitchen. Sometimes we place a hummingbird feeder right near the flowers as well.

In our yard the flower that has been most irresistible to hummingbirds is the cardinal flower (*Lobelia cardinalis*). This is a perennial that thrives in moist, rich soil in sun or part shade and requires mulching in the winter. It blooms from July through September and grows 3 feet high, with spikes of gorgeous crimson flowers. It seems as if the minute the first blossom opens, there is a hummingbird

Herbaceous Plants

Century plant (*Agave americana*)
Carpet bugle (*Ajuga reptans*)
Hollyhocks (*Althaea* spp.)
Columbines (*Aquilegia* spp.)
Butterflyweed (*Asclepias tuberosa*)
Begonias (*Begonia* spp.)
Canna (*Canna generalis*)
Paintbrushes (*Castilleja* spp.)
Spider flower (*Cleome spinosa*)
Dahlia (*Dahlia merckii*)
Delphiniums (*Delphinium* spp.)
Sweet William (*Dianthus barbatus*)
Bleeding hearts (*Dicentra* spp.)
Foxgloves (*Digitalis* spp.)
Fuchsias (*Fuchsia* spp.)
Gilias (*Gilia* spp.)
Gladiolus (*Gladiolus* spp.)
Dame's rocket (*Hesperis matronalis*)
Coral-bells (*Heuchera sanguinea*)
Impatiens (*Impatiens* spp.)
Red-hot poker (*Kniphofia uvaria*)
Lantana (*Lantana camara*)
Blazing stars (*Liatris* spp.)
Lilies (*Lilium* spp.)

Cardinal flower (*Lobelia cardinalis*)
Lupines (*Lupinus* spp.)
Four-o'clock (*Mirabilis jalapa*)
Bee balms (*Monarda* spp.)
Flowering tobacco (*Nicotiana alata*)
Geraniums (*Pelargonium* spp.)
Penstemons (*Penstemon* spp.)
Petunias (*Petunia* spp.)
Phlox (*Phlox* spp.)
Scarlet sage (*Salvia splendens*)
Scabiosas (*Scabiosa* spp.)
Fire pink (*Silene virginica*)
Nasturtium (*Tropaeolum majus*)
Verbenas (*Verbena* spp.)
Yuccas (*Yucca* spp.)
Zinnias (*Zinnia* spp.)

Vines

Trumpet vine (*Campsis radicans*)
Morning glories (*Ipomoea* spp.)
Honeysuckle (*Lonicera heckrottii*)
Trumpet honeysuckle (*L. sempervirens*)
Scarlet runner bean (*Phaseolus coccineus*)
Cypress vine (*Quamoclit* spp.)

waiting, and it is the only flower in our garden that hummingbirds actually fight over.

TREES, SHRUBS, AND VINES

Flowering plants also include trees, shrubs, and vines in addition to herbaceous flowers. These woody plants can also attract hummingbirds; because they are larger and longer-lived, they form the basic framework of your garden.

Group trees or shrubs together to form pleasant clusters and masses of vegetation, then place beds or containers of flowers around or in front of them.

Many vines are superb for attracting hummingbirds. They can grow up trellises or along a fence, and they often bloom for long periods of time. Their flowers are spread out, usually with lots of space around them, making it easy for hummingbirds to feed from them.

Part 3 Birdhouses

BIRDHOUSES ARE FUN AND CAN MAKE YOUR
PROPERTY LOOK LIKE A PRIVATE BIRD SANCTUARY.

As we cut down trees for development and wood, we take away homes for many birds. It is important that we protect the environment we have left. It is also important to provide additional housing for the birds.

In this section we will tell you how to make your property a more attractive environment for nesting birds so that you may have the pleasure of sharing their family life and the knowledge that you are helping to conserve bird populations in this critical time.

Who Uses a Birdhouse?

Some friends of ours wanted to attract their most loved birds, American Goldfinches, to their yard. They had put up some birdhouses, but no goldfinches were using them. They wondered if they had the wrong type of birdhouse. Their intentions were wonderful, but they were missing an important piece of information: American Goldfinches do not nest in natural cavities or manmade birdhouses. They build open nests in shrubs or trees.

A BIRDHOUSE IS NOT FOR EVERYONE

Knowing where birds nest is crucial when you are trying to attract them during the breeding season. Each species has an instinctive pattern of nesting and rarely varies from it.

Before you put up boxes to attract certain birds, learn the bird's nesting behavior. There are four basic types:

Cavity nesters. Only 86 species of birds in North America nest in cavities, such as tree holes or the nooks of buildings. Common examples are woodpeckers, titmice, wrens, and chickadees.

Open-cup nesters. Many other birds build their nests in the open branches of shrubs or trees. These nests are generally cup-shaped and open to the sky. Common examples are American Goldfinches, robins, and mockingbirds.

Ground nesters. Most birds build their nests on the ground, by either constructing an open cup or scraping a shallow depression in the earth. Common ground nesters include towhees, pheasants, and many sparrows.

Underground nesters. A few birds build their nests underground, but practically no backyard birds nest in the ground. A common underground nester is the kingfisher.

You will not find any of the cavity nesters, such as bluebirds, making an open, cuplike nest in a shrub, nor will you find any of the birds that make open nests, such as tanagers, ever using a birdhouse.

When you put up a birdhouse, you are adding a "cavity" to the habitat around your property. Together with food from feeders or plants, a supply of water—and a bit of luck—1 or 2 or 20 birdhouses will attract cavity-nesting birds to settle in and raise a family right in your backyard.

Cavity Nesters of North America

This is a complete list of cavity nesters for North America—86 species in all. Not all of these birds always nest in cavities, but all are known to do so at least occasionally. Those birds that are easily attracted to birdhouses have been marked with an asterisk.*

Eastern Bluebird*
Mountain Bluebird*
Western Bluebird*
Bufflehead*
Black-capped Chickadee*
Boreal Chickadee
Carolina Chickadee*
Chestnut-backed Chickadee*
Mexican Chickadee
Mountain Chickadee*
Brown Creeper
Black-bellied Whistling Duck
Wood Duck*
Peregrine Falcon
House Finch*
Northern Flicker*
Ash-throated Flycatcher*
Brown-crested Flycatcher
Dusky-capped Flycatcher
Great Crested Flycatcher*
Sulphur-bellied Flycatcher
Western Flycatcher
Barrow's Goldeneye*
Common Goldeneye*
American Kestrel*
Purple Martin*
Common Merganser*
Hooded Merganser*
Merlin

Crested Myna
Brown-headed Nuthatch
Pygmy Nuthatch
Red-breasted Nuthatch*
White-breasted Nuthatch*
Barn Owl*
Barred Owl*
Boreal Owl
Eastern Screech-Owl*
Elf Owl
Ferruginous Pygmy-Owl
Flammulated Owl
Northern Hawk Owl
Northern Pygmy-Owl
Northern Saw-whet Owl*
Spotted Owl
Vaux's Owl
Western Screech-Owl*
Whiskered Screech-Owl
Red-breasted Sapsucker
Red-naped Sapsucker
Williamson's Sapsucker
Yellow-bellied Sapsucker
Eurasian Tree Sparrow
House Sparrow*
Starling*
Tree Swallow*
Violet-green Swallow*
Siberian Tit

Bridled Titmouse
Plain Titmouse*
Tufted Titmouse*
Elegant Trogon
Black Vulture
Turkey Vulture
Lucy's Warbler
Prothonotary Warbler*
Acorn Woodpecker
Black-backed Woodpecker
Downy Woodpecker*
Gila Woodpecker
Golden-fronted Woodpecker*
Hairy Woodpecker*
Ladder-backed Woodpecker
Lewis' Woodpecker
Nuttall's Woodpecker
Pileated Woodpecker
Red-bellied Woodpecker*
Red-cockaded Woodpecker
Red-headed Woodpecker*
Strickland's Woodpecker
Three-toed Woodpecker
White-headed Woodpecker
Bewick's Wren*
Carolina Wren*
House Wren*
Winter Wren

OTHER NESTING SITES

Since this section of the book deals with buying or building birdhouses and how to maintain them, we think a little attention should be given here for all those other birds who may use your yard and garden for their nests. The grasses, shrubs, and trees you provide can lure them into setting up housekeeping, too.

Where Other Backyard Birds Nest

On the Ground

Bobolink
Bobwhite
Common Ground-Dove
American Black Duck
Canada Goose

Killdeer
Mallard
Eastern Meadowlark
Western Meadowlark
Ring-necked Pheasant

California Quail
White-throated Sparrow
Eastern Towhee
American Woodcock

In Shrubs

Red-winged Blackbird
Indigo Bunting
Cardinal
Gray Catbird
Evening Grosbeak

Rose-breasted Grosbeak
Mockingbird
Chipping Sparrow
Song Sparrow
White-crowned Sparrow

Brown Thrasher
California Thrasher
Brown Towhee
Yellow Warbler
Common Yellowthroat

In Shrubs or Trees

Brewer's Blackbird
Black-billed Cuckoo
Yellow-billed Cuckoo

Eastern Kingbird
Western Kingbird
Black-billed Magpie

American Robin
Wood Thrush
Red-eyed Vireo

In Trees

American Crow
Northwestern Crow
Inca Dove
Mourning Dove
Purple Finch
American Goldfinch
Lesser Goldfinch

Common Grackle
Great-tailed Grackle
Red-tailed Hawk
Blue Jay
Baltimore Oriole
Hooded Oriole
Orchard Oriole

Great Horned Owl
Eastern Wood Pewee
Western Wood Pewee
Pine Siskin
Scarlet Tanager
Summer Tanager
Cedar Waxwing

On Platforms

Black Phoebe
Eastern Phoebe

Say's Phoebe
American Robin

Barn Swallow
Cliff Swallow

PROVIDING GROUND-NESTING SITES

Some of the common birds that nest on the ground include many ducks, Dark-eyed Juncos, meadowlarks, pheasants, many sparrows, and towhees. Each of these birds needs a different type of groundcover for its nesting.

Some birds, like Bobolinks, meadowlarks, and pheasants, need large areas of tall grasses.

Although the Ash-throated Flycatcher is easily attracted with a birdhouse, this individual has chosen the rotted-out knothole of a tree as its nest cavity.

Most of these will be attracted only to a spot with several acres of meadow.

Other birds, like sparrows and Dark-eyed Juncos, may nest in any small clearing where there are a few tufts of grass in which to hide their nests. They would be happy with a corner of a lawn where the grass is left to grow high.

Many ducks, such as the Mallard—as well as towhees and American Woodcocks—prefer to nest among the open understory of woods, often hiding their nests under the lowest boughs of small trees or blending them in with the fallen, dried leaf litter.

The Killdeer, on the other hand, prefers to be right out in the open with practically no vegetation around at all. It is often attracted to gravel driveways, rocky areas with sparse vegetation, and even flat rooftops.

Thus, to provide habitats for a number of these birds, you may need to cultivate a variety of ground vegetation and cover.

PROVIDING SHRUBS AND TREES FOR NESTING SITES

Shrubs are one of the most important elements in attracting birds to your yard to nest. They not only provide good sites for nests at a height convenient for the birds, but they also produce berries and attract insects on which the birds can feed.

Many shrubs tend to grow in or at the edge of more open areas. This creates what has been called the "edge effect." Wildlife, and birds in particular, are attracted to edge environments because they present the greatest variety of habitats. Creating dense shrub edges at the borders of your lawn, a field, or woods is the best way to attract birds.

Trees are also important but are best when interspersed with open areas and shrubs. Alone, a forest of tall trees will attract very few birds and is a kind of desert for wildlife. The

This female Anna's Hummingbird is incubating eggs in her tree nest.

leaf canopy is high, often there is little growth beneath because of the lack of light, and thus the amounts of food, cover, and nesting areas are inadequate.

When deciding on trees to attract birds, choose a variety of sizes and types. Try to have some smaller trees, such as crab apples, dogwoods, and hawthorns, as well as taller trees like maples, cherries, oaks, and ashes. Plant evergreens for added cover and protection of nesting or roosting birds, and provide decid-

uous trees for good perches. Include trees that produce a variety of foods, such as fruits, seeds, nuts, and cones. For more information on good shrubs and trees for birds, see pages 52 and 62.

PROVIDING FOR PLATFORM NESTERS

There are several common backyard birds that can be attracted to nest on or in buildings if a small shelf or platform is provided. These include the Eastern Phoebe, robin, and Barn Swallow.

Quick Tip

Let a large area of lawn, about 10 × 10 feet, grow tall, and keep tufts of tall turf in other spots to create ground-nesting sites.

The American Robin (male shown here) is comfortable in a variety of habitats from lawns to mountains throughout the North American continent. While they often make nests of grasses and mud in trees, robins, along with some phoebes and swallows, are also attracted to a small platform.

Occasionally, Cave and Cliff swallows may also be attracted to platforms.

Each of these can be found nesting on naturally occurring shelflike projections of buildings, especially underneath eaves or another protected location, such as barn rafters, the tops of front porch lights, roof gutters, and windowsills. By building a small shelf or platform and attaching it to the side of a building or inside an open garage or barn, you can provide the sort of nesting site these birds like.

Of these birds, the robin is the most flexible and would just as soon build its nest in a shrub or tree as on a building. Phoebes often nest near water (under bridges or docks, for example), but they are happy on houses as well and generally are not disturbed by human comings and goings. The Barn Swallow is partial to the interiors of large, open buildings, such as warehouses or barns, although we know of a pair nesting in a neighbor's garage.

If you would like to build a nesting platform, see page 132 for plans.

■ summer range   ■ winter range   ■ all year-round

What's That Bird?

WESTERN TANAGER

ID Clues: About 6 inches long, with a yellow body and black wings with wing bars; the male has red on head or face and under the beak

Habitat: Coniferous or mixed forests

Food: Wasps and other insects in midair; oranges at feeders

Nests: Nest of twigs and rootlets 10 to 65 feet high in tree

Male

PROVIDING NESTING MATERIALS

Each species of bird uses slightly different materials to make its nest. Often, these materials are in short supply, so birds are always grateful if you provide a variety of nesting materials. One easy way to do this is by stuffing a suet holder or string bag with fur, feathers, short bits of string, strands of cloth, and even bits of cellophane. Hang the suet holder or string bag in plain sight; the top of a pole in the middle of your lawn is a good spot.

Another nesting material that many birds use is mud. Choose a part of your yard at nesting season, keep it clear of vegetation, and water it enough to maintain a constant supply of mud. You may attract robins, Barn Swallows, or phoebes.

HOW DO I GET BIRDS TO NEST IN MY YARD?

To answer this question, we must explain how birds choose nesting sites. Older birds that have already nested in previous years usually return to the same areas to nest again. Therefore, they will probably not suddenly "discover" your yard.

This means that it is most likely that young birds that have not nested before will have to first discover your property. Then, they'll have to decide that it is a good place in which to nest. If this happens in the first year, consider yourself lucky.

More likely, what will happen is that as you continually improve your property, pairs of nesting birds will gradually move in and set up nesting territories. Once they start nesting there, it is very likely that they will continue to do so year after year.

It is hard to predict just when a bird will use a birdhouse because there are many factors that affect this: how many cavity nesters there are on your property, what natural cavities are available, and even the age of the birdhouse (birds often prefer older houses). However, there often are not enough cavities to cover the demand, and even older birds need new cavities when previous ones begin to seriously decay. It is possible you may get birds using your birdhouses in the very first breeding season that you put them up.

We have had birds use boxes within days of our putting them up; in other cases, it has taken several years for a birdhouse to be occupied. If a house is not used within two years, change its location and you might have better luck.

Birdhouse Basics

Birdhouses are readily available to purchase, or you may want to build one yourself. If you wish to take the do-it-yourself route, see "Building Birdhouses" on page 122. If you'd rather buy one, you have a wide variety of choices. Birdhouses are sold at lawn and garden, hardware, and gift stores, as well as through mail-order catalogs. See "Resources" on page 289 for a list of catalog companies. Whether you buy or build your birdhouses, there are important criteria to consider. Following these suggestions will ensure that your boxes will be both functional and safe for the birds.

THE IMPORTANT FEATURES

If you meet these basic criteria, then the actual design of the birdhouse can be as simple as an unpainted wood box or as elaborate as a miniature Swiss chalet with flowers painted on the balcony. In general, birds are looking only for the right size cavity in the right location; the other features of the box are more for our benefit and sense of taste.

THE RIGHT DIMENSIONS

Different species of birds require birdhouses of different dimensions. Check the chart on page 106 to see if the house that you are considering meets the requirements of the bird that you are trying to attract. There are three important dimensions to keep in mind.

- The entrance hole should be large enough to admit the bird, but not so large as to admit unwanted species. If you have to choose just one box, choose one with an entrance hole 1½ inches in diameter to benefit the greatest variety of birds.

- The interior area of the house should be large enough so that the bird can build a

Decorating birdhouses is fun and does not harm the birds as long as there's no paint inside the box or near the outside of the hole.

nest sized appropriately to hold its babies, while not so large that the bird would have a difficult time filling it with nesting material. A box about 5 × 5 inches is a safe bet.

- The box should be deep enough so that several inches of space will remain between the top of the nest and the entrance hole, making it more difficult for any predator to reach in and harm the babies. A minimum depth of 6 inches between the entrance hole and the floor is best.

If you are trying to attract a variety of backyard cavity-nesting birds, put up several boxes with different dimensions. For a full discussion of proper dimensions, see "Size Matters" on page 104.

Eastern Bluebirds, like this male (*below*) and female (*top*), use nest boxes placed along the edges of farmland, rural yards, and open woodlands. They are one of our most colorful nesters.

PROPER MATERIALS

Birdhouses should be constructed of materials that have enough insulating quality to protect the birds and the eggs from excessive heat or excessive cold. Wood that is ⅝ to ¾ inch thick is a good choice. Some commercial birdhouses are made of plastic or ceramics, both of which have merits and drawbacks; select carefully according to this and all other criteria. Do not buy metal birdhouses (although Purple Martin houses made of aluminum are acceptable). The box should not be constructed or stained with any materials that could be harmful to the birds, such as lead-based paint, creosote, or pressure-treated lumber. No paint or stain should be in-

side the box or entrance hole or within ¼ inch of the outside of the entrance hole.

PROPER VENTILATION

The box should be well ventilated. Look for or drill holes—or cut slits or cracks—near the top of the sides to let air circulate and help cool it during hot weather.

GOOD DRAINAGE

There should be holes or slits in the bottom of the box so that water will drain out and not accumulate.

A WAY TO CLEAN IT OUT

Preferably, the top, front, or side of the box should open to make cleaning and monitoring possible.

Checklist for a Good Birdhouse

- ☐ Made of wood, but not pressure-treated
- ☐ 1½-inch entrance hole
- ☐ Entrance hole 6 inches above floor
- ☐ Inside dimensions 5 × 5 inches
- ☐ Roof overhang
- ☐ Drainage holes
- ☐ Ventilation holes
- ☐ Inside grooves
- ☐ No perch
- ☐ Muted color, if any
- ☐ Easy way to open for cleaning
- ☐ Way to hang or attach to a support

MUTED COLOR

Birds perceive color. The colors of their plumage have subtle and complex meaning to other members of their species. Birdhouses now come in many colors and designs, and it is difficult to know how these colors affect birds. While under some circumstances birds may nest in brightly colored boxes, to ensure success it is wise to choose boxes decorated with more muted colors that blend with the natural environment. For Purple Martins, white houses help to reflect the heat.

INSIDE GROOVES

On the inside beneath the entrance hole there should be horizontal grooves to help

the young crawl to the entrance when they are ready to fledge.

NO PERCHES

There is no need for a perch on a birdhouse; cavity-nesting birds do not require them. In some cases, perches might make the birdhouse more attractive to unwanted species of birds such as starlings and House Sparrows and might give predators a foothold as they try to reach in for nestlings.

OVERHANG

The roof should overhang the entrance hole by 1 to 2 inches. This protects it from rain and sun.

MOUNTING

There should be a way to hang or mount the box on a tree or post.

SIZE MATTERS

One of the biggest controversies about birdhouses is what size box and entrance hole attracts which birds. In articles or pamphlets on birdhouses, you will see many different dimensions suggested for the same bird.

How are you to know which dimensions are right for, or most attractive to, the birds? Taking a closer look at what these birds do in the wild provides some of the best answers.

Quick Tip

If your birdhouse comes with a perch, saw (or break) it off flush to the box to help thwart nestling predators.

A primary cavity nester at work, this male Red-bellied Woodpecker is tossing chips from his new nest hole. The fungus at the top of the picture shows that this wood has probably already been softened through the growth of the fungus.

After all, what you are trying to do in putting up a birdhouse is to re-create the bird's natural nesting environment.

NOT FUSSY ABOUT TREE HOLES

There are two kinds of cavity nesters: primary and secondary. Primary cavity nesters, such as woodpeckers, some nuthatches, and some chickadees, make their own tree cavities by chiseling out the wood with their bills. Secondary cavity nesters, such as wrens, titmice, swallows, and bluebirds, use ready-made cavities—ones that either are made by a primary cavity nester or occur naturally in the wood through rotting or some accident to the tree.

The only birds that can really control the size of their nest holes are the primary cavity nesters. All secondary cavity nesters, which are in the majority, have to use whatever they can find. Before birdhouses were made, most birds could not be very fussy about what size hole they used for nesting. In fact, they were lucky to find *any* hole that was suitable.

The smallest entrance hole made by a primary cavity-nesting bird is that of the Downy Woodpecker, and it tends to be $1\frac{1}{4}$ inches in diameter. All other holes are larger than this. Therefore, any hole less than $1\frac{1}{4}$ inches in diameter is hard to find in the wild.

NOT TOO SMALL AND NOT TOO BIG

Even though almost any size hole is acceptable in the wild, there are still some important sizing criteria for birdhouse entrance holes. The most important is that the hole must not be too small for the birds to pass through, or so tight a fit that too much feather wear occurs as they come in and out. Therefore, it is better for the hole to be a little larger than too small.

The other important feature of an entrance hole is that it be small enough to keep out the aggressive and ubiquitous starlings, which will otherwise monopolize your nest boxes to the exclusion of smaller native species. The critical dimension is a diameter of $1\frac{9}{16}$ inches. If the entrance hole is $1\frac{9}{16}$ inches or smaller, starlings

Recommended Dimensions for Birdhouses

(All dimensions are in inches.)

Bird	Entrance Hole		Floor Dimensions of Box Interior	Total Height of Box
	Diameter	Height above Floor		
Bluebirds				
Eastern	$1\frac{1}{2}$	6–7	4 × 4	11–12
Mountain	$1\frac{9}{16}$	6–7	$5\frac{1}{2} \times 5\frac{1}{2}$	11–12
Western	$1\frac{9}{16}$	6–7	5 × 5	11–12
Chickadees				
Black-capped	$1\frac{1}{8}$–$1\frac{1}{2}$	6–7	4 × 4–5 × 5	9–12
Carolina	$1\frac{1}{8}$–$1\frac{1}{2}$	6–7	4 × 4–5 × 5	9–12
Chestnut-backed	$1\frac{1}{8}$–$1\frac{1}{2}$	6–7	4 × 4–5 × 5	9–12
Mountain	$1\frac{1}{8}$–$1\frac{1}{2}$	6–7	4 × 4–5 × 5	9–12
Ducks				
Barrow's Goldeneye	$3\frac{1}{2}$–$4\frac{1}{2}$	16–18	10 × 10–12 × 12	24–25
Bufflehead	$2\frac{1}{2}$–3	17–19	6 × 6–7 × 7	17–19
Common Goldeneye	$3\frac{1}{2} \times 4\frac{1}{2}$	16–18	10 × 10–12 × 12	24–25
Common Merganser	4 × 5	16–18	10 × 10–12 × 12	24–25
Hooded Merganser	3 × 4	16–18	10 × 10–12 × 12	24–25
Wood	3 × 4	16–18	10 × 10–12 × 12	24–25
Finch				
House	$1\frac{3}{8}$–2	5–7	4 × 4–5 × 5	9–12
Flycatchers				
Ash-throated	$1\frac{1}{2}$–$2\frac{1}{2}$	6–7	5 × 5–6 × 6	9–12
Great Crested	$1\frac{1}{2}$–$2\frac{1}{2}$	6–7	5 × 5–6 × 6	9–12
Kestrel				
American	3	10–12	8 × 8–9 × 9	14–16
Martin				
Purple	2–$2\frac{1}{2}$	1	6 × 6	6
Nuthatches				
Red-breasted	$1\frac{1}{8}$–$1\frac{1}{2}$	6–7	4 × 4–5 × 5	9–12
White-breasted	$1\frac{1}{8}$–$1\frac{1}{2}$	6–7	4 × 4–5 × 5	9–12

will be excluded. Of course, if you are buying or making a birdhouse for a larger bird, such as a Purple Martin, Northern Flicker, or American Kestrel, then the hole will have to be larger than $1\frac{9}{16}$ inches, and starlings may be able to use the house.

Bird	Entrance Hole		Floor Dimensions of Box Interior	Total Height of Box
	Diameter	Height above Floor		
Owls				
Barred	6–8	14–18	13 × 13–14 × 14	22–28
Common Barn	6–8	4	16 × 22	16
Northern Saw-whet	2 1/2–4	10–12	6 × 6–8 × 8	15–18
Screech	2 1/2–4	10–12	6 × 6–8 × 8	15–18
Sparrow				
House	1 3/16–2	6–7	4 × 4–5 × 5	9–12
Starling				
European	1 5/8–4	6–10	5 × 5–6 × 6	13–20
Swallows				
Tree	1 1/4–1 1/2	6–7	4 × 4–5 × 5	9–12
Violet-green	1 1/4–1 1/2	6–7	4 × 4–5 × 5	9–12
Titmice				
Plain	1 3/8–1 1/2	6–7	4 × 4–5 × 5	9–12
Tufted	1 3/8–1 1/2	6–7	4 × 4–5 × 5	9–12
Warbler				
Prothonotary	1 1/4–1 1/2	5–7	4 × 4–5 × 5	9–12
Woodpeckers				
Downy	1 1/4–1 1/2	8–12	3 × 3–4 × 4	10–14
Hairy	1 3/4–2 3/4	10–14	5 × 5–6 × 6	14–16
Northern Flicker	2–3	10–20	6 × 6–8 × 8	14–24
Red-bellied	1 3/4–2 3/4	10–14	5 × 5–6 × 6	14–16
Red-headed	1 3/4–2 3/4	10–14	5 × 5–6 × 6	14–16
Wrens				
Bewick's	1 1/4–1 1/2	6–7	4 × 4–5 × 5	9–12
Carolina	1 1/2	6–7	4 × 4–5 × 5	9–12
House	1–1 1/2	6–7	4 × 4–5 × 5	9–12

The House Sparrow is another bird that is an aggressive cavity nester and may monopolize birdhouses. In order to exclude it, the entrance hole diameter must be 1⅛ inches or smaller. The problem is that this size is too small for many more desirable nesting birds, such as bluebirds, swallows, and the larger species of titmice and chickadees. For more on House Sparrows and starlings, see pages 257 and 263.

BOXED IN

The other dimension controversy concerns the size of the interior of the box. Which box size is most attractive to which species? If we remember that all secondary cavity nesters have to find a cavity already made, then it is easy to see that there has got to be a fair amount of leeway in what birds will accept. And, in fact, our own surveys as well as other studies have shown this to be true.

There are many important dimensions to a birdhouse, including its entrance-hole diameter and interior size.

A HOLE ANY LARGER THAN 1⁹⁄₁₆ INCHES ALLOWS STARLINGS TO GET IN.

There are two aspects, however, of the interior dimensions of a birdhouse to consider. One is the size of the floor plan, and the other is the distance from the entrance hole to the bottom of the box.

Scientific studies of birds in Europe and North America have shown that smaller floor plans can cause some species of birds to lay fewer eggs in a given brood. At the same time, a house that has too big a floor plan may cause more work for the birds as they try to fill it with nesting material, or it may be so big that they cannot make a properly formed nest. For many birds, the inside dimensions of the box need to be about 5 × 5 inches in order to leave enough room for the eggs and the young to develop and not be overcrowded.

The distance from the bottom of the entrance hole to the bottom of the box should be enough that the birds (except some larger species) can build a nest 2 to 3 inches high and still have 3 to 4 inches of space. In other words, the entrance hole should be at least 6 inches above the floor of the box. This distance provides some measure of safety from predators that may try to reach into the nest box to get the eggs or young. It is also not so great that it will prevent the young birds, in the later stages of nestling life, from reaching the nest hole, looking out, and getting food when the parent lands on the front of the box.

OUR RECOMMENDATIONS

The recommendations for birdhouse dimensions listed on the chart on page 106 are based on a thorough knowledge of birds and their behavior in the wild, as well as surveys—our own and others'—and extensive experience with birdhouses of all makes and sizes.

What we have tried to provide is an easy set of guidelines. We have given a range of dimensions wherever possible. This is, again, in keeping with our knowledge of the great variety of circumstances birds will accept in the wild.

The upper limit for entrance-hole sizes has been kept to 1½ inches for the smaller birds, even though many of them will accept larger dimensions. This is because this dimension excludes starlings. With many of the smaller birds, such as chickadees, wrens, nuthatches, and titmice, our experience is that they often prefer the larger of the dimensions listed. In fact, a hole size of 1½ inches is attractive to all

Birdhouses come in a variety of shapes and sizes. All of these houses are suitable for chickadees, titmice, wrens, swallows, and bluebirds.

of them and is probably the most popular all-around hole size that still keeps out starlings. To build a birdhouse attractive to many backyard birds, see "Our Super-Easy Birdhouse" on page 124.

Remember: To attract a particular bird, you must be in an area of the country where the bird breeds and also have its favored habitat on your property. Range maps for many species, their favored habitats, birdhouse needs, and nesting habits are provided in "Profiles of Common Backyard Birds," beginning on page 159.

Putting Up Your Birdhouses

Once you have a birdhouse—whether you bought it or made it yourself—you need to put it up in such a way that birds will want to use it. Like the old real estate adage, the three most important things to remember are "location, location, and location." Other considerations besides habitat include time of year, height above ground, direction, and the breeding territories for specific birds. For the best chance of occupants, follow the advice here.

WHERE TO PUT IT UP

Different species of birds prefer different habitats, so the first consideration is to place a house in the right habitat for the bird you want to attract. For example, chickadees nest in wooded areas; bluebirds nest in open areas. Do not expect to attract bluebirds in the middle of the woods or chickadees in the middle of an open field.

Placing a birdhouse in an open area like a garden, field, or large lawn will be most attractive to swallows and bluebirds—as well as starlings and House Sparrows. A birdhouse placed at the edge of woods will attract chickadees and wrens; one placed in the woods will attract chickadees, titmice, nuthatches, and woodpeckers.

If you want to attract some of the woodland species, try to place the box within 10 to 15 feet

Birdhouses in open fields are attractive to bluebirds like this male Mountain Bluebird.

of a shrub that can serve as a perch for the birds as they come and go. Birds often like to stop and look around to be sure the coast is clear before they enter the birdhouse. Also, if one parent is in the box feeding the young, the

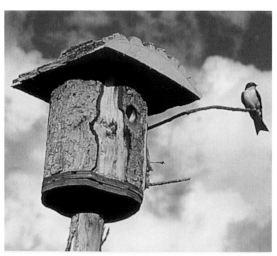

A Tree Swallow checks out the surroundings around this homemade birdhouse, which was made from a hollowed-out log and placed on a pole.

WHEN TO PUT IT UP

The best time of year to put up a birdhouse is late winter or early spring, when birds arrive at their breeding ground and begin to search for suitable nesting spots.

For birds that are year-round residents, such as chickadees, titmice, or nuthatches, fall and winter are also good times. The birds will explore the houses in these seasons and may use them to roost in at night. The following spring they may use them as nest sites as well.

HOW TO MOUNT IT

other parent has a convenient place to wait until the other leaves.

Most suburban properties that have a good mixture of trees, shrubs, and some lawn can attract a wide variety of birds. Use the bird profiles beginning on page 159 to determine which birds will be attracted to your property.

Most birdhouses should be placed about 30 feet from continuous pedestrian activity, although House Wrens or Tree Swallows will readily accept a house in the middle of a vegetable garden. Do not place birdhouses near roads; the birds might be hit by cars as they fly back and forth.

Another placement consideration is to put it where you can see the birdhouse easily so that you can enjoy the birds' breeding behavior. Birdhouses are for your pleasure, too.

Birdhouses need to be attached to a support. Trees are good places to mount them. You can use screws or nails. With screws, you can loosen the attachment a little bit each year to allow for the growth of the tree. Many boxes also can be mounted on poles or posts.

Birdhouses are best mounted on a metal pole. You can also use a wooden post or metal garden U-post. To protect the house from climbing predators like raccoons, use a baffle on the post or pole below the birdhouse. Baffles can be made from large metal cones, stove pipes, or PVC pipe.

Suspension from wires can work well for a smaller birdhouse, such as one for wrens. Hang it from two wires secured to the ends of the birdhouse to prevent it from twirling around.

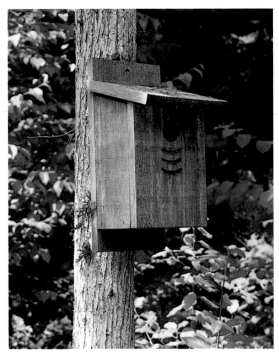

This birdhouse placed on the trunk of a red cedar and near woods is ideal for many cavity-nesting birds, including chickadees, titmice, and nuthatches.

For birds that are particularly tolerant of humans, such as wrens or House Finches, the birdhouse may be mounted on your house or on an outbuilding, such as a barn or shed.

HEIGHT

It is important to keep in mind that there is no exact right or wrong box height for most birds. In the wild, birds accept whatever cavity or suitable excavation spot they find. Most birds will nest in birdhouses placed 4 to 6 feet high. At this height, most people can monitor the nests easily and clean out the box at the end of the year. Houses can be higher (up to 50 feet) and the birds will accept them. We give a range of heights for particular birds in the bird profiles section beginning on page 159.

DIRECTION

The compass direction the birdhouse faces really makes little difference. In a scientific study of the importance of 10 variables to cavity-nesting birds, the volume of the cavity was determined to be more important than any other factor, including the compass orientation of the entrance hole. We have seen most of the smaller cavity-nesting birds use houses that face in any direction.

Having said that, it is preferable to place the birdhouse so that it faces away from the prevailing winds to prevent rain from blowing in. Pointing the entrance hole east or southeast lets in early-morning sun to warm it up after a cool night and also protects the inside from hot late-afternoon sun. In general, try to face a birdhouse in such a way that the birds have ample room to fly to and from the entrance hole.

HOW MANY SHOULD I PUT UP?

There is no limit to the number of birdhouses that you can put up on your prop-

Quick Tip

Mount a birdhouse on the outside of a fence post so that any livestock can't dislodge the box by accident.

erty. Even four or five boxes per acre are not too many.

There is a limit to the number that will be used by the birds. The habitat and territorial needs of each species determine this limit. If you have only open fields or dense woods, then you will attract only the species that prefer those habitats. The more habitats you have, the more birds you will be able to attract—and the more birdhouses you should put up.

The territorial behavior of each species also will limit the number of pairs that will use your nest boxes. A territory is not necessarily the whole area that a bird lives in, just the area that it defends from others of its species during the breeding season. For example, chickadees tend to have breeding territories of about 10 acres, and within that area they will not allow other chickadees to breed. Thus, you are unlikely to have more than one pair of chickadees on your property if it is fewer than 10 acres, unless your property overlaps two chickadee territories. On the other hand, the chickadees will not keep out other cavity nesters, such as titmice

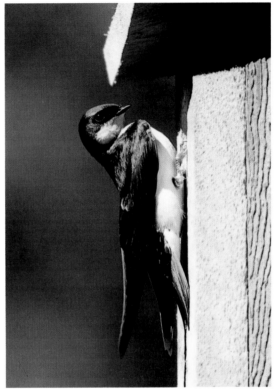

In open areas, Tree Swallows, like this male, compete with bluebirds, House Wrens, House Sparrows, and Starlings for nest boxes.

or wrens, which might choose to nest in the same habitat.

Territory Size of Common Birdhouse Birds

Species	Breeding Territory Size
Bluebirds	2–3 acres
Chickadees	8–10 acres
Nuthatches	20–30 acres
Swallows	10 feet around nest site
Wrens	$\frac{1}{4}$–$\frac{1}{2}$ acre

House Wrens tend to stay within and defend small territories (about ¼ acre); Tree Swallows roam widely but defend just the area right around the nest site (about 10 feet in diameter). Bluebirds have territories of about 2 to 3 acres, so make sure to place their boxes more than 100 feet apart if you want more than one pair to nest.

In our 2-acre field we have 14 birdhouses that are used primarily by Tree Swallows because they do not defend large territories. Overall, we have about 20 birdhouses in various habitats on our 3 acres of our property. Even though we provide all of these houses, only about half of them are used each year. In fact, we rarely know which ones will be used, for it changes from year to year. Plus, many birds nest in the natural cavities that we try to keep in our woods. If a birdhouse is not used for 2 years, we move it to see if a bird will find the new location more attractive.

Q: Will a nest or baby bird be abandoned if I touch it?
A: It is *not* true that visiting or touching a bird's nest or young will make the adults desert the nest. Most birds have a very poor sense of smell, and even when they see you visit the nest, they will return within minutes of your leaving. It is also a myth that opening up a birdhouse will blind baby birds.

KEEPING BIRDHOUSES CLEAN AND READY

Clean out each birdhouse after each nesting (some birds have multiple broods) and again in early spring. This prevents a buildup of mites and other parasites. We use an old pancake spatula and a stiff paintbrush to make this job easier. If your houses are exceptionally soiled, you may want to wash them out with soap; rinse thoroughly.

Repair or replace any boxes that need it before the next spring. Some people prefer to plug up the holes of the boxes during the winter to prevent mice from using them and to deter starlings or House Sparrows, who often become attached to a box and start adding nest material in winter. Remember to unplug holes in early spring when the other birds start looking for nest sites. On the other hand, keeping vacant birdhouses open gives some birds, like chickadees, a place to roost during cold winter nights.

MONITORING THE BIRDHOUSE

Birdhouses should be monitored or checked regularly. This can be both rewarding and educational for you, and it helps to ensure the health and safety of the birds.

Approach the birdhouse in a normal manner and quietly open it. Sometimes we first tap on the box, giving any adult bird inside the opportunity to leave before we open it. On occasion, we have had Tree Swallows and bluebirds calmly remain in the box incubating eggs, in which case we close the box and leave them undisturbed.

WHEN TO MONITOR

During the nesting season, monitor your birdhouses at least once a week. You should not monitor the boxes in bad weather, or when the nestlings are within 4 days of leaving the nest, as this may cause them to leave before they are ready. Check the length of the nestling phase for each bird in the species' profile section so that you will know when the birds will be leaving the birdhouse.

WHEN IN DOUBT, DON'T MONITOR

YOUR BIRDHOUSES.

Nest Identification

Knowing these five common nests will help you to understand and record what has happened in your birdhouses. These houses were opened up after the breeding season for this picture. Here are some clues to identifying each species' nest.

From left to right:
Chickadee or Titmouse: Moss, fur, and other downy materials
House Sparrow: Feathers mixed into a jumble of grasses, cloth, and other odds and ends
Eastern Bluebird: A nicely made nest of grasses and no other materials
Tree Swallow: A nest of grasses that is lined with feathers
House Wren: A nest of solid twigs, sometimes lined with finer fibers

Nest Record Card

Nest box # _____

Species of bird _____

Birds first enter box (date) _____

Start of nest building (date) _____

First egg (date) _____

Total number of eggs _____

First hatching (date) _____

Number of eggs hatched _____

First young fledged (date) _____

Number of young fledged _____

Comments_____

_____

_____

_____

KEEPING RECORDS

We find it fun to keep a record of the nesting progress at each of our birdhouses. We have provided a sample nest record card on this page, which you may copy. Ask yourself: Is the nest complete? How many eggs or young are there? How old are the young?

Here are some clues for watching the babies grow and get ready to leave the nest. Very young birds have almost no feathers, just a little down covering, and they may lift their heads and gape when the nest is touched. Slightly older nestlings have feathers that grow in sheaths that look like quills. Still older nestlings have feathers that have broken out of the sheaths; the birds will cower down in the nest when the birdhouse is opened.

DEALING WITH PROBLEMS

Watching nesting birds successfully raise a brood can be a great joy, and in the majority of cases everything goes smoothly. Occasionally, however, problems occur. It is best to know in advance what these might be and how to deal with them effectively.

If you find dead adults or young, or if you think the young have disappeared because of a predator (rather than simply because it was time for them to fledge), you might feel upset. This is understandable, but do not feel guilty. Remember that similar things occur in nature all the time. By providing safe nest boxes and monitoring them, you are helping the birds to have greater nesting success than they might ordinarily have on their own.

Remove any dead birds from the nest. If all the nestlings have perished, clean out the nesting material; this gives the parents a chance to renest. The urge in birds to repro-duce is strong, and most birds will continue to renest even after a disaster happens. Often, however, they will make a new nest in a different spot. This is why it is preferable to have more than one nesting box available.

Do not attempt to raise young birds yourself; it is against the law. Nestlings are considered abandoned only if you know that both parents have died, or if the young seem extremely weak. If that is the case, contact your local Audubon Society or wild bird rehabilitation center. They are better equipped than you are to handle the situation.

If you suspect predation on a nest, take steps to predator-proof the birdhouse for the next occupant. See "Protecting Your Birdhouses" on page 118.

Protecting Your Birdhouses

Tree holes, the natural habitat for many birds, are a limited resource. To lessen competition among and within species and meet the demand for nesting sites, you can put up several birdhouses of different sizes on your property. But the responsibility doesn't end there: You may also have to take additional steps to control competitors and predators.

COMPETITORS

While your birdhouse seems to you to be just the ticket for a feathered friend, there are other members of your backyard community who think you put it out for them. You'll need to keep a sharp eye out to prevent more aggressive birds, small rodents, and nesting insects from occupying the room you reserved for a bird family.

OTHER AGGRESSIVE BIRDS

House Sparrows and starlings are aggressive species, imported to North America in the 1800s, that nest in holes in manmade structures, natural cavities, and birdhouses. They are the main competitors of native cavity-nesting birds. In some cases, these birds become predators by coming into a birdhouse, killing the owner and/or young, and then taking over the site. Since they are an introduced species, they (and pigeons) are not protected by law, as are our native birds.

Starlings can be excluded from birdhouses with entrance holes 1½ inches or less in diameter, since these are too small for them to enter. If you have put up birdhouses with larger entrance holes and starlings are attracted, repeatedly remove their nesting material every few days or, if necessary, trap and remove the birds.

House Sparrows are more of a problem because they will nest in any bird box with an entrance hole larger than 1⅛ inches in diameter. There are several ways to control these birds.

IT IS LEGAL TO TRAP AND REMOVE HOUSE SPARROWS AND STARLINGS AND DESTROY THEIR NESTS.

As they wait for the day to fly, these Mountain Bluebird nestlings are still vulnerable to attack from a predator.

Since some House Sparrows may claim birdhouses in winter, one option is to keep birdhouse entrances plugged up until spring so the birds do not get a head start. We have also had success in deterring House Sparrows by repeatedly removing their nesting material every 2 days. This requires perseverance, for they often continue to try to renest for weeks.

Placing boxes in habitats that House Sparrows do not frequent is another good solution. For example, House Sparrows rarely nest a mile or more from buildings.

In some cases, when House Sparrows are a persistent problem, people recommend that they be trapped and removed. You must trap the male House Sparrow because if only the female is removed, the male will remain attached to the site and get a new mate.

There are traps for a single box that work by shutting off the hole when the bird is inside. There are also traps for catching larger numbers of birds. (See "Resources" on page 289 for mail-order sources for these.) Take extreme care when using any trap to be sure no native species of bird is caught or harmed because they are protected by law. In areas of dense House Sparrow populations, it may be best not to put up birdhouses.

A white-footed mouse peering out of a knothole. These mice like to occupy birdhouses for a few weeks at a time, especially in winter.

A raccoon emerging from a resting spot. Raccoons can prey on birds' nests, so baffle or grease up birdhouse access routes.

MICE

Small mice can eat bird eggs, but mice seem to be more interested in taking over the birdhouse to live in themselves, especially in the winter. During spring cleaning of houses, remove any mice nests. (The mice themselves generally jump out of the box when it is opened.) The mice will rarely return.

ANTS AND WASPS

Ants and wasps may build their nests in birdhouses and prevent the birds from using them. Control them by spraying with pyrethrum (in no greater than 0.1 percent concentration), a spray harmless to birds that is available at garden and pet stores. Control wasps by checking under the interior roof of the nest box in early spring. If you discover them, carefully scrape off the nests and crush the wasps on cold spring mornings when the temperature is lower than 50°F. The wasps will be too cool then to fly or move quickly. Anyone allergic to wasps should not try this. In the South, putting Tanglefoot, a sticky substance available at garden stores, around the mounting pole may control fire ants.

PREDATORS

Birds can be quite vulnerable when they're nesting. Here are some ideas for keeping

Quick Tip

Keep wasps from building a hive in a birdhouse by putting a thin layer of petroleum jelly on the inside of the ceiling.

out the most common and persistent predators of birds in houses.

RACCOONS

One of the most common predators to visit birdhouses is the raccoon. You will know a raccoon has struck if the nesting material has been pulled from a box—and, of course, there are telltale claw marks on the box.

Birdhouses that are mounted on metal poles are most easily raccoon-proofed with baffles. Attach a 3- to 5-foot length of stovepipe or PVC pipe with a diameter of 4 or 5 inches around the pole directly under the birdhouse. A raccoon will not be able to get a claw hold on the smooth surface. Another effective baffle is a 35-inch-diameter metal cone, or "skirt," attached to the pole directly below the birdhouse, open end down.

CATS AND SQUIRRELS

Another big predator of birdhouse birds is the cat. Cats can be deterred from climbing up to boxes by the use of the baffles mentioned above. Since cats are often more of a problem once fledglings have left the nest, it is wise to keep your cat confined indoors until fledglings are self-sufficient or until they have left the area.

Squirrels occasionally chew at and enlarge the entrances of birdhouses and may eat the eggs. Reinforcing the hole with a wooden block, described below, or a metal plate will deter squirrels from chewing.

SNAKES

In many areas of the country, although less so in the Northeast, snakes are a major predator of nestlings. To deter them, mount the birdhouse on a metal pole that is covered at the base with a 4- to 5-foot-high section of 4-inch-diameter smooth PVC pipe. Spread several shovelfuls of sharp (masonry or concrete) sand around the base of the PVC pipe.

BLOOD-SUCKING FLIES

Blowflies are a species of fly whose young or larvae (small, grayish, ⅜ inch or less) live in birds' nests and at night feed on the blood of the nestlings. During the day, the larvae hide deep in the nesting material. Blowflies are often found in bluebird and Tree Swallow nests. Check by lifting the nest slightly and tapping, being careful of the nestlings. Scrape the chaff from under the nest into your hand. If you discover blowfly larvae, brush them out.

ADDED PROTECTION

The pipes, metal sleeves, and conical baffles described above make a great first line of defense. Putting a baffle over the entrance hole to a birdhouse can add a second layer of protection. Some people like to attach a ¾-inch-thick block of wood with a hole in its middle the same size as the entrance hole. This makes it more difficult for any predator to reach down into the nest.

Building Birdhouses

Although you can buy excellent birdhouses, there are many good reasons to make one yourself. Building a birdhouse can be fun and rewarding, and it may save you money. Many people decide to make building a birdhouse a family project or share it with children in organized groups such as Scout troops, camps, or school classrooms. In this chapter we will tell you all that you need to know to build birdhouses successfully.

GETTING STARTED

To build a birdhouse, you need a plan, some good wood, and several tools and fasteners. Plans for an all-around, super-easy birdhouse (and other houses, too) are presented below. Here's what you will need for assembly.

GOOD WOOD

Various types of wood can be used to build birdhouses, including plywood, redwood, red cedar, western red cedar, and pine. Plywood is the longest-lasting wood. It should be ¾ inch thick and should be *exterior* plywood, which holds up under exposure to rain and sun. The difficulties associated with plywood are that it is sold in large sheets, often 8 feet by 4 feet, and that it splinters, especially when cut with a handsaw.

Among other woods, redwood and cedars are good because they resist rotting. Red cedar and western red cedar are good substitutes for redwood, but these woods are not always available in all regions of the country. This leaves pine as the best and most accessible wood after plywood. Pine is not that expensive and is easy to cut and fasten.

If you have never bought lumber, it is helpful to know how it is measured and how its quality is evaluated. Here is a brief guide to "lumber lingo."

When referring to the size of a board, you say the thickness and width first—thus a "two-by-four" (2×4) is 2 inches thick by 4 inches wide; a "one-by-eight" (1×8) is 1 inch thick and 8 inches wide. You will build birdhouses out of wood that is 1 inch thick and 4 to 8

Quick Tip

Not all birdhouses must be wooden. A dried gourd with a hole drilled in it will attract wrens or Purple Martins.

122

inches wide. You then must specify the length of the board you need (for example, an 8-foot length of 1 × 4).

The thickness and width of a board, however, are measured when the board is first rough-cut. The boards are then planed or smoothed, which means they are slightly thinner and narrower when you buy them. Thus, boards that are referred to as 1 inch thick are actually ¾ inch thick; a 10-inch-wide board is actually only 9¼ inches wide. The lengths of boards are accurate.

Finally, when buying lumber, you should be aware of the grade of wood. With pine, the grade refers to how many knots are in the wood. The more knots, the less valuable and the less expensive. The best grade, which can be expensive, is referred to as *select*, *d-select*, or sometimes *clear* pine. The next best grade is often called *common* pine. This is fine for birdhouses and will help you keep your costs down. Boards of common pine vary tremendously in quality, so look for boards that have the fewest knots.

TOOLS AND FASTENERS

While power tools may make cutting and drilling easier, you do not have to have them. In fact, you can make our super-easy birdhouse with just hand tools. If you need to buy some hand tools, buy good-quality tools. Good tools will last longer and make your job easier. Here is what you will need:

- **Saw:** A handsaw, or a power circular or table saw.
- **Drill:** A small, handheld electric or cordless drill capable of holding a drill bit up to ⅜ inch in diameter at its base. If desired, use a large hand drill called a brace to drill the entrance holes.
- **Drill bits:** Both ¼- and ⅛-inch drill bits for making ventilation holes. For making entrance holes, either a 1½-inch wood-boring bit (a large, flat end with a thin shank), a drill saw bit (a cylinder with saw teeth at one end), or adjustable drill bits that enable you to drill holes of various sizes.
- **Hammer and screwdriver:** A heavy claw hammer and either a flat-head or Phillips screwdriver.
- **Nails or screws:** Galvanized steel (not aluminum) *finishing* nails in 6d or 8d lengths (d stands for "penny," a nail measurement). Or, thin wood screws about 1¼ to 1½ inches long.
- **Fastener:** Any kind of fastener that allows a side or top to open and close easily for cleaning and monitoring the box.

STAINS, PAINTS, AND FINISHES

There is no need to paint or stain a birdhouse. The wood can weather naturally and in most cases will last many years. To make the wood last even longer, we recommend the simplest and safest of preservatives: a little pure linseed oil applied to the outside of the birdhouse. If you do this, wait several days until the oil dries before you put the box up for the birds.

Although there is not much that you have to do to finish off your birdhouse, there are many things that you should definitely *not* do. You should not put any preservative, stain, or paint on the inside of the box, on the inside of the entrance hole, or within ¼ inch of the outside of the entrance hole. This ensures that the birds will not suffer any ill effects from contact with these chemicals.

Also, you should not paint the outside of the box with high-gloss paints or finishes or with bright colors, as they may deter the birds from using it. Dark colors may absorb more heat and make the box too hot for the birds. Martin houses are typically painted white because they are made of thin wood or aluminum, and the white helps reflect the light and keeps the interior of the house cooler.

If you use a paint, finish, or stain other than linseed oil, be sure that it does not contain lead or creosote.

Mounting your birdhouse on a metal garden pole is an easy way to place it exactly where you want it.

THINKING AHEAD

Before you start constructing your birdhouse, consider how you plan to mount it. You can either mount a house on a vertical surface, such as a tree, fencepost, building, or stake, or hang it from a branch on wires.

If you decide to attach the birdhouse to a metal garden stake that already has holes, you can simply drill holes in the back of the house and attach it with bolts and nuts pushed through from the inside. If you plan to use screws to attach the house, be sure there is room to reach inside with a screwdriver, or design the back panel of the box to extend beyond the top and bottom and drill holes in these extended portions.

OUR SUPER-EASY BIRDHOUSE

This birdhouse has been carefully designed so that the dimensions are attractive to a wide vaspecific bird, refer to the birdhouse dimensions listed in the chart on page 106 or under that species' profile later in the book. Those dimensions can also be applied to many of the other plans shown in this chapter.)

BUYING WOOD FOR THE SUPER-EASY BIRDHOUSE

We recommend that you start with common pine. For the super-easy birdhouse, you will need two dimensions of pine boards—1 × 6 inches and 1 × 5 inches. (The real dimensions of these boards are ¾ × 5½ inches and ¾ × 4½ inches, which will work perfectly with the plan.)

To build one birdhouse, you will need 28½ inches of 1 × 6, and 22 inches of 1 × 5. Most lumberyards sell boards only by the foot, so you may have to buy extra. (Consider buying enough for two birdhouses at once.)

The diagrams below show how to cut the pieces you will need from the lumber.

PUTTING IT TOGETHER

The following illustrations and photos show you how to assemble your birdhouse. All you need are a handsaw (or power saw, if you

Here's a finished version of the super-easy birdhouse.

riety of birds: It's a one-size-fits-all birdhouse. We use boxes like this one all over our property and have attracted bluebirds, chickadees, swallows, titmice, wrens, and nuthatches. Starlings can't get in because of the size of the entrance hole. (*Note:* If you are trying to attract only one

---

1 × 5, 22" long

4"	9"	9"
Bottom	Side	Side

1 × 6, 28 ½" long

7 ½"	9"	12"
Top	Front	Back

prefer), a hammer, some nails, and a drill. With cut lumber in hand, do these simple steps:

1. Measure and mark the exact dimensions for each piece of the birdhouse, using the correct section of cut lumber.

2. Cut the pieces as marked.

3. Mark the approximate point where nails go and holes are drilled.

4. Drill the holes.

5. Drive nails partially into the wood where indicated.

6. Place pieces together and finish nailing.

There is no one correct order for assembling the pieces. Some people, however, think it is easiest to first attach the left side of the box to the back, then the bottom to the side and back, followed by the front piece, right side, and the top last.

PLANS FOR THE SUPER-EASY BIRDHOUSE

Bottom

The corners of the bottom piece of the birdhouse must be cut off to allow drainage in case water gets in the box. The gaps also provide some ventilation to the interior of the box.

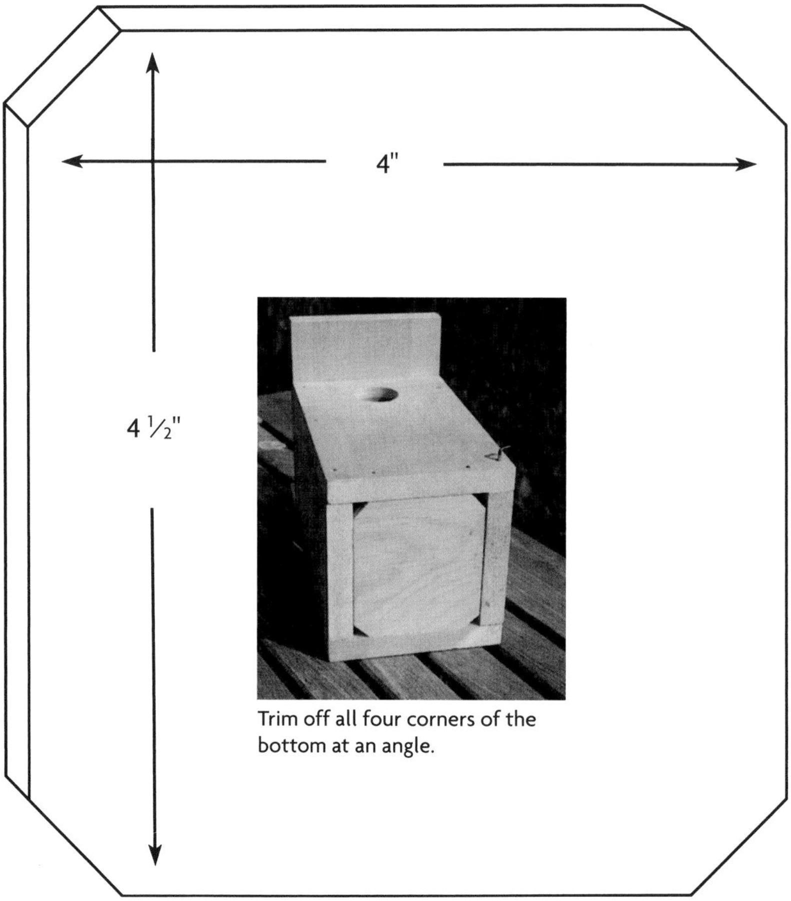

4"

4 ½"

Trim off all four corners of the bottom at an angle.

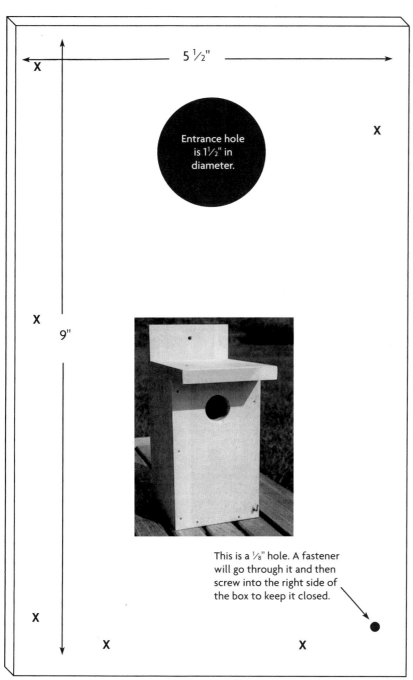

5 ½"

X

X

Entrance hole
is 1½" in
diameter.

X

9"

X

This is a ⅛" hole. A fastener
will go through it and then
screw into the right side of
the box to keep it closed.

X

X

X

Front

On all the illustrations, an X marks the approximate spot where nails are placed. Generally, nails go in ¼ to ½ inch from side edges, and ½ inch from the top or bottom edges.

Since the right side of the box will open, place one nail in it from the right side of the front (as shown) about 1½ inches from the top edge. Another nail will be placed from the back's top left side. The right side will swivel on these two top nails as you open it.

Drill a 1½-inch entrance hole at the spot where the edges of the hole are 2 inches from each side and 1 inch down from the top edge. On the inside, beneath the entrance hole, make several deep horizontal scratches. These will help the young birds hold on as they climb up to the entrance to look out.

Side

You will need two sides, one for the right side and one for the left side.

Drill two holes, each $\frac{1}{4}$ inch in diameter, in the top of both sides of the birdhouse to provide ventilation. Hammer the two bottom nails into the left side of the birdhouse only. The right side will have no nails here since it needs to be opened.

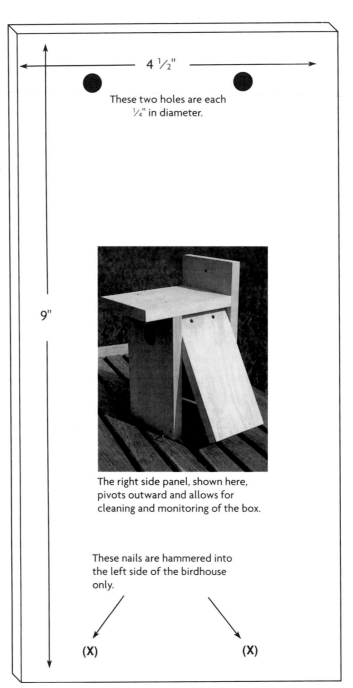

4 $\frac{1}{2}$"

These two holes are each $\frac{1}{4}$" in diameter.

9"

The right side panel, shown here, pivots outward and allows for cleaning and monitoring of the box.

These nails are hammered into the left side of the birdhouse only.

(X)   (X)

Top

The top of the birdhouse is placed flush against the back and overhangs the front of the box to shelter the entrance hole from rain.

The nails attaching the top to the front piece are approximately $\frac{1}{2}$ inch from the side edge and $2\frac{5}{8}$ inches from the front edge. Note that no nails are hammered into the right side of the box so this side is free to pivot when it is opened.

5 ½"

7 ½"

X

X

X

X

X

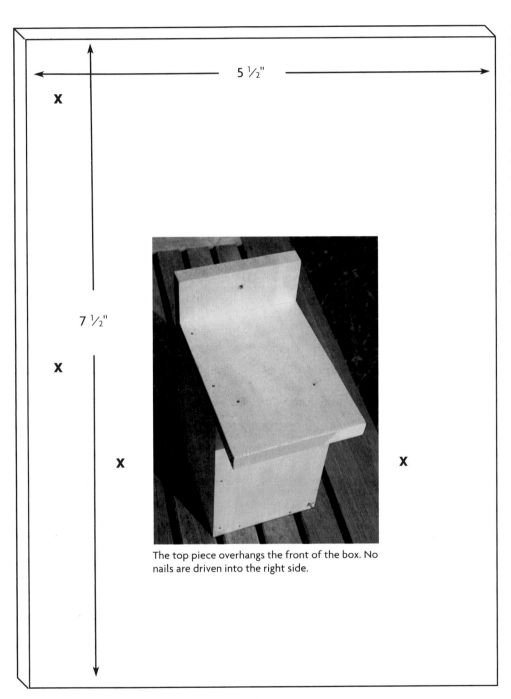

The top piece overhangs the front of the box. No nails are driven into the right side.

Back

The $\frac{1}{4}$-inch-diameter hole at the top of the back is used to attach the birdhouse to a tree or pole. Note there is only one nail on the left side, which needs to be aligned with the top right nail of the front piece so that the right side of the box will pivot. Place this left side nail about $4\frac{1}{4}$ inches from the back's top edge.

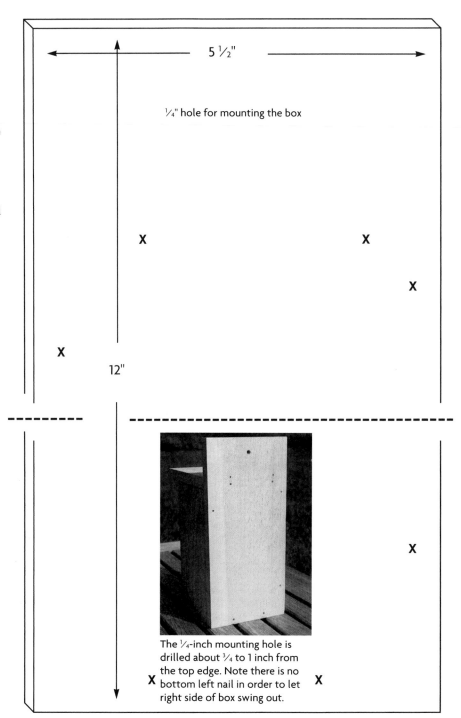

5 $\frac{1}{2}$"

$\frac{1}{4}$" hole for mounting the box

X X

X

X

12"

X

The $\frac{1}{4}$-inch mounting hole is drilled about $\frac{3}{4}$ to 1 inch from the top edge. Note there is no X bottom left nail in order to let X right side of box swing out.

MORE BIRDHOUSE PLANS

The following plans are more advanced in that some power tools are needed. Some require cuts made on angles other than 90 degrees, and these are best done with a table saw. Others involve curved cuts that are best done with a hand saber saw or a band saw.

The various models illustrated here will give you some ideas as to how birdhouse design can be varied to suit your own tastes. The dimensions we have provided are merely rough guidelines to give you a sense of the scale of the house. If you are a novice builder, try one of the simpler designs like the saltbox or hanging house model. If you are an experienced woodworker, we know you are capable of putting together any of these houses with your own touches.

THERE IS NO EVIDENCE THAT BIRDS
ACTUALLY PREFER ONE HOUSE
MODEL OVER ANOTHER.

Detailed dimensions, varied according to the requirements of different birds, are listed on the chart on page 106, and under each species' profile later in the book. If you are trying to attract certain species, refer to those dimensions before beginning. Most of these houses can be made for any of our smaller birds.

The saltbox is named after the typical New England colonial house that looked like a

Saltbox

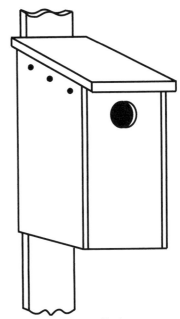

Box dimensions: 6" wide, 6" deep, 10" high

This saltbox model has a small piece of wood that swivels to shut the right side.

Chalet

Chalet dimensions: 6" wide, 6" deep, 10" high

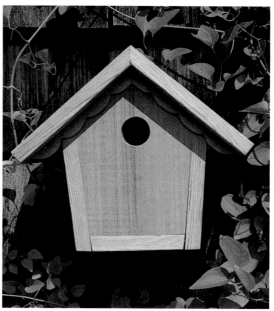

The chalet model shown here has sides that slope in at the base of the house, which looks nice but adds some complicated angles in production.

saltbox with a sloping lid. Its sloping roof, a minor modification of the design for the super-easy birdhouse, has the benefit of shedding rainwater off the box.

The chalet has a pitched roof extending over the sides rather than the front of the house. This is a cute style, one that looks more like human houses. A little ornamentation under the eaves of the house makes it look even more attractive and will not disturb the birds.

The platform is just a modified shelf large enough to hold a bird's nest. It can be as simple as a board nailed to a rafter, or it can be more elaborate, as shown. You might even put a roof over it. The model shown here does not have a roof; it should be hung under an eave, on a porch, or in a shed where it will be protected.

Platform

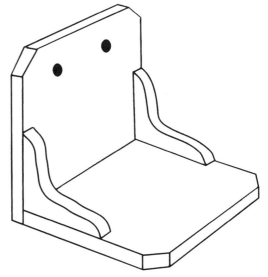

Platform dimensions: 7" wide, 7" deep

The platform may be more attractive to birds without a roof, since this more closely mimics a little ledge that the birds would find in the wild.

This model can be made to look nicer by cutting a design in the angle supports and taking off the corners as shown.

The Peterson house is popular among some bluebird enthusiasts. The small floor area saves the birds time during nest building, for they have to fill less space with nesting material. It is also leaves less room in which blowfly larvae can hide, so it makes cleaning the box easier. The front of the box opens out, pivoting at the base. The entrance hole is slightly oval.

Peterson House

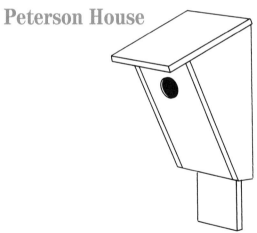

Peterson house dimensions: 5 ¼" wide, 2" deep at base, 10" deep at top

The hanging house is a good one for many smaller birds, such as chickadees, wrens, titmice, and even swallows. Many people call this model a wren house, but the other small birds will use it, too. The only potential problem with this model is that the interior space may be too small and the entrance hole too close to the bottom, thus not leaving enough space for the bird's nest. The distance from the base of the hole to the bottom of the box should be at least 5½ inches. This means that the face of the box, which is a square, should be at least 6 inches on each side.

Hanging House

Hanging house dimensions: 6" cube

The hexagonal house has the advantage of more closely simulating a tree with its rounded cavity and rounded exterior. There is no proof, though, that the birds like it better than any other house. It is more difficult to make because of the angles of the hexagon. The roof can be one piece, as shown on page 134, or it could be a hexagonal turret. Be sure your

Hexagonal House

Hexagonal house dimensions: Each of the 6 sides should measure at least 3 $\frac{1}{2}$" on the outside.

Roost Box

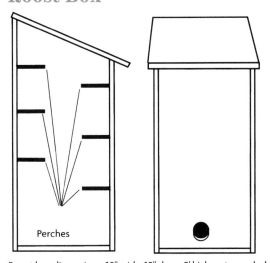

Perches

Roost box dimensions: 10" wide, 10" deep, 2' high; entrance hole 2 $\frac{1}{2}$" in diameter; perches 3" long, $\frac{3}{8}$" in diameter

interior floor area is roughly the same as that for square boxes designed to attract the same species.

The roost box is designed for use in winter, when birds need protection from the extreme cold and often spend the night in tree holes or birdhouses. This design enables several birds to roost in the same spot and, with the opening at the bottom, tends to keep the warmth inside. The perches can be attached either on the sides or on the front and back. When mounting, face the box away from prevailing winds.

Many people love Purple Martins, but not everyone lives near water, where they like to nest. If you have the habitat, making your own **Purple Martin house** can be the ultimate in the craft of birdhouse building.

Purple Martins will accept colonial living conditions as shown in this house. This is a one-story house; more stories can be added. Note that there are nest compartments all around the outside that are roughly 6-inch cubes with 2$\frac{1}{8}$-inch entrance holes. In the center is a ventilation chamber that allows air to pass from the nest compartments out through holes just under the roof. The ledge is important because parents and young birds perch outside the nest at various times in their breeding. The whole structure needs to be mounted securely on a strong pole no higher than 8 feet off the ground so that you can monitor it each week and keep the House Sparrows

Purple Martin House

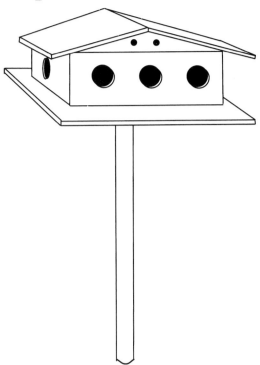

Outside View
This single-floor model, like all designs, requires ventilation holes near the top.

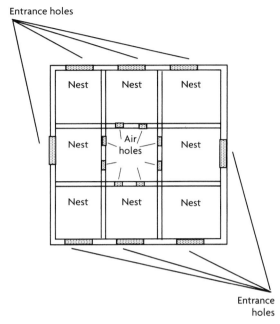

Entrance holes

Entrance holes

Inside View (from above)
Nest compartment dimensions: 6" wide, 6" deep, 6" high; ledge width: 2"; entrance holes: 2 $\frac{1}{8}$" in diameter

out. Martin houses are generally painted white to reflect the heat and keep them cooler. In the long run, it may be better to use one of the modern, commercially available aluminum houses; see the Purple Martin profile on page 255 for more details.

Part 4 Bird Behavior

ONCE YOU ATTRACT BIRDS TO YOUR BACKYARD,
BE SURE TO STOP TO WATCH AND ENJOY THEIR
BEHAVIOR.

By creating feeding stations, garden habitats, and nesting sites, you have gone beyond all those years of barely noticing birds. Birds provide a balance and a perspective to your view of life that is even more pronounced if you take the time to watch birds and observe their behavior. As you begin to do this, you will find that you no longer think of them as simply little feathered creatures but as intricate, living things with their own language, social structures, and complex adaptations for survival.

Watching Bird Behavior

Behavior watching is one of the fastest-growing activities within bird watching. It attracts people who are interested in a bird's whole life; who want to know the what, why, and how of each bird they see; and who generally find each species an endless source of discovery.

The goal of behavior watching is to gain a deeper understanding of any bird you happen to encounter. It takes very little time, is easy to do, and is extremely rewarding; all it requires is focusing on an individual bird and watching what it does. Your watching may be as brief as 15 seconds or as long as 10 minutes. We have been looking at our feeder birds for years, and we continue to discover new things all the time.

KEEP ASKING QUESTIONS

Besides your eyes and ears, the most important thing to bring to your observation of birds is your curiosity. Questions are the driving force behind all learning, and the more you ask, the more you will learn from what you see.

We have found that when it comes to questions, the simpler the better. Also, don't worry too much about not having all the answers—just continue to ask and be open to learning. It was once said that an expert is someone who is afraid to learn something new. In other words, it is better to be a good explorer than to believe you have all the answers: There is always more to learn.

Many of your questions about feeder birds will be answered in the individual profiles on each bird later on in the book, but even scien-

IF YOU WATCH BIRDS CLOSELY, YOU WILL SEE SOMETHING NEW EVERY TIME.

tists and researchers may never have answered other questions that you may have. This is because there are very few people who take the time to observe nature as you can at your feeder. This may sound amazing, but it is true.

ABANDON YOUR ASSUMPTIONS

As you begin to watch birds and ask questions, avoid making assumptions about what you see. If you can avoid making these two assumptions, you will be a much better behavior watcher.

Ask and Learn

Here are some questions you should try to answer as you watch the birds at your feeders. They will help you get started behavior watching and exploring the lives of birds.

Questions about Feeding

Does the bird feed in a flock or alone?
Does it feed on the ground or above ground?
Does it take one seed at a time and then leave to eat it, or does it stay at the feeder and continuously feed?
Does it prefer certain foods?

Questions about Interactions

How does the bird react to others at the feeder?
Is it aggressive toward other birds, or is it tolerant?
Does it make sounds or gestures at other birds while feeding?
Does one member of a flock seem to be dominant over the others?
Does one species seem to be dominant over other species?

This male Red-winged Blackbird is performing a territorial display.

THE "LITTLE FEATHER PEOPLE" ASSUMPTION

Do not assume that birds are like people or that they have motives and emotions like ours. Instead, just watch what they actually do and see how they do it.

For example, a Blue Jay at your ground feeder may pick up a seed, hop over to another Blue Jay that is fluttering its wings, and feed it the seed. Some people might describe this scene by saying that a mother jay fed a seed to a young jay that was begging. But this description makes several assumptions: That the action took place between a parent and young bird, that the young bird was begging, and that the adult was the mother.

In fact, you cannot be sure of any of these conclusions with Blue Jays. You cannot tell male from female by appearance; the bird that was fed may have been demanding food rather than begging; and after a few weeks out of the nest, young Blue Jays look like the adults. It is true that the behavior of a parent Blue Jay and its young as the parent feeds it is extremely similar to this, but so is Blue Jay courtship, in which the male feeds the female.

■ summer range ■ winter range ■ all year-round

What's That Bird?
CALIFORNIA THRASHER

ID Clues: Midsize bird at 10 inches, with dark brown body and pale rusty underparts; holds tail erect when feeding on ground, digging with its curved beak; males and females look alike

Habitat: Coastal chaparral

Food: Lizards, insects, spiders, berries; fruit at feeders

Nest: Nest of twigs and grasses placed in dense bush or small tree, sometimes placed in cactus

Therefore, by making assumptions about birds—assumptions that are in part based on human interactions—we may misinterpret bird behavior; this keeps us from seeing what birds are *really* like.

THE "HE–SHE" ASSUMPTION

One of the most frequent assumptions made by observers, as shown in the previous example, is that a bird is male or female. People either unthinkingly call all birds "he" because this is common usage, or they assume it is a male or a female based on its behavior or the stereotypes we have about gender roles.

Either of these practices can be very limiting to your observations. If you call all birds "he," you may be wrong 50 percent of the time. If you call them "he" or "she" based on your assumptions of the roles of the sexes, you are missing the chance to see birds as they really are.

An easy solution is to call all birds "it" until you are sure they are male or female. In addition, look in the profiles of our common feeder birds and learn in which species male and female look alike and in which they look different.

Maintenance Behavior

Our daily lives consist, in large part, of activities that will maintain us in good health: eating meals, brushing our teeth, drinking beverages, and sleeping, to name just a few. Likewise for birds, maintenance behavior comprises all the actions a bird does to keep itself up. It involves the life-sustaining activities we have discussed in this book—feeding and drinking—and other activities, such as feather care.

FEEDING

Every bird feeds in a slightly different manner, and it can be a lot of fun to watch and discover all of the various methods. For example, chickadees, titmice, and nuthatches usually take one seed from the feeder, then go to another perch—usually a tree branch—to eat it. Birds like grosbeaks, goldfinches, Pine Siskins, and Mourning Doves may stay in one spot as they eat seed after seed.

Some birds typically come to ground feeders; others prefer hanging feeders. This usually reflects what they most commonly eat in the wild. For instance, Mourning Doves feed on fallen weed seeds and will always welcome a ground feeder. Goldfinches eat tree and weed seeds; they will come to your hanging feeder. Birds such as woodpeckers and chickadees,

Q: Can a bird's feet freeze to metal feeder parts in winter?
A: The answer to this common concern is simple. Birds' feet do not have sweat glands, so they will not freeze to metal.

This male White-breasted Nuthatch shows a common behavior: storing seeds in the crevices of tree bark.

which look for insects in tree bark, are more comfortable feeding high off the ground and will frequent suet and hanging sunflower feeders. Some birds, including Blue Jays and starlings, feed on a variety of foods at any level where they can find them; you may see them at any of your feeders.

A few feeder birds have the habit of taking seeds and nuts and storing them for later use. Nuthatches often make repeated trips when they are storing food, and it is easy to spot them leaving the feeder, landing on a nearby tree trunk, and stuffing the seed into a bark crevice. Like squirrels, Blue Jays may store acorns under the ground, which helps replant forests.

DRINKING AND BATHING

If you supply water near your feeders, you will see birds coming to drink and bathe. To drink, most birds collect a small bit of water in their bill and then tilt their head back to let the water run into their throat. The tilting is necessary because birds cannot suck water up through their bill. Of course, there are exceptions: Members of the dove family, including the Pigeon and Mourning Dove, can suck up water, and they continually sip without tilting their head back.

Bathing behavior varies from species to species. Many birds stand in shallow water and, through a complex series of movements—

This male House Finch is getting beak-deep before tilting his head back to get a drink of water.

rolling their head and body and fluttering their wings—trap water in the featherless areas next to their body, and then press the water out through their feathers. Some aerial birds, like swallows, may dive into water and immediately fly up. Still others may jump into water and be briefly submerged before getting out. Some birds bathe in rain or drizzle, in dew on grass, or among wet leaves. Take time to watch bathing behavior; it is fascinating.

On a sunny day you may see a bird adopt a strange pose, its wings spread out and body feathers fluffed. If it remains in this pose for a minute or more, chances are that the bird is sunbathing. Scientists are still studying why birds sunbathe. Two theories are that the rays of the sun help the bird produce vitamin D, and that sunlight is soothing to a bird's skin during molting. Birds usually sunbathe while lying on the ground in an open area, and while doing it they often look as if they are in a trance.

MOLTING

Birds lose and regrow their feathers once or twice a year. This is called molting, and you can observe it while the birds are at your feeders. All feeder birds have a complete molt of their feathers in late summer and early fall, gradually losing and regrowing their feathers in a fixed sequence. The birds start to look unkempt and rather ragged at this time, and there are often blotches of different colors as new feathers grow in. They may also be missing certain tail or wing feathers. Birds that have finished molting have a perfect set of feathers, which are particularly beautiful. Look for evidence of this molt in August and September.

Q: Why do birds pick up ants or other materials and rub their feathers with them?

A: In this behavior, which is striking and not often seen, birds may sit on an ant nest or take cigarette butts or mothballs and use them to rub their feathers. These actions represent a complex behavior generally termed "anting" because it most often occurs with ants. It is believed to help maintain the feathers and/or skin of the bird. Chemicals from the ants or other materials may help rid the bird of feather parasites, a common problem, or soothe the skin as new feathers grow in.

The American Goldfinch's fall and winter coat of feathers is the same for male or female: a grayish yellow or brownish yellow body, with black wings and tail. The wings are marked with a conspicuous white bar.

Some feeder birds have another molt in the spring, but this involves only their body feathers and not their wings and tail. Look for this from March through May. One bird that goes through a spring molt is the American Goldfinch. In winter, the male and female look similar and are more of a gray-yellow than in summer. After they molt in the spring, the female becomes more yellow, and the male turns bright yellow with a black patch on his forehead.

ALL FEEDER BIRDS HAVE A COMPLETE MOLT OF THEIR FEATHERS IN LATE SUMMER AND EARLY FALL, GRADUALLY LOSING AND REGROWING THEIR FEATHERS IN A FIXED SEQUENCE.

Hummingbird Feathers: Like No Others

Anna's Hummingbird (male)

Albino Ruby-throated Hummingbird

One of the many reasons we love hummingbirds is for the beauty of their gorgeous, iridescent feathers. Iridescent hummingbird feathers are the most specialized of all bird feathers. On a male hummingbird's brilliant gorget, or throat patch, only the outer third of each feather is iridescent. This part of the feather contains layers of minute structures called *platelets* filled with tiny air bubbles that partially reflect light, causing the brilliant shining colors of reds, purples, and blues we see on hummers, such as the male Anna's Hummingbird at left.

These iridescent parts of the gorget feathers are also flat, so they reflect light in just one direction. Therefore, in order for you to see the iridescence of the gorget, the sun must strike the feathers in just the right way, or they will appear dusky or even black.

The back feathers of hummingbirds are also iridescent; they are also concave and reflect light from any direction, which often makes both males and females seem as if they are wearing a jacket of jewels.

Even hummingbirds are not immune, however, from mutations that may rob them of their jeweled coats.

The albino Ruby-throated Hummingbird pictured above, like any albino bird, is very rare. Albinism is caused by a genetic change that prevents the formation of dark-colored pigment in feathers. There are different degrees of albinism. Birds may have partial albinism, in which just some feathers are white—or in the rarest forms, may have a total absence of pigment from skin, feathers, and eyes. Albino birds don't live long because they often have poor eyesight, brittle feathers, and therefore reduced flying ability.

Social Behavior

Social behavior is any interaction between birds, including aggression, courtship, flocking, and breeding. Below are some common social behaviors that you are likely to see while birds are at your feeders. The male-female and parent-child social interactions are highlighted in "A Year in the Life of a Bird" on page 150.

FIGHTING FOR FOOD

Most interactions at feeders are aggressive. When you provide a rich, unending source of food in a limited space, birds compete for the food. The more feeders you have and the more spread out they are, the less competition and aggression there will be.

Many feeder birds—such as chickadees, goldfinches, Blue Jays, Pine Siskins, and sparrows—feed in flocks during winter. Because of this, they often compete with other members of their flock for food. Instead of fighting with each other all the time, which takes extra energy and could lead to injury, the birds in these flocks form a hierarchy in which they recognize each other and have agreed who gets food first. When two birds in the flock show up at the same spot, the more dominant one will be allowed to feed first, and the other will either leave or wait without challenging it. Rank in the hierarchy may be determined by one or more factors, including a bird's sex, age, plumage, or individual level of aggression.

BIRD TALK

Birds communicate with each other through gestures and sounds. These gestures and sounds are called displays, and each species has a fixed set of displays that makes up its language. Many of the displays at feeders communicate dominance or subordinance between members of a flock.

CALL TO ARMS

All bird sounds have evolved for communication, and each different sound of a given bird probably has a different function. Birdsongs are usually sung to establish a territory or find

Many of the interactions at feeders are aggressive, such as the head-forward threat of this male American Goldfinch.

With crest high and wing tips down, this Tufted Titmouse looks ready to assert its dominance.

a mate. Birds use a "call," usually nonmusical squeaks or gurgles, for other conversation. Do not expect to determine an exact meaning, in words, of a song or call, for bird sounds are not like sentences or words—they are more like expressions of an emotional state.

Each species also has its own special gestures, which are a part of its language. These generally are unusual postures of the feathers or body. Three common visual displays used by many feeder birds are described below.

Head forward: The bird is horizontal with its bill pointing at another bird. Sometimes its bill is "gaped" (open). An American Goldfinch (see above) or Pine Siskin will often perform this gesture when another bird challenges its perch on a feeder.

Crest raise: The feathers on the top of the bird's head are raised. This is given not only by birds with obvious crests, such as titmice (see above) and cardinals, but also by chickadees, goldfinches, woodpeckers, and sparrows. The display is brief, sometimes lasting only a second. A bird that has just landed at a feeder and is trying to find a space to feed often does it.

Wing droop: The bird's tail is slightly raised and its wingtips are lowered, making them look like points below the tail. This display may be held for several seconds and signals aggression or dominance.

The most obvious sign of dominance is one bird flying at another and displacing it from its perch or spot. This is called displacement or perch taking and is common at feeders.

SOUNDING THE ALARM

Birds have two types of predators: Those that approach on the ground, such as a human, cat,

Q: Why do mockingbirds repeatedly raise and lower their wings in a stiff, mechanical way?

A: This is often seen when the birds are on the ground and is called wing flashing. Although nobody is really sure why the birds do it, there are two theories about its function. The first is that it may cause insects to move and make them more obvious to the feeding bird. When it is given by a lone mockingbird on the ground, the bird probably is looking for food. The other theory is that wing flashing is aggressive, often directed at other mockingbirds and occasionally preceding an attack. We have seen this display in fall when many young mockingbirds travel through areas already occupied by adult mockingbirds.

or snake; and those that approach from the air, such as a hawk. They respond to each of these in a different way.

When there is a ground predator, the birds usually fly up to perches nearby and start to make short harsh calls like "check, check" or "chip, chip." They keep the predator in view and usually keep calling until it leaves.

With an aerial predator, usually the bird that first sees it gives a very high-pitched whistle, causing all other birds in the area to immediately become silent and freeze. When the birds at your feeders become quiet and absolutely still, with only their eyes looking actively in all directions, there probably is a Sharp-shinned Hawk or Cooper's Hawk in the vicinity, for

these are the main aerial predators at feeders. The feeder birds may remain frozen in this manner for several minutes before resuming normal activity. We often have been made aware of these hawks simply through the behavior of our feeder birds.

BIRDS OF A FEATHER (SOMETIMES) FLOCK TOGETHER

In spring and summer, most birds stay in pairs as they go about the various stages of breeding. But in fall and winter, these pairs often break up, and the birds form different social groupings. Below is a list of some of these arrangements and the birds that are most commonly found in them.

Lone birds: Some birds, after breeding, remain as lone individuals throughout winter, usually on a fixed range or territory. Examples: cardinals (occasionally), mockingbirds, Song Sparrows (occasionally), and towhees.

Pairs: A few of the common feeder birds remain together as mated pairs on their breeding territory throughout the year. Examples: cardinals (occasionally), mockingbirds (occasionally), nuthatches, and woodpeckers.

Family group: In some species, the young stay with the parents through the first winter. This is the case with crows, Tufted Titmice, and possibly Blue Jays.

Small flock: Some birds that winter as small flocks may be in family groups; others may not. Birds that form small flocks include cardinals, chickadees, Brown-headed Cowbirds, finches, sparrows, House Sparrows, titmice, and towhees.

Large flock: Many feeder birds stay in large flocks during winter, often roaming widely as a flock. Examples: Red-winged Blackbirds, Mourning Doves, goldfinches, Common Grackles, juncos, Pigeons, sparrows, and starlings.

Mixed flock: Sometimes flocks are composed of more than one species, possibly because several species can benefit from traveling in larger groups, where they gain protection from predators and knowledge of new feeding areas. Examples of mixed flocks include chickadees, titmice, nuthatches, and woodpeckers; juncos and American Tree Sparrows; and goldfinches and Pine Siskins.

HUMMER BEHAVIORS

Many of the social behaviors discussed above are common to hummingbirds, too, with their own special style.

FIGHTING FOR FOOD

Nothing will rile a hummer faster than a trespasser at its own piece of heaven: a feeder with an endless supply of nectar. Any hummingbird that finds a feeder will try to monopolize it by chasing other hummingbirds away.

As new hummingbirds arrive on the scene, they will either challenge the first bird for the whole feeder, or just sneak in when the other bird is away and steal food.

When too many hummingbirds are assembled at one feeder, no individual will be able to defend it, and they may all feed at it with just brief chases occurring every so often.

Certain species seem to be more aggressive at feeders than others, including the Anna's and Rufous hummingbirds. But there are no fixed rules as to who wins at the feeder. The best advice is to watch for yourself and keep track of the interactions.

HUMMER TALK

Hummingbird vocal structures are not as complex as those of most of our songbirds, and they do not produce melodious song. Because of this, their vocalizations are usually just buzzes or chatterings. However, hummingbirds do make many sounds with their wings while flying. This is generally done more by males than females and occurs during visual displays and aggressive interactions.

Hummingbirds use many visual displays to communicate with each other. Some displays are given while perched and others while flying. Perched displays usually involve spreading out of the gorget feathers (the feathers on the neck) in such a way that their iridescence

Fast Fact

Hummingbirds are fiercely aggressive and will attack much larger birds, including jays, crows, and even hawks.

This male Anna's Hummingbird, with gorget in full view and glorious color, may be signaling another hummer to get out of his territory.

Male

What's That Bird?
BERYLLINE HUMMINGBIRD

ID Clues: Tiny, 4 1/4-inch hummingbird with all-green head and throat and brown wings and tail
U.S. Breeding Range: Mountains of southern Arizona (rarely seen)
U.S. Breeding Period: July to August
Nonbreeding Range: Northwestern to central Mexico mountains
Migration: *Northward*, June; *southward*, August

will be seen by the bird to which they are communicating. Another perched display is tail spreading. With the exception of the Blue-throated Hummingbird of the Southwest, this seems to be done more by females and young birds than by adult males because it highlights the white tips of their tail feathers (which are not found on adult males).

Hummingbird aerial displays are of two basic types. One is a shuttle-flight display, where the bird flies back and forth in a short horizontal arc in front of another bird. In these displays the tail and gorget may be spread for added emphasis.

The other aerial display is the dive display, which has been seen performed only by males. In this display the bird does a series of oval or U-shaped dives, often accompanied at certain key points by wing or vocal sounds. Very little is known about the meaning of these displays, except that in most cases they seem to be aggressive. It could be that these displays have different meanings in different contexts, being a part of territorial defense *or* courtship, depending on the circumstances.

A Year in the Life of a Bird

All birds have a yearly cycle of social behavior. Being familiar with this cycle will enable you to place the behavior you see at your feeders within the larger context of a bird's whole life. The most difficult time for a bird to live through is the first year of its life, for it has so much to learn. If it lives for one year, it has a good chance of living for several more. Even so, the average life span for most small birds, such as those at your feeders, is only about 2 to 5 years. Hummingbirds can live up to 12 years, although many live only 3 to 5 years. Larger birds, such as crows, may live 10 years or more.

THE CYCLE OF LIFE

To make bird behavior at your feeders more meaningful and enjoyable, here is a short summary of a year in the life of a typical bird. Clearly this is a generalized account; each bird is slightly different.

START OF BREEDING/MIGRATION

The breeding season for most songbirds starts in late winter or spring when the changing length of daylight, or *photoperiod*, triggers hormonal changes in the birds, which in turn results in changed behavior. For birds that migrate, such as Red-winged Blackbirds, a lengthening photoperiod may result in migration north to their breeding grounds. Other birds that are year-round residents of an area, such as White-breasted Nuthatches, may begin to restrict their movements to a nesting area.

TERRITORY FORMATION

The beautiful singing of birds in spring is one of the supreme delights of nature. Males do most singing, and it generally has two functions: to advertise and defend a territory against other males, and to attract a female to the territory. If other males of the same species try to intrude on the territory, then there are visual displays, chases, and occasional direct fighting. Females arrive in breeding areas after the males, then select and pair with male birds. Once territories are agreed upon among the birds and a bird has a mate, singing is greatly reduced or stops completely. Males may be less vigilant in defending their territory after all their young have left the nest.

A male White-throated Sparrow belts out a lusty song of romance for a mate.

Perhaps this male Evening Grosbeak (*left*) is welcoming a prospective female mate (*right*) to his territory.

COURTSHIP

The magical behavior we tend to lump under the simple name of courtship is far from understood in any animal (probably least of all in our own species). It involves close interactions and displays between males and females, which result in a kind of bonding or mutual benefit that keeps a pair of animals together. An example in the world of birds is a male bird feeding a seed to a female.

In migratory birds, males and females begin to "court"—choose mates and form pairs—shortly after territories have been established. Once paired, the male and female are much more synchronized in their activities and tend to stay together as they move about the territory. It is at this point that birds may investigate a birdhouse by landing on it, cautiously peering in, and then going inside. This investigation may occur over a period of days or weeks and may include several houses or cavities before one is chosen.

NEST BUILDING

Songbirds usually start nest building soon after courtship is completed. In most species, the female does all the building, usually during the morning hours, with the male either guarding the nest site (or birdhouse) or following her to and from the nest as she gathers materials. In the case of the House Wren, the male builds

Bird Feeder Journal

April 21, 11:30 A.M. A male Eastern Bluebird showed up on our property. We followed him around for the whole morning, watching him investigate at least 10 different birdhouses, a few tree cavities, and the neighbor's lamppost (which was minus the lamp, so it was just a hollow 4-inch-diameter pipe). He returned later with a female and tried to interest her in at least 5 different houses by flying to them and singing to her.

A female Mountain Bluebird incubating eggs. She will not move, even though the birdhouse is open and a picture is being taken.

several partial nests; the female chooses one and adds a lining. In other species, like Cedar Waxwings, both sexes participate. Nest building normally takes from a few days to about a week to complete.

MATING AND EGG LAYING

When the nest is complete, egg laying may begin immediately, or the birds may wait several days or more. During this interval the birds will mate.

To mate, the male lands on the back of the female and bends his tail down as she lifts hers up. The anal openings, or cloaca, of the male and female touch, and sperm is transferred. After a few seconds the male steps off the female's back.

The female lays one egg per day, usually early each morning, until the clutch (group of eggs) is complete. Clutch size varies with the species, but four to six eggs is a common number for most small species. (You will find specific information for many feeder birds in the bird profiles, beginning on page 159.) Although it may appear during this time that the nest is abandoned, it probably isn't; the birds generally do not spend very much time at the nest until most of the eggs are laid.

INCUBATION

Incubation does not usually start until the last egg is laid, probably so that all the eggs will hatch on the same or following day. In most

Mountain Bluebird eggs and nestlings at the moment of hatching. The dark streaks are actually wet down.

Mountain Bluebirds in the early days of the nestling phase. They have practically no feathers and still need their mother's brooding to keep them warm.

species, only the female incubates. She actually develops added blood vessels on her breast and may lose some of her feathers at the same spot. This area, called the brood patch, is like a little heating pad that warms the eggs.

During this period the male may bring food to the female, or he may guard the nest while the female takes breaks to feed, stretch, and preen her feathers. In a few species, notably woodpeckers and owls, both sexes take turns incubating. Incubation lasts about 10 to 12 days in small birds.

NESTLING PHASE

A nest of eggs will hatch over a period of a day or two; if you're watching carefully, you'll see outward clues of this occurrence. Your best clue to the onset of this phase is seeing the parents bringing food to the nest. They will make many trips, and it soon keeps both of them quite busy, leaving them barely enough time to take breaks and find food for themselves.

The young are called nestlings because they remain in the nest and are fed by the parents. At first the nestlings' eyes are closed and they barely make a sound. They are tiny and naked except for a few down feathers. They cannot regulate their own body heat, so the female sits over them, brooding them to keep them warm. After several days, their eyes open, they are covered with downy feathers, and they make peeping sounds when fed. Toward the end of the nestling phase the young have grown quite large, are fully feathered, and make loud, begging noises when the parents arrive with food.

For many birds, the nestling phase lasts about 10 days, and sometimes up to 2 or 3 weeks for birds that nest in birdhouses. Instinctively, young birds know when to leave a

A male Northern Cardinal helps feed nestlings, a rare male bird behavior.

box. One by one they exit over a period of hours, or in some cases a day or two. They can fly quite well, often better than their counterparts in open-cup nests.

FLEDGLING PHASE

After the young leave the nest, they are called fledglings. Although they are out of the nest, they are still dependent on the parents for food. Fledglings often sit and call continuously for food, but they also frequently wander around in hot pursuit of the parents. The adults feed them—less frequently than when they were nestlings, and with larger pieces of food. Gradually, the fledglings begin to find food on their own. This phase can end abruptly when the harried parents become aggressive toward the young birds and chase them away.

The fledgling phase lasts from one to several weeks, depending on the species. If the parents begin another brood, the fledgling stage may be shortened, or the male might take care of the first brood while the female is busy with nesting duties.

RENESTING

Renesting may occur after a successful first brood or if the first attempt is unsuccessful. Many birds will keep trying to raise young throughout a season, even after one or two unsuccessful attempts. Birds may or may not use the same birdhouse for subsequent broods.

MIGRATION

The fall migration of birds is always exciting. Bird populations are greatest just before mi-

Two Eastern Bluebirds in the fledging stage. The parents are still feeding them, but soon they will have to fend for themselves.

gration because there are many new young birds from the summer's breeding. The southern migration usually starts after the birds have completed their molt and may be triggered by a diminishing photoperiod. Birds that do not migrate will remain in the breeding area or will move to nearby areas with better food. In winter, most pairs are less exclusive, and many species may gather into small or large flocks (see page 147) until the following breeding season.

A HUMMINGBIRD'S LIFE

Most songbirds and hummingbirds migrate north in the spring to breed, but there are a few hummingbirds that start their breeding migration in different seasons. For example, the

Allen's, Costa's, and Rufous hummingbirds start their northward migration during January and February—what most of us would still call winter. Also, a few hummingbirds, such as Anna's and possibly Costa's, start breeding in December, a good 5 months before many songbirds.

Female hummingbirds set up separate territories from males that will include the nest site. Males are aggressive toward almost all other birds that enter their territories, including, at first, females of their own species. Females defend their breeding territories to a lesser extent, partly because they need to devote much of their time to nest building and raising young. Male territories often shift over the course of the breeding season as flowers fade and come into bloom.

Hummingbirds can also be strongly territorial during migration as they stop along their routes at large patches of flowers or feeders to refuel before continuing on their flight. These resources are very important to them, and they will vigorously defend them.

This can complicate efforts to determine what the hummers are doing in your yard, as several species may be migrating through an area and forming temporary feeding territories, while another species has already established breeding territories in the same spot. This occurs most often along the West Coast, where the Anna's, Allen's, and Costa's hummingbirds are breeding when the Rufous, Black-chinned,

Calliope, and Broad-tailed hummingbirds are migrating through.

Very little is known about the courtship behavior in many of our North American hummingbird species. It is probably very short; you will rarely see male and female hummingbirds spending much time together. After establishing a separate territory, the female comes to the male territory, probably attracted by nectar or nesting material there. At first the male may be aggressive toward her and chase her. Then he may do one or more aerial displays in front of her, such as a dive display or shuttle display, to entice her to select him for mating.

After the male's aerial courtship displays, the female hummer leads the male closer to her territory and initiates copulation, which is done while perched. After copulation, the male returns to his territory and often mates with other females. It is not known whether the first female mates with more than one male, but it is certainly possible.

Unlike songbirds, female hummingbirds start the nest after mating is done. They build their small cup of downy fibers wrapped in spider or insect silk all on their own. Interestingly, a hummer nest is often built on the same spot, right on top of the prior year's foundation. This results in a layered appearance at the base of the nest.

Female hummingbirds are alone again as they in-

A male Calliope Hummingbird with full gorget display flies in front of a female Calliope Hummingbird.

cubate their clutch of eggs and raise the young. The female usually lays just 2 eggs, incubates them for 2 to 2½ weeks, then feeds the hatched babies in the nest for about 3 weeks.

Most hummingbirds spend their non-breeding season south of Canada and the United States. These birds have long migration flights, some going thousands of miles. The Rufous Hummingbird has the longest migration route: up to 3,000 miles from Alaska all the way to northern and central Mexico.

All of our North American hummingbirds make shorter movements just after the breeding season, mostly in response to the sequence of blooming flowers in different habitats. In the West this often means moving to higher elevations in the mountains, where alpine wildflower meadows are at the height of their blooming after the later snow melt.

Fast Fact
Ruby-throated Hummingbirds fly 500 miles across the Gulf of Mexico during migration, bulking up by 50 percent first.

Baby Hummers

What must it be like to be a baby hummingbird, one of the world's smallest birds? The sequence of pictures shows, from left to right, the various stages in the first 2 to 4 weeks of life of two young Ruby-throated Hummingbirds.

The hummingbird nest is covered with lichens and just fits the contours of the female's body, so it keeps all the warmth inside the nest as the female incubates. While males may go into torpor at night to conserve energy, incubating females generally do not.

The young have hatched. Notice how they are all black at first and have no feathers. They cannot control their own body temperature at this stage, so the female must spend a good deal of time brooding them—sitting over them to keep them warm.

The baby hummers have grown feathers. When the female arrives at the nest with food—either nectar or insects—the young tilt their heads back and give high-pitched begging calls. The female places her bill far into their throats and regurgitates food from her crop, a specialized holding area of her digestive tract.

The young have grown considerably and have stretched the nest to almost twice its original size. At this stage the young spend most of their time sleeping or waiting quietly for their mother to return with food.

The young hummers now begin to exercise their wings and legs by standing on the edge of the nest and fluttering.

There is no room left in the nest for the two growing birds; it is about time for them to leave. Notice that their bills are still short. They will continue to grow even after they leave the nest.

Part 5 Profiles of Common Backyard Birds

ONE OF THE REWARDS OF HAVING BIRDS AT YOUR
FEEDERS IS A DEEPER SENSE OF CONNECTION TO
NATURE—A CONSTANT REMINDER THAT THERE IS
MORE TO LIFE THAN ONLY HUMAN CONCERNS.

This section is designed to help you identify your backyard birds. We have included all of the species that are common at backyard feeders over a significant portion of the country. A few of the birds are typically found beyond the ordinary yard, living their lives in fields or on lakes that may be part of your property or just down the road.

Each profile contains a photograph of each species and a description of behavioral traits or other features that make the bird special. The boxes that accompany each species provide clues to identification, typical habitat, favorite foods, nesting needs, and specifics on migration and breeding. For each species, a range map shows the winter range (indicated by blue), summer range (indicated by orange), and year-round range (indicated by green).

Identifying Your Birds

Bird identification involves looking and listening. It is a skill that anybody can learn, and you will get better with practice. You will be amazed at how easy it can be to identify that new bird in your yard with the profiles in this section of the book. You may want binoculars if your feeders are away from the house; in fact, we use them whether the birds are near or far so we can see their beauty in detail.

HOW TO LOOK AT A BIRD

The most common mistake beginners make is not getting enough clues while a bird is in sight. Instead, they run to their identification guide, find they do not remember the bird well enough to locate it in the guide, and then look back for the bird, which has flown away.

Therefore, when you first see a bird, take time to watch it, and pick up as many clues as you can. Try to remember them, repeating them to yourself as you watch the bird. Then go to this book for identification.

The first thing to do when trying to identify a bird is to look at its body.

1. Notice its size. Is it small, like a sparrow? Medium-size, like a robin? Large, like a crow?
2. Look at the colors on its breast, wings, and tail. Is the bird a uniform color? Are there any conspicuous patches of color on the wings or tail? Is there streaking or different colors on the breast?

Then look at its head.

1. Look at the shape and colors of the head. Is it all one color? Is it iridescent? Does it have a stripe through the eye? Does the bird have a crest? Is the shape of the head distinctive?
2. Look at the shape and color of the bill. Is it long or short? Is it conical or thin? Is it all one color?

Another aid in bird identification is the process of elimination. Deciding what a bird is *not* will help narrow down your choices of what it *is*.

Look at the photographs of the birds in this guide during a leisure moment and read the identification clues with them. This will familiarize you with the various species and help you

WHEN YOU FIRST SEE A BIRD, TAKE TIME TO WATCH IT AND PICK UP AS MANY CLUES AS YOU CAN TO IDENTIFY IT.

Buying Binoculars

Binoculars bring birds up close, helping you see their beauty and behavior and getting you close enough so that you can identify them. Here are a few tips about binoculars that will help you get a pair that work for you at the right price and the right quality.

There are two numbers on any pair of binoculars to pay attention to: for example, 7 × 35 or 8.5 × 42. The first number refers to the power of the binoculars to magnify an object, in this case by 7 times or 8.5 times. If you have binoculars more powerful than this, you may have trouble holding the image steady; any less powerful and you will not see the birds clearly or large enough to easily identify them. The second figure—like 35—is the diameter in millimeters of the opening at the far end of the binoculars. The larger the opening, the more light is let through and the clearer you will see the bird. An opening size somewhere between 35 and 42 is good for most purposes.

Finally, avoid a mistake many beginners make. Resist the urge to buy very light and very small binoculars so you can easily slip them in your pocket. Light and small binoculars rarely have the power or let in enough light to be good for bird watching.

identify them when they are at your feeder. Become familiar with all the common birds, and you will be more alert to any similar-looking birds that show up. (These are sometimes highlighted in the box "What's That Bird?" throughout this section.)

Once you have learned to identify a bird by sight, continue to add to your list of ways to identify it—where it feeds, how it flies, how it interacts with other birds, and the sounds it makes. All of these things will help you identify it more easily in the future.

KEEPING A JOURNAL

We like to keep a bird feeder journal to make it easier to remember or compare the many fascinating things that occur at our feeders. What should you record? Anything that catches your attention and interests you. You may want to look at feeding habits, bathing habits, social interactions, breeding behavior, migration timing, or any other part of a bird's life that occurs at or near your feeders. Entries can be very simple, with just these headings:

Date:

Time:

Species:

Observations:

In the case of visual displays, we also try to make a sketch of what it looked like.

We find that looking back over our notes and sketches is extremely rewarding, helping us remember the tremendous variety of things that we have experienced. We encourage all of you to keep your own personal journal of the things you see at your feeders.

BLUEBIRD
A BEAUTIFUL SUCCESS STORY

Bluebirds are some of America's most beautiful birds; whenever we see one, we are in awe. They are a breathtaking sight, with plumage that's truly the color of the sky. Bluebirds nest in cavities and birdhouses in open areas with nearby perches from which they can hunt for insects. They will also eat special bluebird food, available from some feed suppliers, from platform or house hopper–type feeders. They are usually quite tolerant of human presence and are a joy to have nesting on your property along the edges of a field or wooded area.

Once a more common bird, bluebirds severely declined in population due to habitat loss: The House Sparrow and the starling were introduced into the United States in the late nineteenth century, resulting in heavy competition for the existing nesting cavities that bluebirds need. Thanks to the efforts of the North American Bluebird Society and the thousands of people who have put up bluebird nesting boxes, bluebird populations are on the upswing.

THREE KINDS OF BEAUTY

The Eastern Bluebird has a rusty, reddish throat and chest and a white belly. Its range extends over the eastern two-thirds of North America; it is found in suburbs, farmlands, orchards, and open parklands.

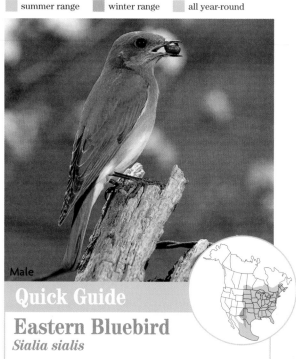

■ summer range   ■ winter range   ■ all year-round

Male

Quick Guide

Eastern Bluebird
Sialia sialis

ID Clues: A small bird at about 6 ½ inches, the male has a blue back, red breast, and white belly; female is similar, but colors duller

Habitat: Farmlands and rural yards, open woodlands

Food: Insects in short-grass areas, berries

Breeding period: March through July

Nests: Natural cavity in tree or birdhouse; nest has base of fine grasses, pine needles, or weed stalks; inner lining of finer grasses

Eggs: Usually 4 or 5 clear blue or white

Incubation: 12 to 18 days, average 13 or 14, by female only

Nestling phase: Usually 17 to 22 days

Broods: 2 or 3

Migration: Migrates to southern part of range

Bluebird Birdhouse

Dimensions

Entrance hole diameter:
For Eastern Bluebird: 1 $\frac{1}{2}$"
For Mountain Bluebird: 1 $\frac{9}{16}$"
For Western Bluebird: 1 $\frac{9}{16}$"
Height of hole above floor: 6" to 7"
Inside floor dimensions:
For Eastern Bluebird: 4" × 4"
For Mountain Bluebird: 5 $\frac{1}{2}$" × 5 $\frac{1}{2}$"
For Western Bluebird: 5" × 5"
Total height of box: 11" to 12"

Placement

Habitat: Open areas with low vegetation and a
nearby perch
Height: 4' to 6' high on a tree, pole, or fence
post

The Western Bluebird has a blue throat, and the brick red color of its chest often extends onto its back. It breeds in western Canada and in the western United States. In some areas, it will nest on the same trails as the Mountain Bluebird. In the western coastal mountain ranges, Western Bluebirds may migrate to the valley floors to find good food supplies in winter. Some, however, winter very near where they nest if the food supply is good.

The Mountain Bluebird is the "all-blue" bluebird, lacking the red breast of the eastern and western species. It breeds in open areas in parklands, mountains, badlands, and ravines, placing its nest in tree cavities, holes in fence posts or utility poles, and birdhouses.

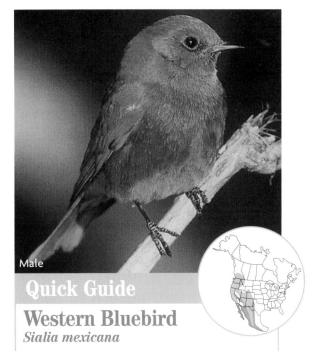

Male

Quick Guide
Western Bluebird
Sialia mexicana

ID Clues: Small bird; male has deep blue throat, gray belly, red breast, and sometimes red on deep blue back; female is grayish on back with blue wings and light red on breast
Habitat: Forest edges and open woods
Food: Insects in open areas and berries
Breeding Period: March into August
Nests: Natural cavity in tree or birdhouse; nest made of dried grass, weed stems, pine needles, twigs, sometimes with hair or feathers
Eggs: 3 to 8, usually 4 to 6, pale blue or bluish white, rarely white
Incubation: 13 or 14 days, by female only
Nestling Phase: 19 to 22 days, usually 20 to 21
Broods: 1 or 2, rarely 3
Migration: Some birds are resident year-round; others migrate to southern part of their range

Swallows often compete with bluebirds for nesting spots as they favor similar habitats—open areas near woods or fields. However, they will easily live close together: While this male Tree Swallow may be using this fence-post hole, a bluebird might take up residence in a box mounted on the next post.

HABITAT NEEDS

You can help make a difference in the success of these beautiful birds by maintaining a "blue-bird trail," which is simply several bluebird houses placed along edges of fields, fence lines, or trails where they can be easily moni-tored while driving or hiking.

Birdhouses on a bluebird trail should be placed about 100 yards apart in open (not heavily wooded) areas that have short or

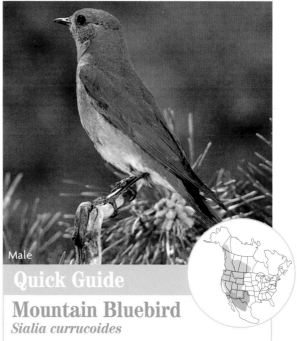

Male

Quick Guide

Mountain Bluebird
Sialia currucoides

ID Clues: Only all-blue bluebird, paler on the breast and belly than on the back and head; female is grayish brown with a white belly, except in fall, a reddish hue on throat and breast

Habitat: Mountain meadows, rangeland, sagebrush, coniferous woods

Food: Insects while hovering or from perches, berries

Breeding period: March into July

Nests: Natural cavity in tree or birdhouse; nest made of strips of bark, dried grass, and other dry plant material

Eggs: 4 to 7, rarely 8 or 9, pale blue or sometimes white

Incubation: About 14 days, by female only

Nestling phase: 17 to 21 days

Broods: 1 or 2

Migration: Migrates to southern part of its range

sparse ground vegetation. Bluebirds like having small trees, shrubs, or other perches within 5 to 100 feet of the box. If you don't have the right habitat for bluebirds on your own property, consider putting a bluebird trail on conservation property in your town or in other appropriate areas—with the permission of the landowner.

To maintain a bluebird trail, the boxes must be monitored. (See Part 3 for more information on building, protecting, and monitoring your boxes.) Some of the events you will likely see while monitoring boxes on your trail are described below.

NESTING HABITS

The nesting habits of the three bluebird species are similar. The male bluebird searches for a territory that includes a good nesting site. He courts a female with sweet warbled notes and by doing a wing-wave—raising and quivering one or both wings. He may feed her tasty morsels as further enticement.

After the female selects a nest box, she does the nest building. Nest building can be completed in several days, or it can sometimes take her more than a week.

MALE BLUEBIRDS COURT FEMALES

WITH SWEET WARBLED NOTES AND A

WING-WAVE.

Both parents will feed the young, but the light shades of blue and red indicate this bird is the female Eastern Bluebird.

FAMILY LIFE

After an incubation period of about 14 days, the eggs hatch. For the first several days, the female keeps the tiny and practically naked babies warm by brooding them, while the male brings all of the food. When the young have more feathers and are able to regulate their own body temperature, both parents make food trips.

The babies grow rapidly, more than doubling their weight in a week. Their eyes open on the fourth to seventh day, and they have tail feathers showing by the eighth day. By the fifteenth day they are completely feathered, and they leave the nest when they are 17 to 22 days old. (Do not monitor the box after the fourteenth day; the young may leave prematurely.) For 2 to 4 weeks, the parents continue to care for the fledglings until they become proficient flyers and are able to feed themselves.

Fledgling bluebirds of all three species have grayish blue backs and brownish spots on white breasts. After a partial molt in early fall, they resemble the adults.

The female may begin a second and, rarely, a third brood in the same or in a different box. Sometimes one or more of the young from a previous brood remain with the parents and help raise the nestlings of the following brood by bringing them food.

After breeding, family groups of bluebirds remain near their nesting areas into autumn, and then they drift southward when cold weather sets in. In winter, they travel in flocks to find and eat fruits and whatever insects they can uncover.

CARDINAL
WINTER'S POSTER BIRD

Sometimes it seems as though every Christmas card with a nature scene has a cardinal perched on it somewhere. It's easy to understand why: The brilliant red coat of the male cardinal is familiar to nearly everyone and always stands out sharply amid a snow-covered background. A philosopher might say cardinals symbolize the beauty and hope of nature even in the harshest of times.

The male's beautiful red coat of feathers also gave this species its name. The word *cardinal* originally meant "important" and later referred to the high-ranking official in the Roman Catholic Church. It then became associated with the bright red color of the cardinal's robes. With feathers so reminiscent of papal robes, it makes sense that cardinal became the name of the bird. (Of course, its full name is Northern Cardinal.)

A BEAUTIFUL SONG

We were awakened one early spring morning by the most beautiful singing in our yard. As we listened, we realized it sounded like a duet, with one bird singing a certain series of phrases and another bird repeating those phrases exactly. It sounded a little like: "Whoit, whoit, whoit . . . whoit, whoit, whoit . . . what-cheer, what-cheer, what-cheer . . . what-cheer, what-cheer, what-cheer."

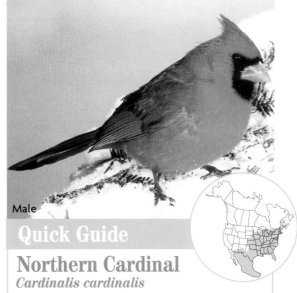

Male

Quick Guide
Northern Cardinal
Cardinalis cardinalis

ID Clues: The male is a medium-size (8 ½-inch) all-red bird with a crest and an area of black surrounding its red bill

Habitat: Shrubs near open areas, open woods, suburban yards

Food: Insects, spiders, seeds, berries; sunflower seed at feeders

Breeding Period: Mid-spring through summer

Nests: Nest of twigs, bark strips, leaves, rootlets in dense shrubbery or branches of small trees

Eggs: 2 to 5, buff-white with dark marks

Incubation: 12 or 13 days

Nestling Phase: 9 to 11 days

Broods: 1 to 4

Migration: Generally a year-round resident

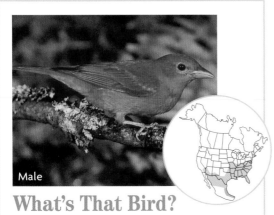

Male

What's That Bird?
SUMMER TANAGER

ID Clues: All 7½ inches are uniformly bright rose-red with darker red wings and tail
Habitat: Pine-oak woods, willows and cottonwoods along streams
Food: Insects, especially bees and wasps; fruit and berries
Nests: Nest of weed stems, bark, grasses 10 to 35 feet high in tree

We knew cardinals were in our yard, but since both male and female cardinals can sing, we did not know whether this was the duet of a mated pair or birds of the same sex. When done between male and female, it is part of courtship activities and strengthens the bonds between the pair. When sung between cardinals of the same sex, it can mean each is defending its own territory.

Cardinals in different areas of the country may use different phrases in their songs, and cardinals in Missouri might sound different from cardinals in Ontario. Since cardinals rarely travel great distances from where they were born, it's easy to see why birds in the same area sound alike.

HABITAT AND FOOD PREFERENCES

If you have the right habitat in your yard, you should be able to attract cardinals. They like to live in generally open areas that have both trees and berry-producing shrubs. They usually build their nests in dense thickets or low shrubs or vines an average of 4 to 5 feet off the ground. Cardinals also sleep in these dense

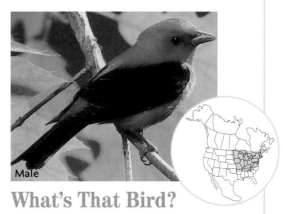

Male

What's That Bird?
SCARLET TANAGER

ID Clues: About 7 inches of scarlet-red body set off by black wings and tail
Habitat: Large tracts of mature deciduous forests
Food: Caterpillars and other insects in tree canopy; some wild berries
Nests: Nest of twigs, grasses 5 to 75 feet high in tree

tangles. Some of their favorite plants include honeysuckle, evergreens, privet, and multiflora rose.

Cardinals prefer feeding stations that offer seed on a tray, on a platform, or just scattered on the ground. Although they relish sunflower seed, they do eat a variety of other foods, including cracked corn, millet, safflower seed, and nutmeats. When eating sunflower, they manipulate the seed with their tongue until it lies sideways in their powerful bill, crack it open, eject the hull with their tongue, and swallow the seed. We most often notice cardinals feeding just after dawn or at dusk.

The adult female cardinal, like the male, is a medium-size bird with a crest. It has an olive-to-buff-brown body, reddish wings and tail, and a bright red bill. A fledgling is similar to the adult female but has a gray-to-black bill instead of a red one.

SEEDS AS KISSES

Through most of the winter, males are usually dominant over females at the feeder. Then a change occurs, and a lovely ceremony starts to take place in late winter and continues on through midsummer. You will see the male pick up a bit of food, go over to the female, and place it in her bill. It looks like they are kissing.

This is called courtship feeding, or mate feeding, and is a good sign that the birds are paired and about to start their breeding season.

PAIRS GIVE WAY TO FLOCKS

During the breeding season—middle of spring through summer—you will have either pairs or lone birds visit your feeder. But in winter, cardinals often join flocks in areas of abundant food and stay together until breeding starts. The flocks contain both males and females and can reach 50 or more birds. In northern areas, where the cardinal may have just recently moved in, winter flocks are less likely to occur because the overall population of cardinals is still low.

Bird Feeder Journal

May 20, 9:00 A.M. The cardinals are nesting in the catbrier, very close to where cardinals nested 2 years ago. She is incubating four eggs. He takes sunflower seed from the feeder, flies near her, and sings softly. She comes off the nest, and he feeds her.

CHICKADEE
AMERICA'S FAVORITE FEEDER BIRD

The chickadee is one of America's favorite feeder birds. On the dreariest winter days, watching them at our feeders always cheers us up. Observing their constant activity and hearing their tiny calls, we just can't help being intrigued and entertained.

Chickadees are remarkable because they have one of the most complex social structures of any feeder bird; they also have one of the largest "vocabularies" of calls. These two may be related—they may need a greater range of communication to keep order in their complex flock structure.

SONGS AND CALLS

Chickadees make more than 15 different sounds, but these are their most common:

"Chickadeedeedee"—Often given at disturbances or when one bird becomes separated from the rest of the flock. Given all year.

"Tseet"—A short, high, soft call given between members of a pair or a flock to help them keep in contact. Given all year.

"Feebee"—The song of the Black-capped Chickadee; a two-note whistle, with the second note lower than the first. The Carolina Chickadee song is made up of four notes that sound like "feebee feebay." Given by males to advertise territory and attract mates.

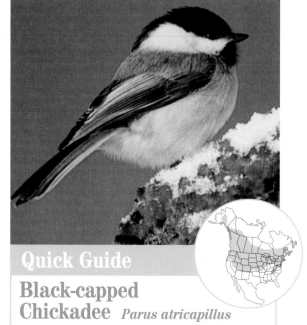

Quick Guide

Black-capped Chickadee *Parus atricapillus*

ID Clues: 5¼-inch bird with gray body, rusty edge of breast, black cap and bib, and white cheeks; whiter on wing edges than Carolina Chickadee; males and females look alike

Habitat: Woods, farmlands, suburbs

Food: Insects, seeds, berries; suet and sunflower at feeders

Breeding period: April to July

Nests: Can excavate cavity in rotted wood of standing tree or use existing hole or birdhouse; nests of wood chips, moss, hair, feathers, insect cocoons, other downy fibers

Eggs: 6 to 8, white with red-brown speckles

Incubation: 12 days, by female only

Nestling phase: 16 days

Broods: 1 or 2

Migration: Generally a year-round resident, but young birds may migrate south

CAROLINA OR BLACK-CAPPED?

There are four species of chickadees. The Chestnut-backed and Mountain Chickadees live only in the West and are easy to distinguish. The Carolina Chickadee lives only in the East, and the Black-capped Chickadee lives all over North America.

From the range maps, you can see that there are areas, especially in the mid-Atlantic states, where both the Carolina and Black-capped Chickadees live. If you live in one of these areas, you may want to distinguish between the two species, but trying to do it by sight is difficult. When the two birds are together, you can see that the Black-capped is slightly larger, has a longer tail, and has more white on the edge of its wing feathers. Everybody agrees that the males' songs differ markedly in the two species, and this is the best clue.

WATCHING CHICKADEES FEED

Chickadees tend to take one seed from a feeder, fly away to a nearby perch and eat it, and then fly back for another. They usually carry the seed away in their bill, and then hold it down on a branch with their foot as they peck at it. In the wild, they feed on tiny seeds and insects.

Chickadee flocks have a fairly stable hierarchy throughout winter, and in general the most dominant bird is allowed to feed first. The dominant birds visit the feeder one at a time while other chickadees wait nearby. A domi-

Quick Guide

Carolina Chickadee
Parus carolinensis

ID Clues: Nearly identical but slightly smaller than Black-capped at just under 5 inches; feathers on wings may appear all gray; males and females look alike
Habitat: Woods, farmlands, suburbs
Food: Insects, seeds, berries; suet and sunflower at feeders
Breeding period: April to July
Nests: Can excavate cavity in soft, rotted wood of standing tree or use existing hole or birdhouse; nests of wood chips, moss, hair, feathers, insect cocoons, down from cinnamon fern
Eggs: 6, white with red-brown speckles
Incubation: 11 or 12 days, by female only
Nestling phase: 13 to 17 days
Broods: 1 or 2
Migration: Generally a year-round resident

nant bird may also fly to the feeder and displace a less-dominant bird.

Quick Guide

Chestnut-backed Chickadee *Parus rufescens*

ID Clues: Small bird, about 5 inches with black cap, black throat, and white cheeks; only chickadee with a chestnut-brown back; males and females look alike

Habitat: Coniferous or mixed woods

Food: Insects and seeds; sunflower and suet at feeders

Breeding period: March to July

Nests: Can excavate cavity in soft, rotted wood of standing tree or use existing hole or birdhouse; nest of moss, hair, feathers, other downy materials

Eggs: 6 or 7, white with light reddish speckles

Incubation: About 11 or 12 days, by female only

Nestling phase: About 13 to 17 days

Broods: 1 or 2

Migration: Generally a year-round resident

Chickadees have amazing acrobatic abilities, enabling them to hang upside down underneath delicate twigs. This allows them to feed on insects on the tips of branches and also to find insects on the underside of branches when the tops are covered with snow.

CHICKADEES CAN HANG UPSIDE DOWN UNDER THE MOST DELICATE TWIGS, ALLOWING THEM TO FIND INSECTS ON THE UNDERSIDE OF SNOW-COVERED BRANCHES.

BUILDING TERRITORIES AND MATING BONDS

Just before breeding in spring, the males become more aggressive and territorial; they begin to outline large areas, roughly 10 acres, which they defend with chases and song. Thus, if you have a breeding male in your yard, he will keep out most other chickadees except his mate. The other chickadees have to move elsewhere to breed.

Part of chickadee courtship is the male's feeding of the female. He gets an insect or seed and flies to the female, who gives a high, thin call that sounds like "teeship teeship," then she quivers her wings and takes the food from the male. This is called mate feeding. It continues from the beginning of courtship through the incubation period.

Male

What's That Bird?
COMMON YELLOWTHROAT

ID Clues: Small, 5-inch bird with
brownish body, yellow throat and
upper breast; distinctive black mask
with grayish white border

Habitat: Dense brushy habitats near wet
areas

Food: Insects, spiders, seeds gleaned
from ground or shrubs

Nests: Nest of grasses 1 to 2 feet high in
shrubs

Quick Guide
Mountain Chickadee
Parus gambeli

ID Clues: Small gray bird with black cap, black
throat, and white cheeks; distinguished by
the white eyebrow going through the black
cap; males and females look alike

Habitat: Open coniferous forests in mountains

Food: Insects, seeds, berries; suet and
sunflower at feeders

Breeding period: April to July

Nests: Can excavate cavity in soft, rotted
wood of standing tree or use existing hole
or birdhouse; nests of wood chips, hair,
feathers

Eggs: 7 to 9, pure white, sometimes with faint
spots

Incubation: About 14 days, by female only

Nestling phase: 17 to 20 days

Broods: 1 or 2

Migration: Generally a year-round resident

CARVING OUT A HOME

In general, chickadees look for tree holes made
by woodpeckers—or other natural cavities—in
which to build their nests. They are also good
at making their own cavity as long as the wood
is soft or rotted so that they can excavate it
with their short, thin bills.

If you go out some morning in early spring,
you may be lucky enough to see a pair excavating their nest. The birds do it together, each
taking a turn pecking out the wood and then

Two Black-capped Chickadees, probably a mated pair, may be thinking of excavating at the end of this birch stub. Chickadees often excavate in the rotted wood of dead birches.

Chickadee Birdhouse

Dimensions
Entrance-hole diameter: 1 $\frac{1}{8}$" to 1 $\frac{1}{2}$"
Height of hole above floor: 6" to 7"
Inside floor dimensions: 4" × 4" to 5" × 5"
Total height of box: 9" to 12"

Placement
Habitat: Suburban or rural locations with a mixture of trees and open areas
Height: 5' to 10' high on a tree or post

The female does all the egg incubating while the male brings her food. One of the most engaging breeding behaviors is the fledgling phase. For a few weeks, the young—with their bright, new feathers; high-pitched voices; and already adult size—look adorable as they follow their parents about, begging for food. On the other end of the spectrum are fairly

carrying a beakful of sawdust 10 to 20 feet away to drop it.

Trees that typically rot in the center, such as birches, are excellent places for chickadees to excavate. This is one good reason for leaving dead branches or standing dead trees on your property—they provide much-needed nesting spots for hole-nesting birds such as chickadees. In addition, all four species of chickadees commonly use birdhouses.

Bird Feeder Journal

April 30, 10:30 A.M. We have been watching a pair of chickadees excavate a nest hole in the top of a 2-foot-high rotting gray birch stub in our woods. Earlier this morning, as our son was clearing some brush, he accidentally dragged the brush over the stub, and it fell over. We decided to tie it together with string and stake it up. The chickadees called excitedly as we did this, but within minutes of our having resurrected the stub, the pair resumed their excavation as if nothing had happened! They successfully raised a brood from this nest.

ragged-looking chickadees at your feeder in late summer: adults whose feathers are molting and worn out from all that going in and out of the nest hole to feed their young.

FORMING FLOCKS

From March to August, chickadees live in pairs on large 10-acre territories. In August, when they are finished breeding, they gather into small flocks of about six to ten birds. These flocks are composed of adults who bred in the area and young birds from other areas.

Each flock stays within and defends a territory of about 20 acres and chases out other chickadee flocks that enter. Thus, if your feeder is in a chickadee territory, you will have the same birds feeding there from August to March. Sometimes a feeder is near the border of two chickadee flock territories. When both flocks show up at once, you will see many chases and hear scolding calls. In spring, the most dominant pairs of the flock breed in the area of the winter territory, and the others are forced out to breed elsewhere.

COWBIRD
THE BUFFALO BIRD

Before people started clearing the forests of the eastern and western United States, the Brown-headed Cowbird's range followed closely that of the buffalo herds, which roamed the Great Plains. The birds are believed to have followed the herds throughout the summer, eating insects that the buffalo stirred up with their movements, as well as ticks and other parasites off the animals' backs. They may also have followed herds of antelope throughout the same region.

Several things may have affected the coast-to-coast expansion of the Brown-headed Cowbird's range. One was the fencing off of large areas of the West and introduction of cattle, from which the Brown-headed Cowbird could obtain food in the same way it did from the wild buffalo herds. In addition, the clearing of land to the East and the addition of cows and cattle there probably enabled this bird to extend its range eastward.

DISTINGUISHING MALE, FEMALE, AND JUVENILE

The male and female look quite different. The male has a brown head, but the rest of his body, wings, and tail are black with a greenish, glossy iridescence. The female has fairly uniform gray-brown plumage with slightly darker wings and tail. The juvenile cowbird is similar in

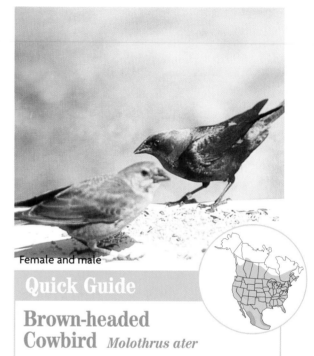

Female and male

Quick Guide

Brown-headed Cowbird *Molothrus ater*

ID Clues: A medium-size bird, about 7 inches long; the male has a brown head and black body with iridescence; the female is uniformly grayish brown with no markings

Habitat: Pastures, edges of woods, forest clearings, lawns

Food: Grains, grasses and weed seeds on the ground; insects

Breeding Period: Spring to mid-June

Nests: No nest

Eggs: 1 per host nest, white with dark marks

Incubation: 10 to 13 days

Nestling Phase: 9 to 11 days

Broods: Unknown

Migration: Migrates to central and southern parts of its range

appearance to the female, but has a brown-streaked breast.

The Brown-headed Cowbird belongs to the family Icteridae, which includes blackbirds, orioles, and meadowlarks. Their body shape is similar to that of these cousins, but their bills are noticeably shorter and more conical.

PROTECTING FEEDING SPACE

The next time a small group of Brown-headed Cowbirds visits your ground feeder, take a moment to watch them and you will likely see some actions that reveal which bird is dominant. Generally each bird maintains a distance from the others, but if one bird is approached too closely, it will fluff out its feathers, raise its wings, and thrust its head toward the intruding bird. This makes the other bird back away.

If there is a standoff, then both birds may briefly point their bills up in the air as another way to settle who controls the disputed area.

Bird Feeder Journal

May 12, 3:00 P.M. Several male Brown-headed Cowbirds have landed at the ground feeder and are displaying to each other. They are doing the bill-tilt display almost to the point of not getting time to feed. They have now flown up to the top of a nearby tree and are doing topple-over displays. It is almost comical, for they all look as if they are going to fall off the branches. Each bird ends its display by wiping its bill several times across the branch.

This "bill tilt" seems to communicate which of the two is the dominant bird, and the other moves slightly away.

COURTSHIP DANCE

Courtship behavior begins when the birds arrive in spring and lasts until mid-June. If you see a group of males and a female at your feeder, watch for acts of courtship to break out. A group of males usually competes among themselves for dominance, and the winner gets the female.

To compete, males use the bill tilt and another interesting gesture called topple-over. This move looks both complex and a little comical. The male fluffs his body feathers, arches his neck, spreads his wings and tail, and seems to fall forward while singing a song, which sounds like "bublucomseee." He may then vigorously wipe his bill back and forth on the ground or on a perch.

THE PROBLEMS OF BEING A PARASITE

The Brown-headed Cowbird makes no nest of its own; rather, it lays its eggs in other birds' nests and lets the other parents raise its young. Thus, it is considered a parasite. This habit may be a result of the bird's background of following the buffalo herds and not having time in any one place to build its own nest and raise young. It seems like a pretty good arrangement for the Brown-headed Cowbird, so you might wonder why more species don't do it and why

Male

What's That Bird?
PROTHONOTARY WARBLER

ID Clues: A small, 5½-inch bird with all-yellow head and breast and blue-gray wings; male is bright golden yellow and female is greenish yellow

Habitat: Wooded swamps and wetland areas; trees along streams and rivers

Food: Insects and spiders found in crevices of logs and tree trunks

Nests: Tree cavities or birdhouses; nest of twigs, moss, lichens, fine grasses, leaves

ready nests so she can deposit her eggs in them. The next problem is that many other birds can recognize the larger egg when it is laid in their nest; they either take it out, abandon the nest, or build a new nest on top of it. Hence, Brown-headed Cowbirds have a very low success rate for their eggs. It has been estimated that a female Brown-headed Cowbird lays about 40 eggs per season with only two or three young surviving to adulthood. This, however, is enough to expand the population.

WHAT HAPPENS TO THE BABY?

If a Brown-headed Cowbird egg is laid in a nest and the host parent, often a warbler or vireo, does not notice it, then the baby is on its way. It usually hatches slightly earlier than the other eggs, and it grows very fast in its first few days. These two adaptations give it an advantage over its nest mates, for it is larger and able to get more of the food the parents bring to the nest; this may slow the development of the other young. In many cases, a baby Brown-headed Cowbird crowds one of the host species' young out of the nest, and it dies.

The parents feed the nestling Brown-headed Cowbird as if it were one of their own, even though it is bigger and looks different from the other nestlings. The Brown-headed Cowbird is usually the first to leave the nest and to be fed by the parents outside the nest. It is indeed a strange sight to see a Yellow Warbler adult feeding a fledgling that is twice its size. How a

we are not overrun with Brown-headed Cowbirds.

The reason is that it is not as easy as it seems. First of all, the female Brown-headed Cowbird must find other birds' nests just when the other birds are laying eggs; she then removes one egg from that nest and lays her own egg in its place. Like other birds, she lays one egg a day and, therefore, must find four or five

young Brown-headed Cowbird then proceeds to join its own species is still a mystery.

FLOCKS ARE THE NORM

Brown-headed Cowbirds generally feed together in small or large flocks, depending on the season. In fall and spring, when they are in the process of migrating, they feed in large flocks in fields or agricultural areas. Each night they go to large communal roosts that may contain thousands of birds of several species, such as Red-winged Blackbirds and Common Grackles. During the summer, they may still go to communal roosts, but these are usually smaller—only several hundred birds.

CROW
A CAUTIOUS YET FEARLESS BIRD

American Crows display a curious mix of behaviors. They give careful, quiet protection to feeding areas and nesting sites, yet they are loud and undaunted in chasing away predators.

BEHAVIOR AT FEEDERS

One of our favorite activities is watching the behavior of crows around our feeders.

FEEDING WITH CARE

American Crows are undoubtedly the most wary of feeder birds. They usually land in nearby trees and take a good look in all directions before landing at your ground feeder. Even while some crows are feeding, one or more may remain in the trees, possibly acting as lookouts. If your feeders do not have open space around them, the crows may not come to visit at all.

Crows eat just about any kind of seed, but especially cracked corn and sunflower seeds. In the wild they feed on seeds, insects, fruit, earthworms, carrion, and garbage.

AGGRESSIVE DISPLAYS

For most of the year, crows seem to live in small groups of about four to seven birds, most likely parents and young from the previous year or years. Each of these groups may occasionally defend their area against other groups, especially in spring when breeding begins. One

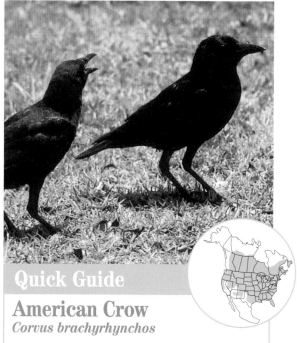

Quick Guide

American Crow
Corvus brachyrhynchos

ID Clues: A large, 18-inch, all-black bird with a large bill and dark eye; males and females look alike

Habitat: A variety of habitats from country to city

Food: Wide variety, including seeds, insects, cracked corn, nuts, fruit, earthworms; opportunistic eater of carrion and garbage

Breeding Period: Late winter to early summer

Nests: Bulky nest of sticks lined with bark, grass, and moss placed high in treetop or trunk fork

Eggs: 4 or 5, bluish green with brown marks

Incubation: 18 days

Nestling Phase: 21 days or more

Broods: 1

Migration: Migrates to southern part of its range

way crows show aggression is by chasing each other in the air. In another method, one group of crows circles high above another group.

When the crows are on the ground, they may perform several other aggressive displays. One is cawing—their loud and distinctive call—with an exaggerated bowing of the head and body and with the wings partially opened; another is wiping the bill back and forth across a branch; and a third is repeatedly flicking the wings and tail.

SECRETIVE NESTER

We once had some crows build a nest within 20 yards of our house, but we knew nothing about it until we heard the young nestlings calling for food. The crow is so secretive around its nest that it is difficult even to see it building the nest. Nests are often located in the tops of evergreens, which also makes them hard to spot.

The best time to discover a nest is when the young are several days old and start to call as the parents bring them food. From then on, the older they get, the louder they get. When the nestlings receive food, their caws change to garbled sounds that make it seem as if they are strangling, although they obviously aren't.

MOBBING HAWKS AND OWLS

One of the best ways to discover the presence of a hawk or owl in your area is by the actions of the crows. When you hear several crows giving loud, harsh, drawn-out caws and see

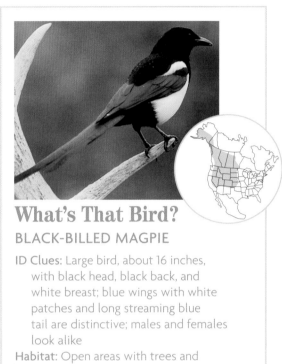

What's That Bird?
BLACK-BILLED MAGPIE

ID Clues: Large bird, about 16 inches, with black head, black back, and white breast; blue wings with white patches and long streaming blue tail are distinctive; males and females look alike

Habitat: Open areas with trees and shrubs, farmlands, gardens, parks

Food: Insects, berries, bird eggs, carrion, mostly on ground; suet and mixed seed at feeders

Nests: Large domed nest of thorny twigs in top of tree or shrub

them repeatedly diving into the top of a tree, chances are there is a hawk or owl there. Crows typically show no fear and harass, or "mob," these birds of prey whenever they find them. The mobbing may continue for 5 or 10 minutes before the bird of prey flies off to a new spot. When it takes flight, the crows follow and dive at it in flight and continue to caw. After 10 or 15 minutes of this the crows usually stop, but they may come back later and repeat the mobbing.

Why crows do this is still not clear. It is true that some hawks and owls can catch and eat crows and, to some extent, the mobbing may discourage a hawk or owl from settling in an area with crows. It is likely that mobbing helps teach young crows who their predators are. In most cases, little damage is done, and the hawk or owl ignores the crows.

CROW CONVENTIONS

Roosting, especially in fall and winter, is typical of crows all across the country. The birds start in the afternoon, fly along fixed routes, stop briefly at pre-roost sites where they gather with other flocks, and then move on to the final roost. Communal roosts are usually located in some protected spot, such as a group of evergreens or dense trees. A roost can be in the city or the country, and crows may fly as far as 50 miles each day to join it.

CROWS ARE UNDOUBTEDLY THE
MOST WARY OF FEEDER BIRDS.

The final roost can contain from a few hundred to 100,000 crows, with the larger roosts usually occurring more in the South. In the morning, the crows leave and go back to where they feed during the day.

Why roosts form is something still being investigated by scientists and bird watchers. Much more careful observation of their behavior near and at roosts is needed to answer this question. For a few theories on why roosts form, see the profile on the starling on page 263.

Bird Feeder Journal

December 18, 4:00 P.M. Every winter afternoon we see the crows in our area fly off in the same direction, and then return early the next morning. Today we decided to follow them in our car. It was not easy keeping them in view, but after several miles, we saw them join with other crows and the flock got larger with each mile.

After 20 miles of driving, we noticed all the crows were heading toward a parking lot in a shopping center. We were amazed, for we saw thousands of crows streaming in from about three different directions. They gathered in the tops of trees and, around sundown, all went into a group of pine trees covering about a half-acre. Amazingly, once they were settled in this roost, it was hard to see or hear a single bird.

DOVE
STRONG WINGS AND SOFT COOS

There are many varieties of doves in the world, and at least two are common coast-to-coast visitors to rural, suburban, or urban feeders. The Mourning Dove and Rock Dove (commonly known as Pigeon) have similar traits but their own special flair.

MOURNING DOVE

People often think the name of this bird is spelled *morning* dove. Indeed, it is active early in the morning, but its name actually refers to its most common call, which has a mournful sound. It is given almost exclusively by the male in spring and summer and is a series of slow, drawn-out coos that sounds a lot like "ooahoo oo oo oo." The male Mourning Dove is, in fact, not mourning at all, but is trying to either attract a mate or defend a small area around his nest.

The only other call you will hear is a shortened version of the series of coos that sounds like "ooahoo." While it can be given by male or female during courtship or territorial conflicts, it is most often given by the male as he calls the female to the nest site as they are choosing a site or actually building the nest.

LARGE CROP AND LOOSE FEATHERS
Mourning Doves feed almost exclusively on small seeds that have fallen on the ground.

Quick Guide
Mourning Dove
Zenaidura macroura

ID Clues: A medium-size, 12-inch bird with a long pointed tail, smooth beige head and breast, and grayish wings and back; adult has a black dot on the cheek; males and females look similar

Habitat: Almost any open habitat, including suburbs

Food: Seeds and some insects; mixed seed on ground

Breeding Period: Late winter to late summer

Nests: Flat nest of twigs, grass, weeds, pine needles on support of tree, shrub, or cactus 3 to 30 feet high

Eggs: 2, white

Incubation: 14 or 15 days

Nestling Phase: 12 to 14 days

Broods: 2 or 3

Migration: Generally a year-round resident but also will migrate to southern part of its range

Unlike the adult, this Mourning Dove fledgling has no black dot on its cheek and has fine, buffy edgings to its wing feathers.

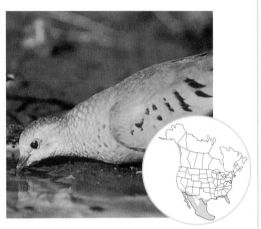

What's That Bird?
COMMON GROUND-DOVE

ID Clues: Small, 7-inch pinkish gray bird with scalloped effect on head and breast; reddish bill has black tip; short tail is often raised; males and females look similar
Habitat: Open areas at edge of vegetation; suburbs
Food: Seeds, insects, berries; mixed seed on ground
Nests: Nests on ground in open area, beach, field, woods

They are fairly large birds, and though they are fast fliers when in the air, they are a bit slow on takeoff. This makes them vulnerable to predators such as Sharp-shinned and Cooper's hawks, as well as cats, which may catch them while they are feeding.

Two adaptations help protect the Mourning Dove from predation. One is its large crop (the storage area in its throat), which enables it to take in large amounts of seeds in a short time and then retire to safety as it slowly releases the seeds into its stomach for digestion. The other adaptation is its loose feathers, which come out easily when the bird is grabbed by a predator. This often allows it to escape, leaving the predator with just a mouthful of feathers.

MOVES AROUND THE FEEDER
Whenever you have several Mourning Doves at your ground feeder, you are bound to see some interesting behavior. In winter you might see one bird run toward another while holding its head and tail in a horizontal plane, or you might see a bird quickly raise and lower one or both wings. These actions are performed by dominant birds in a flock and usually force other birds to move away from choice feeding spots. Wing-raising may even be directed toward squirrels that are feeding too close to the dove;

when this happens, the dove may lower its wing so quickly that it makes a clapping sound.

In fall and winter, you will notice that Mourning Doves alternate between feeding and retiring together to a nearby tree to sun, preen, and sit. During this time they are probably beginning to digest the large numbers of seeds they have just taken into their crop.

MATING MOVES

Throughout spring and summer, when Mourning Doves are more involved with courtship, you will see different behavior near your feeders. A male will run and hop short distances after a female, bow down so his head touches the ground, lift up, puff out his chest, and give his "mournful" call.

Males and females will perch together in pairs, and the male does what is known as perch-cooing: He sits erect, puffs out his iridescent throat feathers, bobs his tail, and gives the long coo. He may also bow and coo in front of the female on the branch. She often moves a short distance away, and he follows. This can continue all day.

Bird Feeder Journal

June 8, 2:00 P.M. A Mourning Dove is at the birdbath. It is drinking differently from other birds. Instead of taking a little bit of water and then tilting its head back to swallow, the Mourning Dove can actually sip up water through its bill. It keeps its bill in contact with the water as it drinks.

Several clues help you know when the birds are about to mate. First, you will notice two birds perched right next to each other. One bird preens the head of the other, and they may hold each other's bills and bob their heads up and down. Next, the male usually steps on the back of the female, and they mate. Afterward, both birds preen for a while before flying away. Copulation usually occurs on the male's territory, so the pair's nest is probably nearby.

PIGEON (ROCK DOVE)

Rock Dove is the name many experts use for the bird everyone else calls Pigeon; today it is one of the most common birds of city streets and rooftops. We are not near enough to an urban center to have Pigeons at our feeders, but when we go to the city, we always enjoy taking a moment to sit on a park bench and watch their behavior. It is a fascinating display that thousands of people walk by every day and never even notice.

BRED FOR BEAUTY, SPEED, AND DISTANCE

As you look at Pigeons, you can see many variations—sometimes shimmering—in their colors. These are a result of selective breeding by people who wanted to show them for beauty or race them for sport.

Indeed, Pigeons are among the best fliers in the bird world, and anyone who has watched them swoop around on the winds of a city street can appreciate this. Their excellent flying abilities are probably due to their original environment, along cliffs and rocky outcroppings, especially near the sea, where gusts of wind necessitate strong flight to land on the narrow cliff faces.

PIGEONS ARE ONE OF THE WORLD'S FASTEST FLIERS; THEY HAVE BEEN CLOCKED AT UP TO 82 MILES PER HOUR.

Such cliffs are also the habitat of the Peregrine Falcon, probably the fastest of all birds. Since the Peregrine catches Pigeons in midair for food, it may be that some of the Pigeon's aerial skills evolved to avoid the Peregrine's attacks.

It is believed that as early as 4500 B.C. in the Middle East, people may have bred Pigeons for their speed and homing abilities to carry long-distance messages, such as results of battles or the outcome of early Olympic games. Pigeons were used even as recently as World War II to carry messages.

Homing is the ability of a bird to return to a known spot—its home—from various distances. Any bird that migrates performs amazing feats of homing, as it makes long journeys between a wintering ground and a breeding ground each year. Pigeons are able to home up to 1,000 miles. By studying Pigeons,

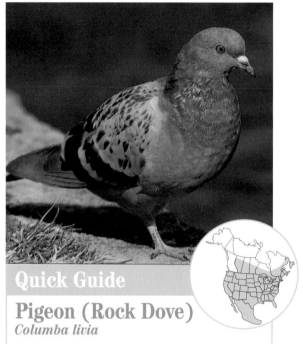

Quick Guide

Pigeon (Rock Dove)
Columba livia

ID Clues: A medium-size bird of 13 inches with various hues of gray, brown, or white feathers; white marking at base of upper bill; iridescence on neck shows in good light; males and females look alike

Habitat: Cities, parks, bridges, steep cliffs

Food: Grains, seeds, crumbs or garbage scattered on ground

Breeding Period: Any month, but especially March to June and August to November

Nests: Saucerlike nest of roots, stems, leaves on building ledges, bridge beams, rafters

Eggs: 1 or 2, white

Incubation: 18 days

Nestling Phase: 25 to 29 days

Broods: 2 to 5

Migration: Generally a year-round resident

researchers believe birds may use several methods of finding their way home. Among them are remembering certain landmarks, orienting themselves to the sun and the stars, and even sensing the earth's magnetic field.

AN AMERICAN HOME

Pigeons originally lived in Europe and the Middle East. They were first introduced into North America around 1606, in Nova Scotia. Over the next 50 years they were brought to both Massachusetts and Virginia, and now, of course, they can be found all across North America.

They have flourished for a number of reasons. Human activity and cars do not disturb them. They are generalists in their feeding behavior, surviving on the tidbits of food they find in cities. Buildings and bridges are so similar to their native nesting habitat of rock ledges that they readily accept them as nest sites.

FLIGHT DISPLAYS

Pigeons in normal flight are quiet and use strong, shallow wing beats, but around their nests they may execute a very different kind of flight. As they take off, they use deep wing beats, making their wings slap together in a clapping sound. Once they are aloft they will alternate this clapping flight with glides in which their wings are held in a V over their back and their tail feathers are spread wide. Although its function is unclear, you can look for this behavior around bridges and buildings where pigeons breed.

FASCINATING GROUP BEHAVIOR

Whenever we see a group of Pigeons feeding together, we take a moment to look at and enjoy several fascinating behaviors, as Pigeons are anything but ordinary. One behavior is called *bowing*, and it usually occurs just after a bird has landed among other pigeons. The bird puffs out its neck feathers, lowers it head, and turns in half- or full circles. Bowing is seen most often among males asserting their dominance or attracting a female.

Sometimes a bird that has been bowing in front of its mate continues into another behavior called *tail drag*, lifting its head high and dragging its spread tail feathers along the ground. It is a striking sight and can last for several seconds.

Finally, you may see two birds running in tandem through or away from the other feeding birds; one bird seems to push the other along. This is called *driving;* the male is behind the female to drive her away from his competition.

DUCK
BEAUTIFUL WATER BIRD

Although most of us never think of ducks as perching or nesting in trees, there are several North American species that regularly do so. These include the Wood Duck, Bufflehead, Common Goldeneye, and Common and Hooded mergansers. The Wood Duck and Hooded Merganser are found throughout the East and Northwest; the others breed primarily in the Northwest, Canada, and Alaska.

Through hunting and habitat destruction, Wood Ducks became extremely rare in the early 1900s. A conservation effort was begun in the 1930s and 1940s to preserve duck habitats, especially tree cavities, and to put up nesting boxes. This effort was extremely successful, and we are lucky enough to have a healthy population of Wood Ducks today.

You can help continue the success of duck conservation efforts and attract more beautiful birds to your nearby ponds and lakes by providing houses for our cavity-nesting ducks.

WHY SOME DUCKS NEED A HOUSE

Cavity-nesting ducks are totally incapable of creating or even enlarging a nesting hole in a tree. Therefore, they are entirely dependent on what they can find—and they need to find a large cavity because they are big birds. Large cavities are made only by Northern Flickers and Pileated Woodpeckers or are formed natu-

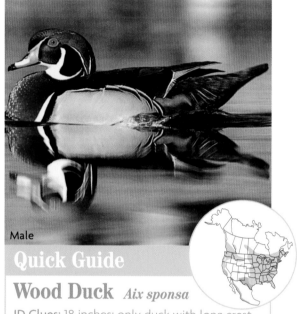

Male

Quick Guide
Wood Duck *Aix sponsa*

ID Clues: 18 inches; only duck with long crest that drapes down the back of the head; male in breeding plumage is unmistakable because of bright colors on head, white throat, and chinstrap; female is brownish gray with a prominent white eye ring that tapers to a point

Habitat: Wooded swamps, rivers

Food: Aquatic plants, minnows, frogs

Breeding Period: April through June

Nests: Large natural cavity in tree or birdhouse; lined with wood chips and down from the female's breast

Eggs: 8 to 10, ivory to buff

Incubation: About 29 to 31 days, by female only

Nestling phase: 1 day

Broods: 1

Migration: Generally migrates south or to coastal areas in winter

Duck Birdhouse

For all ducks except Bufflehead

Dimensions

Entrance hole (oval):

For Wood Duck and Hooded Merganser: 3" high, 4" wide

For Common Goldeneye: 3 ½" high, 4 ½" wide

For Common Merganser: 4" high, 5" wide

Height of hole above floor: 16" to 18"

Inside floor dimensions: 10" × 10" to 12" × 12"

Total height of box: 24" to 25"

Placement

Habitat: Swamps, shallow lakes, or woods near water, preferably facing water and with no obstructions near entrance hole

Height: At least 4' high when nest is placed over water and at least 10' high over land

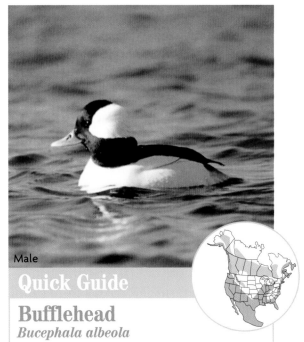

Male

rally from old, rotting trees. A young forest or one without these specific woodpeckers is not going to provide nesting sites for ducks.

FEATHERING THE NEST

Ducks do not seem to bring nesting material into the nest; rather, they line cavities with down and feathers plucked from their breasts. Generally there is only a little down when egg laying starts, but later more and more is added. During the incubation period, the female covers over the eggs with the down each time she leaves the nest. You'll know a tree cavity is occupied by a nesting duck when you see bits of down clinging to the nest hole entrance or scattered on the ground below.

Bufflehead Birdhouse

Dimensions
Entrance-hole diameter: 2 ½" to 3"
Height of hole above floor: 13" to 14"
Inside floor dimensions: 6" × 6" to 7" × 7"
Total height of box: 17" to 19"

Placement
Habitat: Swamps, shallow lakes, or woods near water, preferably facing water and with no obstructions near entrance hole
Height: At least 4' high when nest is placed over water and at least 10' high over land

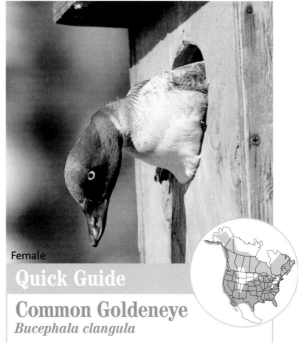

Female

Quick Guide

Common Goldeneye
Bucephala clangula

ID Clues: 18 inches; male has dark head, white flanks, and round white spot in front of golden eye; female has dark brown head and white collar on grayish body
Habitat: Lakes and marshes
Food: Crustaceans, mollusks, aquatic insects
Breeding Period: May into July
Nests: Lined with feathers from the female's breast
Eggs: 8 to 10, olive to light green
Incubation: 30 to 32 days, by female only
Nestling phase: 1 day
Broods: 1
Migration: Migrates in winter to large rivers and coastal areas

A GIANT LEAP OF FAITH

Imagine yourself a young duckling. You hatch out of the egg in a dark cavity inside a tree or nest box, and the next day, from your nest you hear your mother calling outside. You are drawn to the nest entrance for your first look out and discover that you are anywhere from 3½ to 60 feet above the ground. Mom is telling you to jump, and you can just barely walk, let alone fly.

This situation is typical for all of the cavity-nesting ducks. On the second day of their lives, the young jump out of the nest, fall through the air, and, after one bounce off the ground (which never seems to hurt them), they are ready to follow their mother to water (if they are not already in it).

A SINGLE-PARENT FAMILY

As with many ducks, the male of a cavity-nesting pair leaves after the female starts to in-cubate the eggs and has little to do with raising the young. The ducklings can feed and generally fend for themselves within a day of hatching, so the female's only duty is to keep

This young Wood Duck is just about to take the plunge from the nest to the ground. Because of its light weight and downy cushioning, it will not get hurt.

Male and female

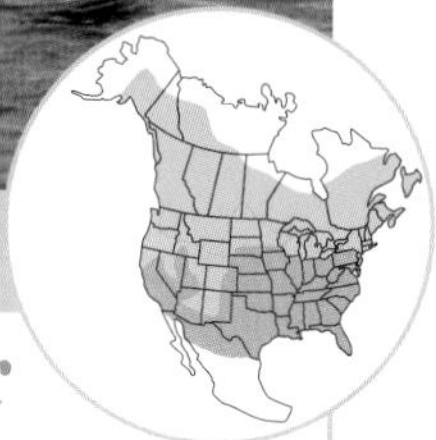

Quick Guide

Common Merganser

Mergus merganser

ID Clues: A large, 25-inch duck with long, tapered red bill; male has dark green head, dark back, white breast and sides; female is grayish with distinctive red-crested head
Habitat: Wooded lakes and rivers
Food: Fish, crustaceans, and mollusks
Breeding Period: April through June
Nests: Lined with feathers from the female's breast
Eggs: 8 to 11, buff
Incubation: 28 to 35 days, by female only
Nestling phase: 1 day
Broods: 1
Migration: Generally migrates south in winter

them safe from predators. The female is better able to do this because she is more camouflaged than the brightly colored male.

After about 2 weeks, the ducklings are quite independent but still stay with either their mother or another family of ducks. Little rafts of baby ducks bobbing along with an adult female or two are a common sight in early June.

SPECIAL FEATURES OF DUCK HOUSING

Several special features are required for duck birdhouses. Young ducklings have to climb to the entrance hole to jump out. To be able to do this, they need a rough surface inside the front of the nest box that they can grab onto. Attach wire mesh on the inside front, or score the inside with horizontal saw cuts to provide footholds. Fill the duck birdhouse with 2 to 4 inches of wood chips to keep the eggs from rolling around and to provide insulation.

When placing the house, try to angle it slightly forward so it is easier for the ducklings to climb out. Also be sure that the entrance is clear of obstructing branches: Ducks are big birds and need an open path to the nest hole. Once a duck has started to incubate the eggs, do not monitor the nest—the duck may leave.

PROTECTION FROM RACCOONS

Because ducks nest in large cavities near water, they are particularly vulnerable to raccoons, which feed at water edges, climb trees, and can reach into the large duck nest holes.

One way to minimize raccoon problems is to place your duck houses out on poles in the water, which is not particularly easy. One way to do it is to walk out to the center of the water in winter—only if the ice is safe to walk on—poke a hole through the ice, and pound the pole into the pond or lake bottom. Mount the house 4 to 6 feet above the water.

Houses placed on trees at the water's edge should be 10 to 20 feet high. You can protect the duck houses by putting baffles around the bases of poles or wrapping sheet metal around the trunks of trees. For more information, see "Protecting Your Birdhouses" on page 118.

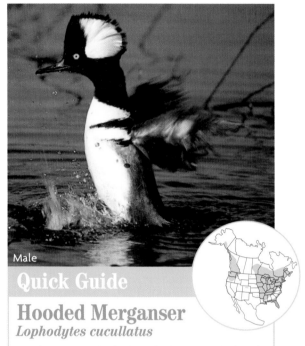

Male

Quick Guide

Hooded Merganser
Lophodytes cucullatus

ID Clues: 18-inch duck with short, thin bill and crested head; male has large white patch within his crest, black back, brown flanks with black diagonal line through sides of white breast; female is dusky color with reddish brown crest

Habitat: Wooded lakes and rivers

Food: Small fish, frogs, crustaceans, mollusks, aquatic insects

Breeding Period: April through June

Nests: Lined with feathers from the female's breast

Eggs: 10 to 12, white

Incubation: 32 or 33 days, by female only

Nestling phase: 1 day

Broods: 1

Migration: Generally migrates south in winter

EVENING GROSBEAK
BEAUTIFUL, MAGICAL VAGABOND

People are often mystified about why Evening Grosbeaks seem to mob their feeders some years and other years are nowhere to be found. It is important to remember that birds live in or travel to various locations based largely on the food supply. Evening Grosbeaks live in flocks and feed on tree seeds. The production of tree seeds varies from year to year and region to region, which means Evening Grosbeaks have to move about to take advantage of local seed abundance that will sustain the flock.

The Evening Grosbeak was once a relatively unknown western bird. From 1850 to 1890, they wandered farther and farther eastward—all the way to Massachusetts—by following the widespread planting and varying seed production of their favorite tree, the popular shade tree called box elder or ash-leaved maple (*Acer negundo*). Increasing numbers of feeders holding sunflower seeds, another favorite, also aided in their expansion.

Male

Quick Guide

Evening Grosbeak
Coccothraustes vespertinus

ID Clues: Just over 7 inches long, with huge conical beak; male has bright yellow body, black tail, and wings with large white patches; black head has bold yellow streak above eyes

Habitat: Mixed and coniferous woods, open areas with trees and shrubs, suburbs

Food: Tree seeds, fruit, nuts, insects, tree sap; sunflower seed at feeders

Breeding Period: May to July

Nests: Nest of twigs, lichens, roots 20 to 100 feet high in tree

Eggs: 3 or 4, pale blue-green, lightly speckled

Incubation: 11 to 14 days

Nestling Phase: 13 to 14 days

Broods: 2

Migration: Migrates to southern United States

Bird Feeder Journal

April 4, 10:00 A.M. A flock of 18 Evening Grosbeaks flew overhead. Their beaks have changed from yellow to the most incredible pale jade green. Yesterday at our feeder 10 were crowded on the platform, and we saw a male put sunflower seeds in a female's beak three times!

A female Evening Grosbeak has a grayish tan body with black-and-white wings and tail and no yellow.

Male

What's That Bird?
BLACK-HEADED GROSBEAK

ID Clues: 7½-inch bird with black head, orange underparts, white wing patches

Habitat: Deciduous forests, thickets, pine-oak and pinyon-juniper woodlands

Food: Tree seeds, berries, insects, spiders; sunflower seed at feeders

Nests: Nest of twigs and rootlets 4 to 25 feet high in shrub or tree

STRIKING BEAUTY

On the male Evening Grosbeak, the contrast of black tail and wings with large white patches against a bright yellow body is striking; add the bright yellow thunderbolt streak just above each eye and this bird is breathtaking. In early spring an amazing, magical thing also happens: Their beaks turn from yellow to a beautiful light green. It is a gorgeous sight.

A friend of ours has likened the heads of male Evening Grosbeaks to space helmets and calls the birds space cadets. Some people say they look like oversize goldfinches. We simply say they are stunning to look at—and their beautiful "sleigh-bell" calls are a joy to hear at our feeders.

FEEDER BEHAVIOR

When the grosbeaks arrive, they can eat large quantities of sunflower seed and dominate the feeder. They seem to prefer feeders with ledges, tray-type feeders, or seed on the

Male

What's That Bird?
ROSE-BREASTED GROSBEAK

ID Clues: 8-inch bird with black head and back and white breast; distinctive red triangle on breast

Habitat: Deciduous woods, mixed shrubs and trees

Food: Insects, seeds, tree buds, fruit; sunflower seed at feeders

Nests: Nest of twigs 5 to 25 feet high in tree

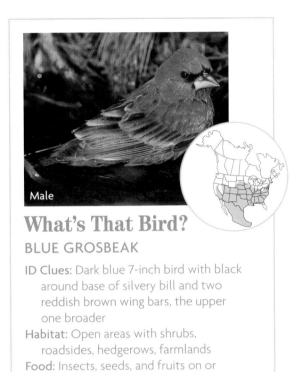

Male

What's That Bird?
BLUE GROSBEAK

ID Clues: Dark blue 7-inch bird with black around base of silvery bill and two reddish brown wing bars, the upper one broader

Habitat: Open areas with shrubs, roadsides, hedgerows, farmlands

Food: Insects, seeds, and fruits on or above ground

Nests: Nest of rootlets and grasses placed in shrub or tangle of vines

ground. When feeding on the open ground, they are more harmonious. When a number of them crowd together, as on a feeding tray, they can be very aggressive, opening their beaks and lunging at one another.

Besides having a great fondness for sunflower seed, Evening Grosbeaks eat a variety of other seeds, buds, and fruits. They eat the seeds of the box elder tree with great skill, manipulating the seed in their powerful beaks and quickly extracting the seed as the winged pod flutters to the ground. They eat the seeds of many other kinds of trees, such as sugar maples, pines, and tulip poplars, and will eat the buds of elms and other trees and shrubs. When they eat fruit, such as cherries, you can actually hear them crushing the cherry stones with their powerful mandibles. They will eat snow and the sap from trees, and they are attracted to the road salt that is left on gravel and sand after the winter.

COURTSHIP AT FEEDERS

Evening Grosbeaks may linger at feeders until May before returning to northern states and Canada to breed, and at this time you may see some of their courtship behavior. Males feed females as part of their courtship. The female or male may bob or sway in front of the other, or the female may quiver her wings and give short calls as she receives food. In an elaborate display, males will spread and vibrate their wings and pivot back and forth.

FINCH
NEARLY IDENTICAL COUSINS

The Purple Finch and House Finch are both in the genus *Carpodacus* and thus are close relatives. They have similar songs, breeding behaviors, and appearances, so people often are confused as to which birds they have at their feeders. Distinguishing between the two species can be difficult due to individual variation within each species. We get both types of finches at our feeders, and so we enjoy this challenge all the time.

WHICH FINCH IS IT?

The females are easier to tell apart than the males; you need to just look at their heads. The female Purple Finch has a broad white eyebrow stripe. The female House Finch has no distinct markings on her head; it is completely covered with fine brown streaks. Interestingly, the female Purple Finch is lightly streaked on her breast, while her House Finch counterpart is heavily streaked on her breast and belly.

One way to distinguish the males is the reddish coloration of their heads and body. The male Purple Finch has a deep raspberry red all over his head, back, rump, and breast. The red or orange-red of the male House Finch is limited, falling mainly on his forehead, chest, and rump. Their red feathers are tipped with gray after their fall molt; the gray wears off by spring to reveal the brighter colors underneath.

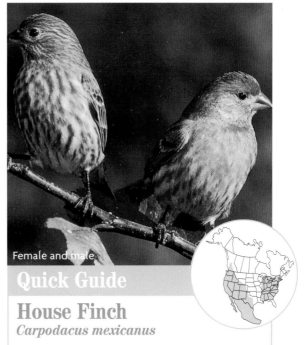

Female and male

Quick Guide

House Finch
Carpodacus mexicanus

ID Clues: 5½-inch brown bird; male has red to red-orange head and upper breast, heavy brown streaking along flanks; female has unmarked head and heavily streaked breast and belly

Habitat: Urban areas, suburbs, parks, canyons, semiarid brush

Food: Seeds, blossoms, buds, fruits; sunflower seed at feeders

Breeding Period: March into July

Nests: Nest of twigs and grasses placed in trees, shrubs, or natural or artificial cavities like hanging plant baskets; birdhouses

Eggs: 4 or 5, white to pale buff

Incubation: 12 to 14 days, by female only

Nestling Phase: 11 to 19 days

Broods: 1 to 3

Migration: Generally a year-round resident

We think the best way to tell the males apart is by the brown streaks along their flanks (the sides of their belly). The Purple Finch has faint or no brown streaks along his flanks; the House Finch has thick brown streaks.

If you happen to have a mix of finches at your feeders, you may see that Purple Finches are somewhat larger and stockier than House Finches and have a more pronounced notch at the tip of their tails.

THE BEST WAY TO TELL THE MALE FINCHES APART IS THE PRESENCE OR ABSENCE OF BROWN STREAKS ALONG THEIR FLANKS.

SONGS AND CALLS

House Finch song occurs most often in spring and summer, but bits of it may be heard on warmer days in fall and winter. Males—and occasionally females—sing a lovely, rich warbling song. The song is only a few seconds long, but the bird tends to string several songs together in a row, making them sound almost continuous. The song ends with a harsh "chee-urr" sound, and this last sound will help you distinguish House Finch song from the similar song of the Purple Finch. The Purple Finch's song, given only by the male, is a long musical warbling tune without the harsh end note.

Male

Quick Guide

Purple Finch
Carpodacus purpureus

ID Clues: 6-inch brown bird with raspberry red covering head, back, breast, and belly; little or no brown streaking on flanks
Habitat: Mixed woods, coniferous forests, lower mountain slopes, suburbs
Food: Seeds, tree buds, berries, insects on or above ground; sunflower seed at feeders
Breeding Period: March into July
Nests: Nest of twigs and grasses 5 to 60 feet high in tree
Eggs: 3 to 6, light green-blue with dark marks
Incubation: 13 days
Nestling Phase: 14 days
Broods: 1 or 2
Migration: Generally migrates south to U.S./Mexico border area

The normal call note of the House Finch sounds just like the "cheerp" of a House Sparrow. The normal call note of the Purple

Finch, given as the birds are in flight, is a distinctive short, metallic "tick."

FEEDER HABITS

Both finches generally remain in small flocks through winter, and both are attracted to seeds at feeders, especially sunflower seed. In the wild, House Finches feed on seeds from trees and weeds and are comfortable feeding at either hanging or ground feeders. The Purple Finch is more accustomed to feeding on tree seeds and may be more used to feeding above the ground.

Courtship displays are often seen at feeders as well. Like other songbird species, the male gets food and brings it to the female, who quivers her wings as she takes it. This mate feeding begins in late winter and spring and continues through the incubation phase.

HABITAT HABITS

House Finches are very comfortable around urban dwellings and live in both the city and suburbs. They will also breed in these areas—they are willing to place their nest just about anywhere. Once nesting is over, both the young and the adults tend to go to areas where there are abundant seeds to feed on; thus, they may be less prevalent at this time. But during winter or summer they remain in the same general area; they migrate only a short distance or not at all.

The Purple Finch is less of a city bird, preferring to nest in mixed woods or conifers. It

The female Purple Finch is a small brown bird with a white eyebrow stripe and sparse streaking on the breast.

breeds along the West Coast, across Canada, and in the northeastern states. In fall it migrates south for the winter and may visit feeders anywhere in the eastern United States. However, it cannot be counted on as a winter visitor—flocks will stop and stay at any available food on their way rather than head for a certain spot each year, as most other winter birds do.

EASTWARD, HO!

House Finches are native to the western states, and although they are now common in the East, their presence there is a recent occurrence. In 1940 a few pet dealers in California captured House Finches and shipped them to New York City to be sold as "Hollywood finches." Catching and shipping the birds was illegal, and when agents of the U.S. Fish and Wildlife Service discovered the scheme, they began to arrest the New York dealers who had the birds. To avoid being arrested, some dealers released the House Finches, and the birds survived and reproduced in the wild. They have now spread throughout most of the eastern states, marching toward the Midwest.

NESTS MAY BE ANYWHERE

One of the reasons for their rapid expansion in the wild is that House Finches have proved to be very adaptable birds. They have become increasingly accustomed to human habitats, to the point that they are now considered common dooryard birds.

Finches have the added flexibility of being both open-cup and cavity nesters. Because of this, they can build their nests in any nook or on any ledge of a building; in urban areas they compete with House Sparrows for nesting sites. They have also been found nesting in tin cans, tree holes, and stovepipes; on the ground;

House Finch Birdhouse

Dimensions
Entrance-hole diameter: 1 ⅜" to 1 ½"
Height of hole above floor: 5" to 7"
Inside floor dimensions: 4" × 4" to 5" × 5"
Total height of box: 9" to 12"

Placement
Habitat: Near human habitations in urban or rural settings
Height: 4' to 10' high on a tree, post, or building

and on branches of cacti, trees, and shrubs. A common nesting spot in the East is in baskets of plants hanging on people's porches.

House Finches sometimes appropriate the nests of other birds, either after they are abandoned or even while the other birds are still using them. They commonly use nests originally built by orioles, phoebes, Cliff Swallows, and robins. The range expansion and adaptability to a variety of nest sites are not necessarily good for other cavity nesters. It means that there will be more competition for nest holes—an already scarce commodity.

NEARLY DECIMATED BY DISEASE

The House Finch range expanded rapidly after the 1940s. The corresponding population expansion, however, fell rapidly among eastern birds in just a few years as this bird endured an epidemic of conjunctivitis—a disease that

Bird Feeder Journal

July 16, 3:30 P.M. A flock of 10 House Finches were gathered on our garden path that is covered with wood chips. One started to sunbathe by crouching down with tail and wings spread over the ground and its body tilted to one side. Soon four others joined in the sunbathing, while the other 5 finches pecked at things on the ground. Sunbathing lasts for about 1 minute.

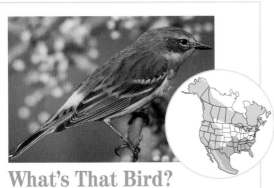

What's That Bird?
YELLOW-RUMPED WARBLER

ID Clues: Small, 5 ½-inch brown bird with bright yellow rump and patch in front of wings; males and females are similar, but female has duller color

Habitat: Coniferous or mixed forests

Food: Insects and some berries; suet and fruit at feeders

Nests: Nest of twigs and grasses 5 to 50 feet high

causes swollen, crusted eyes. House Finch numbers crashed from 300 million in the winter of 1993–94 to 180 million by about 2001. While 5 to 10 percent of eastern House Finches are thought to still suffer from the condition, the rapid spread of the disease has leveled off and the House Finch is no longer in extreme risk of such huge population declines.

The disease, which also afflicts Purple Finches and American Goldfinches, can be spread to healthy birds when they contact a feeder touched by an infected bird. To help prevent infection, clean your feeders every 2 weeks with a solution of 1 part bleach to 10 parts water, and rinse thoroughly.

The House Finch epidemic was first recorded and continues to be monitored by backyard bird watchers like you who participate in a bird survey project known as Project FeederWatch, a joint effort between Cornell University and the National Audubon Society. Look in "Resources" on page 289 for how you can join this important, easy-to-do program.

GOLDFINCH, PINE SISKIN
SPOTS OF SUNSHINE

Some spring morning you will walk outside and feel blinded, as if by a ray of sunshine, by the bright yellow of a male American Goldfinch sitting at your feeder or chirping a long warbling song from a treetop nearby. Or maybe you will catch a fleeting glimpse of brilliant yellow as a Pine Siskin streaks by you on his way to your feeders. The American Goldfinch and Pine Siskin are two branches of the same genus, *Carduelis*; each brings a small spot of sunshine to our yards.

GOLDFINCH

After a winter season of drab colors, the male American Goldfinch molts into a vibrant yellow and black, undoubtedly to help him attract a female or advertise the boundaries of his territory. Perhaps it is also to bring us the joy of spring.

CHANGE OF SEASONS, CHANGE OF COLORS
American Goldfinches molt twice a year. In fall, after breeding, they have a complete molt. At this time the male loses his bright yellow colors and grows in feathers that make him look grayish yellow. The female also changes from her dull brownish yellow plumage to this grayer color. Both grow new feathers for their black wings with white wing bars. Thus, in winter it is impossible to distinguish between male and female American Goldfinches.

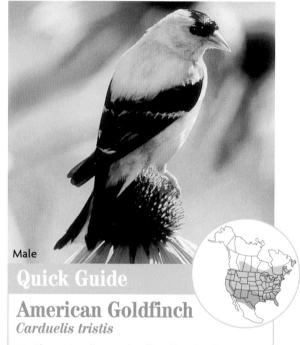

Male

Quick Guide

American Goldfinch
Carduelis tristis

ID Clues: Small, 5-inch, all-yellow bird in spring and summer with black cap, tail, and wings with white wing bars

Habitat: Open areas with some shrubs and trees, farms, gardens, suburbs

Food: Seeds, berries, insects; sunflower and thistle at feeders

Breeding Period: June to September

Nests: Nest of plant fibers and caterpillar webbing 4 to 20 feet high in tree

Eggs: 3 to 7, light blue

Incubation: 12 to 14 days

Nestling Phase: 11 to 15 days

Broods: 1 or 2

Migration: Generally year-round residents; some migrate to southern part of United States.

In spring, American Goldfinches molt all their body feathers, but not their wing feathers. At this time both acquire their summer plumage. The male's bright yellow color may make him an attractive potential mate, and the female's more camouflaged coloration may allow her to be more secretive around the nest.

COME SIT AND EAT

If you watch American Goldfinches at your feeders, you will immediately notice that they feed in a very different manner than many other birds. Chickadees and titmice, for instance, come to the feeder, take a single seed, and fly off. American Goldfinches land on the feeder and continue to eat seed after seed. This method may stem from their eating habits in the wild, where they land on a composite flower head or a birch and eat many seeds right at that spot.

Watch them closely and you will notice that they can take off the outer hull of a seed while

Male

What's That Bird?
LESSER GOLDFINCH

ID Clues: Just 4 ½ inches long with black back and cap, yellow underneath, and white patch on wings
Habitat: Woods edges, roadsides, gardens, parks
Food: Seeds, flower buds, berries; sunflower and thistle at feeders
Nests: Nest of bark strips, moss, plant stems 2 to 30 feet high in shrubs or trees

Bird Feeder Journal

January 5, 2:00 P.M. A flock of about 25 American Goldfinches has been visiting our feeder over the past 2 weeks. They are aggressive at the perches, for they cannot all fit on at once. When they start feeding, the seed level in our hanging feeder starts dropping at an alarming rate!

March 21, 11:00 A.M. A flock of about 50 Pine Siskins has arrived in our yard and found our hanging feeders with hulled sunflower seeds. There are too many to all feed at once, so the birds are very aggressive, pushing each other off perches. Last year we saw no siskins at all!

keeping it in their bill and do not depend on holding it in their feet and pecking at it like the chickadees. They are able to do this because the conical shape of their bill is specially adapted for seed eating. This bill shape is typical of all finches, including House and Purple finches and Evening Grosbeaks.

WHAT THEY EAT

In the wild, you will find American Goldfinches feeding wherever there are lots of seeds;

This female American Goldfinch tends the nest wearing her spring and summer plumage, as you can see by her yellow breast, brownish olive back, black wings and tail, and white wing bars.

generally they take seeds right off a plant rather than feeding on ones that have fallen below. They like to feed on birch and alder seeds in winter. Spring through fall they eat composite weed seeds such as thistle, sunflower, dandelion, ragweed, mullein, evening primrose, and goldenrod.

At feeders, American Goldfinches are partial to sunflower (hulled) and thistle seeds.

THE GOLDFINCH-THISTLE MYTH

It is often said that American Goldfinches do not nest until the thistles have bloomed and gone to seed because the thistle down is needed for its nest. This is not true; American Goldfinches often build nests long before thistle is in bloom, and they use all types of

other fibers in their nests. We have seen them build with fibers from milkweed stalks, salsify seed tops, and other downy materials.

The reason American Goldfinches nest late (starting in July) is probably that they feed their young on the seeds of composite flowers, such as thistle or sunflower, which ripen in late summer.

PINE SISKIN

A finch with a strange name, the Pine Siskin likes to wander in large flocks in search of food and, like the American Goldfinch, tends to sit in one spot and eat continuously. You might have hundreds of these birds at your feeders one year—particularly if you live in the East or Midwest—and possibly none the next. If they do arrive, they likely will be noisy and aggressive eaters.

RUNNING IN FLOCKS

From fall through early spring, Pine Siskins remain in large flocks ranging in size from 50 to 1,000 birds, with flocks of around 200 birds being quite common. As the flock moves about to feed, it may join with other species, such as redpolls, American Goldfinches, and crossbills. These mixed flocks are not permanent associations, just a result of birds being attracted to similar food sources, such as the seeds of birches and alders.

In spring, Pine Siskins become more aggressive; the large flocks begin to break up into smaller groups of five to ten birds. These flock sizes are retained even through the breeding season, for although a breeding pair defends a small area right around its nest, they may let other Pine Siskins land or nest in the same tree. When the pair leaves the nest site, it often joins other Pine Siskins to feed.

SISKIN SOUNDS

Pine Siskins have a flight call and flight pattern similar to the American Goldfinch. Their flight call is a three-syllable "ti-te-ti," and their flight is undulating. When flying, Pine Siskins tend to remain in a tight flock, fly quite high, and then drop down quickly when they land.

Once a flock lands, it tends to be noisy, and the various calls used include an upward slurred whistle, which sounds like "sweeet." A harsh, distinctive call that will help you recognize the bird sounds like "zzzzzz" and has been compared to escaping steam.

Like their American Goldfinch cousins, you will also hear Pine Siskins sing continuously from the treetops for several hours in the morning. Their song is a jumble of chirps and "sweeet" notes, somewhat canary-like, interspersed with their harsh "zzzzzz" sound.

EATING HABITS

Pine Siskins seem to love hanging feeders or trays where there is either hulled sunflower or thistle. They can be very aggressive at feeders to both other Pine Siskins and other species that are about their same size (goldfinches) or

Quick Guide

Pine Siskin
Carduelis pinus

ID Clues: Small, 5-inch, brown-streaked bird with a long, fine-pointed bill and touches of yellow on the wings and tail; males and females look alike

Habitat: Coniferous or mixed woods, shrub thickets, suburbs

Food: Conifer seeds, weed seeds, insects, flower buds, nectar; sunflower and thistle at feeders

Breeding Period: Late winter to early spring

Nests: Nest of grasses and twigs placed 3 to 50 feet high in tree

Eggs: 1 to 5, light green-blue with dark marks

Incubation: 13 days

Nestling Phase: 14 or 15 days

Broods: 1 or 2

Migration: Migrates in wandering fashion throughout southern United States

even a little larger (titmice). When being aggressive, they assume a common display called the head-forward threat, in which they lean forward, point their opened bill at the intruder, and may slightly raise their wings.

Pine Siskins are primarily seed eaters, favoring the seeds of conifers, birches, alders, eucalyptus, and a wide variety of weed seeds along roads and in fields. The birds are very adept at crawling out on fine branches or even hanging upside down to reach tree seeds.

Some of their other feeding habits might be considered unusual. These include eating the leaves and flowers off young plants and even vegetable shoots, and occasionally eating salt and ashes, especially in winter when the birds are drawn to road salt.

COURTSHIP DISPLAYS

Pine Siskin courtship starts early in January and February, while the birds are still in their winter flocks. Like many other birds, the male often takes food in his bill, flies to a crouching, fluttering female, and gives it to her. You may also see the male Pine Siskin use a display flight to court a mate. Leaving from a perch near the female, he flies up in circles with tail spread and a rapid fluttering flight, singing continuously as he circles higher. Soon he stops circling and drops down to perch near the female, often then repeating the action.

GRACKLE
IRRIDESCENT BLACK CAN BE STRANGE

The Common Grackle is a frequent visitor at backyard feeders from the East Coast to the Rockies. It may help you to know you really can tell the males and females apart. The male and female Common Grackle look similar in that they are both black with iridescent heads; however, the male is larger, has a longer tail, and has more iridescence.

There are several other tricks for telling them apart. During the breeding season the female is almost always in the lead when the two fly. Also, a flying male folds his tail vertically into a V just after takeoff and just before landing. This is a display done only during the breeding period, and it may advertise the bird's sex and breeding readiness.

The first young grackles appear in late spring and early summer. They have dark brown plumage (different from the black of the adults) and dark eyes, strikingly unlike the bright yellow iris of the adults.

SONGS BRING OUT THE RUFF-OUT

The song of the Common Grackle will never make the record books as most melodious; it sounds more like a squeaky gate. It is given by the male or female and is often written as "reedeleek," "scoodeleek," or "ch'gasqueek." Males often sing when near other males, and paired males and females may alternate singing.

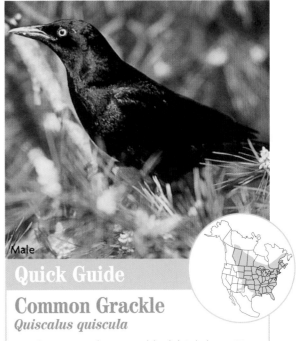

Male

Quick Guide

Common Grackle
Quiscalus quiscula

ID Clues: A medium-size black bird about 12 inches long with iridescence on head, back, and belly and a bright yellow eye; female has shorter tail and less iridescence

Habitat: Open areas with some trees; parks, urban yards, farmlands

Food: Seeds, insects, fruit, crustaceans, fish; mixed seed at feeders

Breeding Period: March to June

Nests: Nest of grass and mud in tree

Eggs: 4 to 7, pale greenish brown with dark marks

Incubation: 13 or 14 days

Nestling Phase: 12 to 16 days

Broods: 1

Migration: Some are year-round residents; some migrate to the southern United States

One thing to look for when the male or female is singing is a visual display called ruff-out. In this display the bird spreads its tail, opens its wings a little bit, and ruffles out its head and body feathers. Part of what the ruff-out does is heighten the effect of the iridescence on the bird's feathers, and it is always accompanied by song.

HEADS UP AT THE FEEDER

Watch the Common Grackles at your feeder, and every so often you will see them point their bills up as if they were looking at the sky. (They are not really looking at the sky; when birds do that they tilt their head to one side.) This display, called bill tilt, is part of their language. It is usually done between two males or two females when they are competing for dominance over a mate or at a feeding site. The display is held for several seconds, and then the birds resume feeding. Bill tilting is especially likely to occur when new birds arrive on the scene.

STRANGE ANTICS

Common Grackles have several unusual behaviors that people often see around their feeders or in their yards. One is the occasional killing of other small birds, especially House Sparrows. Some people have actually seen grackles drown House Sparrows in the birdbath. Generally just one individual in a given area picks up this behavior, but it is startling.

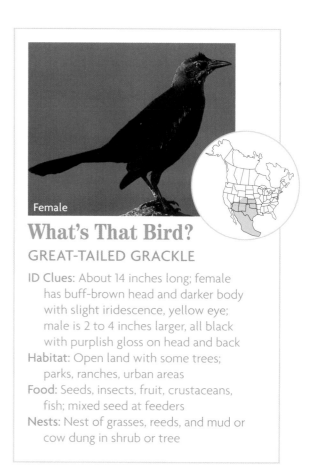

Female

What's That Bird?
GREAT-TAILED GRACKLE

ID Clues: About 14 inches long; female has buff-brown head and darker body with slight iridescence, yellow eye; male is 2 to 4 inches larger, all black with purplish gloss on head and back
Habitat: Open land with some trees; parks, ranches, urban areas
Food: Seeds, insects, fruit, crustaceans, fish; mixed seed at feeders
Nests: Nest of grasses, reeds, and mud or cow dung in shrub or tree

Another behavior is referred to as anting. Here, the bird rubs different materials over its feathers, possibly to rid itself of feather parasites or to soothe its skin. Sometimes the bird uses ants, and thus the name of the behavior. The ants may be squeezed and rubbed through the feathers, releasing formic acid, or the bird may spread its feathers over the ants and let them crawl about. Birds may also use different substances for anting, such as mothballs or cigarette butts. Many other species of birds practice anting, but Common Grackles are the birds most often seen doing it.

A third unusual habit involves feeding. Common Grackles are often seen taking food—crackers, stale bread, even dry dog food—and carrying it to water, such as a birdbath, where they soak it before eating it. Occasionally food "prepared" in this way is fed to fledglings.

LOOKING FOR THE REAL NEST

Soon after they arrive on their breeding grounds and are seen at your feeder, Common Grackles will begin breeding behavior. This is the time to look for signs of nest building—and even these habits seem a little strange.

Common Grackles often nest in suburban areas, and they usually choose to build their nests in evergreens. A good clue is when you see either the male or female flying into these spots with long strands of grass trailing from its beak. This is a preliminary stage of nest building, done sporadically and lasting from 1 to 4 weeks. These grasses are not, however, used in building the nest that the birds will ultimately use, and it is not known why the birds transport them to the nest site.

After this stage, the real nest building takes place—all by the female; the male merely follows her around. The nest may be placed where the strands of grass were laid. It is constructed in about 5 days, and it contains grasses and mud. When finished, it looks like a large version of a robin's nest.

Bird Feeder Journal

October 14, 3:00 P.M. Hundreds of Common Grackles have temporarily descended into our woods and are feeding on the ground. Their noise is astoundingly loud. The birds are walking through the woods and flipping over leaves in search of insects or other food. Every so often they all suddenly fly up and silently perch in the trees. Then gradually they drop down to feed again and continue their raucous sounds. A spectacular sight.

June 1, 5:00 P.M. The first young Common Grackles for the year have shown up at the feeder. They are brownish and have dark eyes. They are not feeding on their own yet, just following the parents to the feeder and then soliciting food from them (even though it is right in front of them, free for the taking). They make a harsh, grating sound and flutter their wings as they receive food.

HUMMINGBIRD
HUMMERS ARE SPECIAL

As with one's first love, we will never forget the first hummingbird in our garden. These tiny, marvelous bundles of energy always have amazed us in so many ways: their jewel-like colors, their fantastic flying abilities, and their diminutive size. For example, a Ruby-throated Hummingbird is only 3¾ inches long and weighs just 3 grams—one-tenth the weight of a first-class letter!

There are 16 species of hummingbirds that breed in the United States. In the East, there is only the Ruby-throated Hummingbird, although on rare occasions one of the western species may wander off course into the East. West of the Mississippi, the *common* hummingbirds that come to feeders are the Allen's, Anna's, Black-chinned, Broad-tailed, Calliope, Costa's, and Rufous hummingbirds. We will look briefly at each of these species below; first, we'll describe some attributes all hummers share.

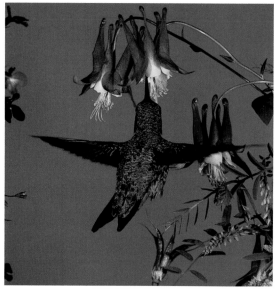

A male Ruby-throated Hummingbird searches for some nectar.

WINGED JEWELS

The iridescence on hummingbirds' feathers makes them sparkle like jewels, even though it covers only the outer third of the feather. When light strikes these feathers, it is reflected and intensified when viewed from a certain angle. That is why, for example, a male Ruby-throated Hummingbird's throat patch will appear to be brilliant red if the light is shining directly on it.

When viewed from a different angle it will look dusky orange, green, or violet, and when no light is reflected it will look black.

FAST AND AGILE

Hummingbirds can fly in every direction: up, down, sideways, and even upside down, which they may do briefly to escape. When they hover, their wings move backward and forward, rotating at the shoulder as the tips trace a horizontal figure eight.

Hummers are among the fastest small birds, reaching speeds of up to 60 miles per hour in

Identifying Hummingbirds

When you are first starting out, identifying hummingbirds can be tricky. The birds are small, look similar, and move quickly. On the positive side, they are readily attracted to feeders, and their bodies remain still as they hover to feed. Here are some ways to identify and distinguish the hummers that may come to your yard.

Which Hummingbirds Are in My Area?

This book looks at the eight major species of hummingbirds that breed in North America. They are Allen's, Anna's, Black-chinned, Broad-tailed, Calliope, Costa's, Ruby-throated, and Rufous hummingbirds.

Only one of these species, the Ruby-throated Hummingbird, lives in the Midwest and the East. The other seven all live in the West. This list will help you narrow down which hummers are found in your area.

East and Midwest
Ruby-throated

Western Mountains
Black-chinned
Broad-tailed
Calliope
Rufous

West Coast
Allen's
Anna's
Black-chinned
Broad-tailed
Calliope
Costa's
Rufous

Southwest
Allen's
Anna's
Black-chinned
Broad-tailed
Calliope
Costa's

Tips to Identify the 8 Major Males

The males of the eight major species are quite distinct from one another. These males all have bright iridescent feathers on their gorgets (throats) that show only when light reflects off it in just the right way; in other lights the feathers look black.

Allen's: Rufous color on sides and tail, all-green back; orange-red throat

Anna's: Rose iridescence on top of head and throat

Black-chinned: Black chin, then a band of purple iridescence

Broad-tailed: Red throat, green back and body

Calliope: Separate streaks of purple iridescence

Costa's: Purple iridescence on top of head and throat

Ruby-throated: Red throat, green back and body

Rufous: Rufous color on back, sides, and tail; orange-red throat

Looking at Females and Young

The females of the major species have clear or slightly marked throats and all have white tips on their outer tail feathers; the males' tail feathers are all dark. Immature males usually have plumage halfway between that of the male and female and white tips to their tail feathers.

forward flight. They can also fly long distances in their migration to Central America, including 500 miles across the Gulf of Mexico. Fortunately, an adult Ruby-throated hummer can store up to 2 grams of fat, enough to make this over-water crossing.

AERIAL ACROBATICS

Hummingbirds save their best aerial acrobatics for defending a territory, attracting a mate, or intimidating other hummingbirds (or people near feeders). Each species of hummingbird has flight patterns that are unique to that species. Here are a few samples.

In its visual display, a male Ruby-throated Hummingbird flies along a wide, shallow arc, as though suspended by a wire. He usually is oriented toward the sun so that its rays reflect his iridescent red throat. He may pass close to the female, and his wings and tail will produce a loud buzzing at that point.

When displaying, the male Anna's Hummingbird will rise up more than 150 feet, pause, sing (a thin grinding sound) briefly, and then zoom down over the female, making a loud popping noise with his tail feathers as he swoops over her.

The display flight of the Rufous Hummingbird is a diagonal loop. It moves quickly going downward and more slowly going up, accompanied by a loud whirring of its wings.

RED IS THEIR FAVORITE COLOR

Someone once said, "Hummingbirds like any color, as long as it's red." We have actually seen them at flowers of every color, including the greenish yellow flowers of the buckthorn shrub, but they do have a definate preference for red flowers.

Hummingbirds are not born with this preference but learn through trial and error that red means good food. Many of these red flowers offer quantities of nectar with exactly the concentration of sugar that hummingbirds prefer—about 20 to 25 percent.

EATING NECTAR

Hummingbirds have a higher metabolism than any other bird and must eat enormous amounts of food to fuel themselves. Nectar is an easily digested source of quick energy for hummers. It has been estimated that they consume 50 percent of their weight in sugar each day. Hummingbirds also get proteins, fats, and minerals by eating small insects and spiders that they find on flowers they visit or on other vegetation.

To save energy when feeding, a hummer will perch instead of hovering if it can. Hummingbirds also save energy at night, particularly when it is cold, by going into a state of torpor. Their metabolic rate drops to one-fifth of the

Fast Fact

The wings of a Ruby-throated Hummingbird beat 78 times per second in regular flight; up to 200 times per second in a dive.

normal rate, their heartbeat and breathing slow down, and their body temperature lowers.

TINY NESTS

A female seeks out a mate; then, after mating, she alone builds a nest. She lays two white eggs and raises the young alone. The nestlings will remain in the nest for about 21 days as the mother feeds them regurgitated nectar and insects. She will fiercely defend a territory around her nest from intruding hummers and occasionally other birds.

Hummingbird nests are the tiniest in the bird world, no bigger than a half-dollar. They usually blend in so beautifully with their surroundings that they can be impossible to spot. The nests may be adorned with such materials as insect cocoons, fern scales, spider skeletons, and lichen. They are flexible enough to actually stretch along with baby hummingbirds as they grow.

AT YOUR FEEDER

Depending on the area of the country that you live in, you may attract one or several species of hummingbirds; sometimes you may be lucky enough to host many individuals of each species. Hummers can be fiercely competitive over food sources, and you may see lots of aggressive behavior as they compete for feeders or flowers. They will swoop and dive at one another and may make a variety of clicking or buzzing sounds. You may also find that some hummers seem to frequent the feeder, while others visit only briefly and then leave.

ALLEN'S HUMMINGBIRD

The Allen's Hummingbird is named in honor of Charles Andrew Allen, a California naturalist in the early 1900s.

SCRAPPY LITTLE HAWK CHASER

During the breeding season, males defend territories in mixed shrubs and woods located in coastal canyons or at the edges of small openings in wooded areas. Territories are often located in small, isolated openings that are shielded from one another by taller vegetation. Therefore, there are fewer territorial squabbles between neighbors in this species.

Males usually perch on a twig that gives them a good view of their land and from which intruders are chased out (to the accompaniment of the hummer's chirping sounds). Allen's Hummingbirds have even been seen chasing Red-tailed Hawks and American Kestrels from their territories.

SHY NESTER

You may not find Allen's Hummingbirds nesting around your home; they prefer more isolated habitats. Females nest in wooded areas, often using live oaks or pines, and usually pick nest sites well away

Fast Fact

A hummingbird's egg is less than $^1/_2$ inch long, half the size of a jelly bean.

from male territories, possibly to avoid interference by the males.

The nests of Allen's hummingbirds are somewhat larger than those of other hummingbirds and may straddle a branch rather than being built right on top of it. They can be placed from a few inches to 50 feet above the ground and are built in tangles of low vines or trees. For lower nest sites, hummers choose wild blackberry bushes or the fronds of ferns.

Moss, dried weed stems, willow down, dried leaves, dog or horse hair, a few feathers, and insect or spider silk are some of the materials that make up the body of the nest. Lichens often cover the outside. The remains of a nest from a previous year may form the base of a nest in the following year.

When first starting to build her nest, the female hovers over the nest site as she carefully applies spider silk and plant materials. These form a sticky base on which to build the nest rim. When she places the final downy material on the floor of the nest, she may pack it down by rapidly tamping her feet.

In some cases, the female starts laying eggs while the nest is still just a shallow cup; in other cases the nest is more complete. She usually continues to add material to the nest right up until the young leave.

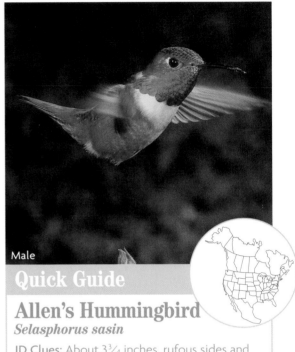

Male

Quick Guide

Allen's Hummingbird
Selasphorus sasin

ID Clues: About 3¾ inches, rufous sides and tail, all green back, orange-red throat
Habitat: Woods, thickets, gardens, parks
Food: Flower nectar, insects; sugar-water at feeders
Breeding Period: Mid-February to early July
Nests: Moss, plant down, spider silk, hair, lichens, 1 to 50 feet high
Eggs: 2, pure white
Incubation: 15 to 17 days
Nestling Phase: 22 to 25 days
Broods: 1 or 2
Migration: Migrates to Central Mexico: *northward*, January through March; *southward*, mid-May through September

NORTH BY COAST, SOUTH BY MOUNTAINS
Allen's Hummingbirds breed along the West Coast, from California into southern Oregon.

Almost all of the population is migratory, leaving the United States for central Mexico after breeding and then returning the next

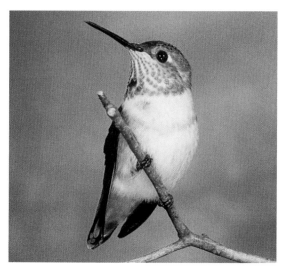

This female Allen's Hummingbird has the typical coloring: rufous on the sides and tail and flecks of iridescence on the throat.

year. However, on the Channel Islands, located just off the southern coast of California, there is a population of Allen's Hummingbirds that is slightly larger than the mainland birds; members of this subspecies are year-round residents.

The migration of Allen's Hummingbirds occurs substantially earlier than those of most other hummingbirds—their northward journey starts as early as January and their southward trip in mid-May. Their route is roughly oval, with the birds moving rapidly up the West Coast and more leisurely south along the foothills of the Sierras. With this route they take advantage of the habitats with the greatest number of blooms during their migration.

It is believed that adult males leave the breeding grounds first, followed after 2 weeks by adult and juvenile females, who are followed in turn about 2 weeks later by the juvenile males.

ANNA'S HUMMINGBIRD

In the early 1800s, a French nobleman named Prince Francois Victor Massena collected many specimens of North American hummingbirds. After Prince Massena introduced him to French society and bought one of his portfolios, John James Audubon commented in his writings on the beautiful wife of the Prince, Anna de Belle Massena. Another French naturalist then thought it fitting to name this species in her honor.

ONE OF THE EARLIEST BREEDERS

The Anna's Hummingbird breeds all along the West Coast and inland into southwestern Arizona. Unlike most of our other hummingbirds, the Anna's Hummingbird is a year-round resident throughout most of its large range. After breeding it usually wanders only slightly in search of areas with favorable flowers on which to feed.

By early December the Anna's hummingbird has returned to its breeding ground, and in some cases it has laid eggs before the first of the year. This makes it one of the earliest breeding birds in all of North America, earlier even than the Great Horned Owl, which is traditionally thought of as the earliest breeder.

WILD ABOUT GOOSEBERRIES

One of the few wild plants in bloom during December, when the Anna's Hummingbird starts breeding, is gooseberry (*Ribes malvaceum*), which starts to bloom soon after fall rains begin. A month or so later another gooseberry (*R. speciosum*) takes over as the main flowering plant in the wild.

Scientists believe that the gooseberries and Anna's Hummingbird may have co-evolved. Both species have gained from their relationship: The hummingbird gets a source of food in winter that enables it to breed earlier than other birds and before migrant species of hummingbirds return, and in turn the plant gets the undivided attention of an effective pollinator.

In many cases, male Anna's territories are centered around gooseberry plants, and the most dominant males claim territories around gooseberries with the most blooms. It may even be that females judge males on the basis of the quantity and/or quality of these plants in the male's territory.

Many introduced species of plants in the West have also aided the winter breeding of Anna's Hummingbirds, particularly eucalyptus trees (*Eucalyptus* spp.). Many other introduced garden plants also bloom early in the season and are helpful sources of food.

TERRITORIAL BEHAVIOR

The breeding season starts with the males moving to a favorable area and defending a ter-

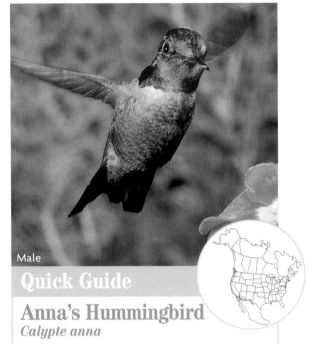

Male

Quick Guide

Anna's Hummingbird
Calypte anna

ID Clues: 4 inches, entire head and throat covered by rose-colored iridescence; green back

Habitat: Open woods, shrubs, gardens, parks

Food: Flower nectar, insects; sugar-water at feeders

Breeding Period: December to June

Nests: Downy plant fibers, lichens, spider silk; placed in variety of locations, often near houses

Eggs: 2, pure white

Incubation: 14 to 19 days

Nestling Phase: 18 to 23 days

Broods: 1 or 2

Migration: Does not migrate, but shifts to local areas with more food; may expand range to the north and south

ritory that contains nectar-rich flowers and several good perches from which he can watch

The female Anna's Hummingbird has a green back, grayish underparts, and occasionally traces of red on the throat.

fore he climbs higher. Once at the top of his climb he starts on a rapid descent, aiming directly down on the intruder. At the bottom of his dive he veers up while giving a loud "speeek" sound. To make his display even more dramatic, the male orients his dive so that he is angled toward the sun, heightening the effect of his beautiful, iridescent throat feathers as they shine toward the intruder.

In another unusual display, the male leans forward and ruffles out the feathers of his crown and gorget at an intruder. If the intruder does not get the message to leave, the male may fully extend his crown and gorget feathers until they are expanded into a brilliant red disk facing the intruder.

over his area. This territory is usually about a quarter-acre in size. From the perches within it the male sings, chases out intruders, and starts his display flights.

Through much of the day the male perches and sings one of the most complex songs of any of our hummingbirds. It sounds like "bzz-bzz-bzz chu-ZWEE Dzi! Dzi! Bzz-bzz-bzz." All of the other hummingbirds in North America have much less complex songs that are more like simple buzzes or trills.

Anna's Hummingbirds have one of the most spectacular aerial displays of any of our North American hummingbirds. The dive consists of the bird's flying 6 to 12 feet high, hovering, and calling several sets of "bzz bzz bzz" phrases be-

BABY FOOD

As any good parent knows, a diet of sugar and water is not enough for a growing youngster. This applies equally to baby hummingbirds. Studies of female Anna's Hummingbirds during breeding have discovered that, over the course of the day, she changes what she feeds her young. In the morning, she starts out by feeding nectar to her hungry nestlings. By the afternoon, insects are the main food she brings back to the nest.

Why does this feeding sequence occur? One possible explanation is that after their long night, the young need the instant energy derived from nectar to enable them to keep warm as the female goes off to collect food. It is also

true that insects are less active in the cooler morning air and thus harder to collect. This pattern of feeding the young also has the advantage of giving the nestlings added protein late in the day that will help them get through the cooler nights.

BACKYARD GARDENS HELP

In May and June, male Anna's Hummingbirds begin to undergo their molt, lessen their defense of their territories, and may wander extensively in search of rich sources of nectar. This may bring them to gardens where flowers are blooming.

Anna's Hummingbird has been expanding its range for the past 50 years to the north, south, and east. Much of this expansion may be due to pressure within the breeding range from a growing population. The expansion and growing population may also be affected by increased suburban plantings that provide food for the birds where it would otherwise not be available.

BLACK-CHINNED HUMMINGBIRD

The Black-chinned Hummingbird has the most extensive breeding range of any of our western hummingbirds: from Texas, where it is the most common hummingbird, all the way up into British Columbia.

Throughout this range the birds are drawn to lowland areas and often nest along streams or creek beds that support stands of willows

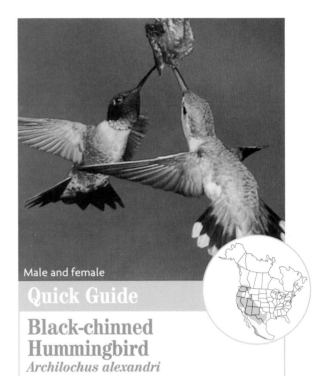

Male and female

Quick Guide

Black-chinned Hummingbird
Archilochus alexandri

ID Clues: Only 3¾ inches; male has green back, black chin bordered by band of purple iridescence; female has green back and clear white breast and throat
Habitat: Dry lowlands and foothills
Food: Flower nectar, insects; sugar-water at feeders
Breeding Period: April through August
Nests: Downy fibers, spider silk; placed in drooping branches of trees or shrubs
Eggs: 1 to 3, pure white
Incubation: 13 to 16 days
Nestling Phase: About 21 days
Broods: 1 or 2
Migration: Migrates to western portions of central Mexico and southern and coastal Texas: *northward,* Mid-March to mid-May; *southward,* Mid-August into November

and alders. The willows are especially important because their blossoms offer lots of nectar, attract swarms of insects, and produce fluffy down, which the hummingbirds use in nest construction.

Other habitats used by Black-chinned Hummingbirds for nesting include the bases of small canyons where sycamores grow, and suburban areas where feeders and lots of nectar-rich flowers are available.

TERRITORIAL SQUABBLES

Like many of our other hummingbirds, the Black-chinned male and female lead fairly separate lives. Males arrive on the breeding ground first and set up territories around prime feeding areas. Depending on the richness of the flowers, these may be as small as 10 feet or up to 100 feet in diameter. They are generally situated in open areas that are surrounded by taller vegetation.

When territorial disputes heat up, the hummingbirds engage in displays, chases, and actual fights. In fights the two birds hover facing each other, often only an inch or two apart, and each tries to get above the other and strike down on it. This may result in quite a sight: both birds rising up together. Bodily contact with bills, wings, or feet can occur, and fights can last a minute or two.

The female defends her own separate area that includes a nest site, perches, roosting site,

and some places to feed. A male or female may change the location of its territory during the breeding season in order to take advantage of new flowers coming into bloom.

During migration, Black-chinned Hummingbirds stop and feed often and will vigorously defend temporary feeding territories from other hummingbirds.

TWIRLING BUILDER MAKES ROOM FOR MORE

One careful observer was lucky enough to watch a female Black-chinned Hummingbird build her nest. He noticed the female twirling about inside the nest as she pressed her breast up against the edge to mold it into the right shape. To mold the outside, she perched on the edge, leaned over, and smoothed it with her bill. It took 4 days to build the nest.

Unlike most of our other hummingbirds, the Black-chinned hummer does not tend to coat the outside of the nest with lichens. The resulting nest is beige in color, like the down material the hummer has gathered from willows or from the undersides of sycamore leaves.

Like several other species of North American hummingbirds, the Black-chinned Hummingbird can build successive nests right on top of one another. The nest is placed in shrubs or trees—5 to 10 feet above ground—and usually overhangs an open space, such as a stream, path, or road.

Interestingly, all of our other North American hummingbirds lay just two eggs per clutch, but the Black-chinned Hummingbird occasionally lays only one or up to three eggs.

BROAD-TAILED HUMMINGBIRD

If you are camping, hiking, or just traveling in any of the large mountain ranges of the West, such as the Rockies or the Sierras, then be on the lookout for the mountain hummer: the Broad-tailed Hummingbird. It breeds in the mountains from Arizona and New Mexico all the way up to Idaho and Montana at elevations from 4,000 feet to as high as 12,700 feet.

Broad-tailed Hummingbirds often nest along mountain streams, dry creek beds, or springs, and they can be seen feeding on the flowers of alpine meadows. These hummers, in fact, follow the abundance of flowers from one area to another during their breeding season. This means leaving the lower elevations where flowers first bloom for higher, moister elevations where new flowers begin to bloom later in the season.

In the morning the birds may also be seen bathing in or drinking from the clear, crisp pools or shallows of mountain streams. They may bathe by standing in very shallow water and then fluttering their wings, or they may dip their feet and bellies into the water while hovering above it.

WING WHISTLE

Many hummingbirds create sounds with their wings while flying, but those of the Broad-tailed Hummingbird are among the loudest and

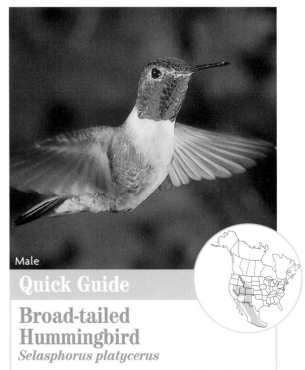

Male

Quick Guide

Broad-tailed Hummingbird
Selasphorus platycerus

ID Clues: 4 inches, green back and head, red throat

Habitat: Open mountain woodlands and meadows

Food: Flower nectar, insects, spiders, tree sap; sugar-water at feeders

Breeding Period: March to July

Nests: Downy plant fibers, bark bits, lichens on horizontal limbs 5 to 15 feet high

Eggs: 2, white

Incubation: 16 to 17 days

Nestling Phase: 21 to 26 days

Broods: 1 or 2

Migration: Migrates to mountains of Mexico: *northward*, March into May; *southward*, August into October

most constant. The movement of air through the ninth and tenth primary feathers of the

A female Broad-tailed Hummingbird has slight amounts of rufous coloring on sides and tail; her throat is speckled.

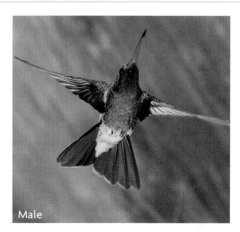

Male

What's That Bird?
BROAD-BILLED HUMMINGBIRD

ID Clues: 4 inches, green on back and belly with large blue patch on throat and blue tail; bright red bill with black tip

U.S. Breeding Range: Southeast Arizona, southwest New Mexico, western Texas

U.S. Breeding Period: Mid-April to August

Nonbreeding Range: Northern and central Mexico

Migration: *Northward,* March to April; *southward,* September to October

wings creates the sound. It occurs only in the male and is a high-pitched, continuous buzzing, much like a cricket, and can be heard 75 to 100 yards away (so you often hear the male before you see him). Researchers believe the wing whistle is an important part of aggressive behavior in males and that without it they would not be as effective in defending territories.

PROTECTING THE HOME FRONT

Male Broad-tailed Hummingbirds defend territories from early to midsummer. Territories vary in size from a third of an acre to over an acre and contain two or more good perches from which the male watches over his territory. Many times they contain small mountain willow species that are in bloom in early summer. The females are attracted to these areas by nectar, insects, and the dispersal fila-

ments of the willow seeds that the birds use in building their nests.

Territorial interactions seem to be most common in the morning. In one study, only 20 percent of the males in an area actually owned territories. The others were competing with them for these spots. Territories are defended against other hummingbirds, both male and female, of any species, as well as against other much larger birds such as grosbeaks, kingbirds, and even Sharp-shinned Hawks.

UNUSUAL COURTSHIP

For hummers, courtship and mating usually occur after first trying to chase the female away. On one occasion, several Broad-tailed hummers were seen performing dive displays for a single female. This is similar to behavior in some other birds, where males compete for dominance in an area to which females are attracted. The dominant male then gets to mate with the female. Such behavior, though, is unusual among our North American hummingbirds and has been seen only once for this hummer.

NESTING BEHAVIOR

Female Broad-tailed Hummingbirds choose nest sites where there is some protection from rain or sun, such as places where there will be branches of dense foliage over their nest site. Interestingly, females will reuse nest sites in successive years when their previous nesting attempts were successful.

The nests are generally placed on horizontal limbs about 5 to 15 feet above ground, though nests have been recorded in unusual places such as among roots, 2 feet above a rushing stream, and on a light fixture next to a front door. In one case, a Broad-tailed hummer had two nests at once: one with fledglings she was feeding, and another where she was incubating a single egg.

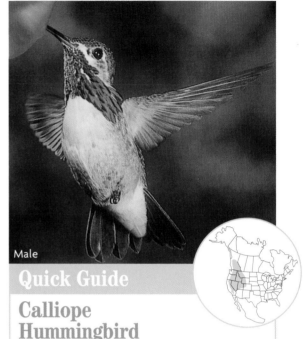

Male

Quick Guide

Calliope Hummingbird
Stellula calliope

ID Clues: 3 inches, green back, white breast; separate streaks of purple iridescence on the throat

Habitat: Open mountain woodlands and meadows

Food: Flower nectar, insects; sugar-water at feeders

Breeding Period: Mid-May through July

Nests: Plant down, bark, lichens, insect and spider silk; often placed on horizontal branch of a pine tree with overhanging protection

Eggs: 2, white

Incubation: About 15 days

Nestling Phase: 18 to 23 days

Broods: Probably only 1

Migration: Migrates to Central Mexico: *northward*, March through May; *southward*, Late July through September

CALLIOPE HUMMINGBIRD

Its scientific name means "little star." The Calliope Hummingbird has lovely streaks of purple iridescence on its throat and is the smallest bird in North America. Most of our other hummingbirds are 3½ to 4 inches long, but a Calliope hummer is just 3 inches long. Just for comparison, a typical first-class letter weighs about an ounce; a Calliope Hummingbird weighs less than one-tenth of an ounce.

FOLLOWING THE FLOWERS

Calliope Hummingbirds breed throughout most of the West, except for the Southwest and the Pacific Coast. However, when they migrate north in March and April, their route is primarily along the Pacific Coast, where more flowers are in bloom.

The Calliope hummer definitely prefers to breed at higher elevations and in this regard is similar to the Broad-tailed Hummingbird. As the summer progresses, Calliope Hummingbirds often move up mountain slopes to take advantage of the succession of blooming from lower to higher elevations. These birds frequently live as high as 8,000 feet and sometimes up to the timberline at around 10,000 to 11,000 feet. Their southward migration is an inland route along mountain ranges to take advantage of later-blooming flowers.

CAMOUFLAGED NEST

The Calliope Hummingbird is well known for camouflaging its tiny nest. Nests have been found in pine trees, nestled and well-hidden among groups of pinecones on the branches. They may be as low as 2 feet above ground and as high as 70 feet. In many cases they have overhanging protection, provided by another limb or dense greenery. Old nests may be reused in successive years, serving as the base for new ones. Up to four nests have been seen piled on top of one another.

Nests are frequently situated with an eastern exposure, possibly to take advantage of the early warming rays of the sun after cold mountain nights. They are also often located in woods that are adjacent to meadows where males defend territories.

COLD-WEATHER NESTER

To survive the cold night temperatures in the mountains, the males can go into a state of torpor at night, but incubating females must keep their body temperature up to keep the eggs warm and the young developing. On the last feeding trip away from the nestlings before the female settles down for the night, she does not feed the young. She is probably reserving the food energy for her own body so that she can keep the nestlings warm. She also sinks way down into the nest, whose high walls and dense downy lining help retain her heat.

THE YOUNG BIRDS

The female lays two eggs; there is up to a 3-day interval between layings. The female may continue to add to the nest during the time that she is laying and incubating.

For the first 11 or 12 days after hatching, the baby hummingbirds are brooded fairly constantly by the female; they have no feathers yet and cannot regulate their own temperature. For the second half of the nestling phase, they can conserve heat and brooding stops.

TERRITORIAL SEPARATION

As with most hummingbirds, the males and females defend separate territories. Females may visit males to mate and then return to their own nesting and feeding areas. Male territories are in open areas with flowering plants and contain several perches from which the birds get a good view of their areas and can spot any intruders. Female territories and nesting sites, however, are more likely to be in or at the protected edge of woods.

Since all other species of hummingbirds are larger, the Calliope Hummingbird is at a disadvantage during aggressive encounters; the Black-chinned Hummingbird, which nests in the same area, usually dominates it. However, the Calliope hummer has been known to hold its own against other hummers on its own feeding territory.

COSTA'S HUMMINGBIRD

Named for a French nobleman naturalist of the early 1800s, Louis Marie Pantelion Costa, the Costa's Hummingbird is the one hummer that

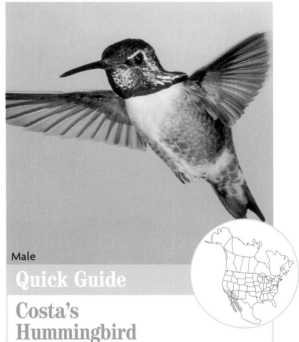

Male

Quick Guide

Costa's Hummingbird
Calypte costae

ID Clues: 3½ inches, green body and sides; purple iridescence on entire head and throat

Habitat: Dry environments with sparse vegetation; dry chaparral

Food: Flower nectar, insects; sugar-water at feeders

Breeding Period: Mid-February through June

Nests: Downy fibers, dry leaves, feathers, spider silk; 1 to 8 feet high

Eggs: 2, pure white

Incubation: About 16 days

Nestling Phase: 20 to 23 days

Broods: 1, possibly 2

Migration: Shifts farther south within its range to southeastern California, southwestern Arizona, and Baja, Mexico: *northward,* late January to February; *southward,* September and October

This female Costa's Hummingbird is brooding her eggs. Spotting on the throat (faintly visible here) may form a small, distinctive red patch.

prefers the driest climates and environments. It is often found along dry washes where streams have laid down large areas of stone and gravel or in large expanses of dry chaparral.

LARGE LAND OWNERS

Costa's Hummingbirds form territories in areas where there is low vegetation interspersed with a few taller stalks of plants, such as yuccas, on which the birds can perch and watch for intruders. Flowering plants in these habitats are sparse, therefore the males must defend large territories in order to have enough nectar to meet their needs. These territories can be very big by hummingbird standards, ranging from 2 to 4 acres.

During the nonbreeding season, Costa's and Anna's hummingbirds often share the same ranges and habitats. This results in conflicts over nectar resources such as flowers and hummingbird feeders. If there are conflicts between the two species, the larger Anna's hummers seem almost always to be dominant over the Costa's.

What's That Bird?

BUFF-BELLIED HUMMINGBIRD

ID Clues: About 4 inches, green back and throat, buff breast, distinctive red bill; males and females look alike
U.S. Breeding Range: Southern Texas
U.S. Breeding Period: March to July
Nonbreeding Range: Gulf coast of Mexico, Texas, and Louisiana
Migration: *Northward,* June to July, after breeding; *southward,* August

Interestingly, some displays of the Costa's hummer when defending its territory are similar to those of the Anna's. For example, to threaten another hummingbird, a perched male turns toward the intruder and spreads out his beautiful, iridescent violet-blue gorget.

NEST BUILDING

Females build their nests near males' territories at the edge of taller shrubs or at the edge of an opening in the vegetation. This allows the female to spot possible dangers around the nest as she tends her babies.

In desert areas, look for nests in cacti, sage, and dead yucca stalks; in canyons, in a variety of shrub and tree species. The nests are usually 1 to 8 feet above the ground.

DIFFERENT BROODS IN DIFFERENT HABITATS?

Costa's Hummingbirds begin the breeding season in desert regions, where they live from mid-February to mid-April. After this, they leave these regions and reappear in chaparral habitats in late April. They may make this shift to take advantage of certain plants that come into bloom at different times in the different regions. It may be that they have a second brood in these chaparral areas, but further study is needed before we can know for sure.

RUBY-THROATED HUMMINGBIRD

Hummingbird identification in the eastern half of North America is easy: If you see a hummingbird, it is a Ruby-throated Hummingbird. Only this one species lives throughout the eastern half of the United States and most of southern Canada. All of the other 15 species of hummingbirds that regularly occur in North America live in the West.

Why do no other species of hummingbirds exist in the East? There are two possible explanations. The first is that the milder climate along the West Coast favors the development of more hummingbird flowers and a longer flowering season. The second possible explanation is that the lack of nectar-rich wildflowers in parts of the Midwest (in some areas of the Midwest there are no hummingbirds) has kept western and eastern hummingbirds separate.

Of course, do not forget to look closely to be sure of your identification—just because the Ruby-throated Hummingbird is the only breeding hummingbird in the East, you may occasionally see one of several western species that wander to the East, especially in late fall.

EVERYBODY OUT

Male Ruby-throated Hummingbirds usually return to the breeding area ahead of females and start to establish territories around nectar-rich flowers. Their territory size varies with the density of flowering plants and the amount of nectar they provide, but an average size is about a quarter-acre. If the flowers finish blooming, the male may shift his territory to another spot with more flowers.

Female Ruby-throated Hummingbirds also defend territories around the nest and sometimes around food sources as well. Following breeding and during migration, both male and female defend temporary territories around good nectar sources as they build up fat reserves for their long migration. The birds can be extremely aggressive around these resources. We have regularly seen them chase titmice, chickadees, American Goldfinches, and even Blue Jays, even though these other birds do not use nectar.

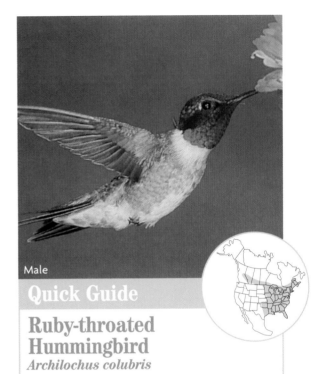

Male

Quick Guide

Ruby-throated Hummingbird
Archilochus colubris

ID Clues: 3¾ inches, green head and back with red throat
Habitat: Wood edges, streams, parks, gardens
Food: Flower nectar, insects, spiders, tree sap; sugar-water at feeders
Breeding Period: Late March into August
Nests: Plant down, bud scales, lichens, spider/insect silk on a small horizontal limb 10 to 20 feet above ground
Eggs: 2, pure white
Incubation: About 16 days
Nestling Phase: 14 to 31 days
Broods: 1 or 2
Migration: Migrates to southern Mexico and Central America: *northward*, Late February to mid-May; *southward*, Late July to late October

The female Ruby-throated Hummingbird has a green back and clear white breast and throat.

GATHERING DOWN

The female builds the nest from plant down, adding bits of lichens or bud scales to the outside. Ruby-throated hummers build nests in coniferous or deciduous trees at the edge of streams, meadows, or roads, often 10 to 20 feet high on a small, downward-sloping, lichen-covered branch. A female may continue to add material to her nest throughout the period that she is incubating the eggs.

TOO MUCH IN THE SUN

The female lays two eggs and, when it is cool, she sits tightly over them to keep them warm. When it is hot, she may simply stand by the side of the nest or perhaps try to shade the eggs from the sun.

After an incubation period of about 16 days, the young hatch. One strange feature of the Ruby-throated nestling phase is the wide range of times reported for its length—from 14 to 31 days—far longer, at 31 days, than for any of our other hummingbirds. There is as yet no clear explanation for this range, but it may have to do with varying weather conditions and availability of food.

ACROSS THE WIDE GULF

Ruby-throated Hummingbirds winter in southern Mexico and Central America. To get there, most of them must fly their tiny bodies more than 500 miles across the Gulf of Mexico. Ruby-throated hummers are up to the task; they increase their body weight by 50 percent, storing energy as fat to burn while crossing. Ruby-throated Hummingbirds that breed in the central United States and Canada take the land route through Texas to Mexico.

THE SAPSUCKER CONNECTION

The northward migration of Ruby-throated Hummingbirds does not coincide with the peak blooming of many flowers that they could feed on. In fact, they arrive in northern areas often up to a month before many such plants have even begun to bloom.

Then how do they survive? They are very resourceful in their feeding habits and do not rely only on flower nectar. In many cases, they subsist on insects, or they feed on sap that drains from sapsucker holes.

Sap is remarkably similar to flower nectar: It contains a concentration of sucrose similar to that of flower nectar, and it has traces of amino acids. Thus, sap is a perfect substitute for nectar in areas where nectar-rich flowers are few and far between.

It is now believed that the range of hummingbirds that nest in the North, such as the Rufous Hummingbird in the West and the Ruby-throated Hummingbird in the East, is controlled not by the range of suitable flowers but by the range of the sapsucker, especially the Yellow-bellied Sapsucker.

FOLLOWING JEWELWEED SOUTH

Although Ruby-throated Hummingbirds do not seem to follow blooming flowers as they migrate north, they may be very dependent on jewelweed during their march south. They are especially fond of spotted touch-me-not (*Impatiens capensis*), which blooms later than other jewelweed species. It could be that the later time of blooming is an adaptation of this species to take advantage of hummingbirds as pollinators.

RUFOUS HUMMINGBIRD

The Rufous Hummingbird is the most northern hummer. It breeds in the Northwest, from northern California, Oregon, Washington, Idaho, and Montana right up through British Columbia and well into southern Alaska. It is the only hummingbird that regularly appears in Alaska.

The general appearance and behavior of the Rufous is extremely similar to the Allen's

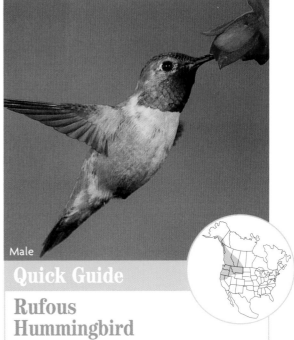

Male

Quick Guide

Rufous Hummingbird
Selasphorus rufus

ID Clues: 3¾ inches, rufous sides, tail, and back; back sometimes tinged with green; orange-red throat

Habitat: Woods edges, thickets, parks, mountain meadows

Food: Flower nectar, insects, spiders, tree sap; sugar-water at feeders

Breeding Period: April to July

Nests: Downy plant fibers, moss, lichens, placed in a variety of locations and heights

Eggs: 2, white

Incubation: Unknown

Nestling Phase: About 20 days

Broods: 1, maybe 2

Migration: Migrates to southern Mexico: *northward*, February to May; *southward*, June to October

Hummingbird. Both have red to red-orange iridescent throats, but only the Rufous hummer has a rufous-colored back.

NUMEROUS NESTS

The nests of Rufous Hummingbirds can be located quite close to one another and are extremely abundant. One study found as many as 105 nests within a 100-acre forest of Douglas fir, western red cedar, western hemlock, white birch, and broadleaf maple. In this study, a very interesting trend in nest location was also discovered: In spring Rufous Hummingbirds build their nests low and in the conifers, whereas in summer they build them high and in the deciduous trees.

In early spring, the most constant temperatures occur low to the ground in the coniferous areas; in fall, they occur in the upper layers of deciduous trees. Thus, these birds minimize the effects of the environment on their nests by choosing different nest sites in different seasons.

TAPPING THE SAP

Rufous Hummingbirds, like Ruby-throated Hummingbirds, have been known to defend certain trees where sapsuckers have made sap-collecting holes through the bark. The hummingbird eats the sap and defends the tree against other intruding hummingbirds. In fact, birds defending trees seem to stay perched more than birds defending patches of flowers and therefore use less energy getting their food. Because sap is similar in sugar concentration to flower nectar, these trees are important feeding places for the Rufous hummer during migration.

THE MOST AGGRESSIVE HUMMER

During migration, when Rufous Hummingbirds defend temporary feeding territories, they are the most aggressive of all species and regularly displace Anna's, Black-chinned, Broad-tailed, and Calliope Hummingbirds from flower patches. They may be able to do this due to their greater wing loading—more weight per area of wing.

Greater wing loading means the hummer can be more agile but not as efficient a flyer. This is a strange adaptation for a bird that has the longest migration route of any of our hummers, but it may be a result of how the Rufous Hummingbird feeds during migration. It takes a long flight, followed by a short stop of a few days at nectar-rich flowers to build up fat reserves; then it takes off on another long flight. Nature seems to have favored the Rufous hummer with the ability to acquire a territory easily, even during a short stop, rather than giving it increased efficiency during the migration flight itself.

There are two types of Rufous hummers searching for temporary feeding territories: challengers and robbers. Challengers try to take over a territory by giving chattering calls and fighting with the territory owner. Robbers take a different tack: Their strategy is to quietly sneak in and rob some nectar until they are spotted. Once seen, robbers immediately leave. Because of their bright colors, it is hard for males to be robbers; females and immatures, however, tend to be less aggressive and are usually robbers.

Interestingly, where migration routes or ranges overlap, there may be many species of hummingbirds defending territories in the same patch of flowers. In one patch of bladderpod in southern California in late spring, 15 hummingbirds, including Costa's, Rufous, and Allen's, were all seen defending separate territories within an area 100 feet by 50 feet.

THE LONGEST MIGRANT

The Rufous Hummingbird has the longest migration route of any North American hummingbird, up to 3,000 miles. Its spring route north is almost exclusively along the coast, while its post-breeding route is inland along the Rocky Mountains. They usually migrate south in two waves: adult males first, followed in a week or more by the females and immatures.

For some reason, the Rufous hummer is the most common vagrant species of hummingbird east of the Mississippi. (A vagrant is a bird that has wandered or been blown out of its normal range.) The Rufous Hummingbird has been seen from Nova Scotia to the tip of Florida, mostly in November and December. So if you live in the East and see a hummingbird in late fall, look closely: It may be a Rufous hummer.

JAY
A BIRD OF STUNNING TROPICAL BEAUTY

The Blue Jay is one of the most beautiful of our feeder birds. Its colors are particularly brilliant in fall and early winter because it has just undergone its yearly late summer molt and all its feathers are fresh. The black barring across the throat and bright white spots on the wings stand out against the different hues of blue on the back, tail, and wing feathers. You could easily spend a lot of money traveling to the tropics to see a bird this stunning. Why not enjoy it right in your own backyard?

EAST AND WEST

The Blue Jay is found all across eastern, southern, and midwestern states. The western and Pacific states have several other species of jays. These include the Steller's Jay, the Gray Jay, and the Western Scrub-Jay. The Western Scrub-Jay is the most common at feeders and in residential areas, while the other two species remain more in the woods and mountains. The Western Scrub-Jay's behavior is similar in many ways to that of the Blue Jay, as described below.

LOOKING FOR LOVE

On a sunny day in late winter, you are likely to see flocks of Blue Jays flying from tree to tree; once they land, they tend to hop higher and higher in the branches. They will give a great

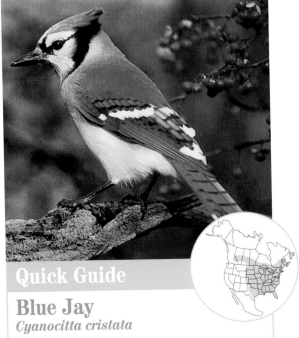

Quick Guide

Blue Jay
Cyanocitta cristata

ID Clues: Medium-size, 12-inch bird with blue head, back, wings, and tail; black collar and necklace; gray belly; crest that may be raised or lowered; males and females look alike

Habitat: Woods and suburbs

Food: Acorns and other nuts, fruit, insects, bird eggs; sunflower and mixed seed at feeders

Breeding Period: March to July

Nests: Nest of twigs and bark in trees

Eggs: 4 or 5, greenish blue with brown spots

Incubation: 17 days

Nestling Phase: 17 to 19 days

Broods: 1 or 2

Migration: Generally a year-round resident

variety of calls: One is bell-like and sounds like "toolool, toolool;" another sounds like a squeaky gate, or "wheedelee." The birds may also bob up and down. When the birds get to the top of the tree, they all fly off to another tree, calling "jaay, jaay," and then start over again. This is Blue Jay courtship—a female in the lead and several males following and competing for her.

Another courtship feature is mate feeding in spring and summer, where the male picks up a seed, goes to the female, and feeds it to her. As she receives the seed, she may fluff out her body feathers or rapidly flutter her wings, and she almost always gives a soft call that sounds like "kueu, kueu, kueu" or "kuetkuetkuet."

LOUD ONLY WHEN NECESSARY

We generally think of Blue Jays as always being raucous, but this is far from the truth. In fact, once their courtship is completed, paired birds become incredibly secretive as they build their nest and start to raise young.

Of course, the Blue Jay's loud voice comes in handy when it gives its excellent imitation of hawk calls. Blue Jays in our yard mimic several different Red-tailed Hawk and Broad-winged Hawk calls. Sometimes there is a hawk in the area, usually circling overhead, when it gives these calls. It is not really known why Blue Jays mimic hawks, but it may serve as an alarm to all birds in the area.

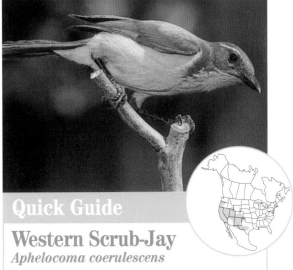

Quick Guide

Western Scrub-Jay
Aphelocoma coerulescens

ID Clues: About 10 inches, with blue wings, tail, and head; olive-gray back and belly; no crest; males and females look alike

Habitat: Varied; brushy country, desert scrub, orchards, canyons

Food: Insects, acorns, bird eggs, frogs, berries; sunflower seed at feeders

Breeding Period: March to July

Nests: Nests of bulky sticks in low tree or shrub about 2 to 12 feet high

Eggs: Usually 4 to 6

Incubation: 16 days

Nestling Phase: 18 days

Broods: 1 or 2

Migration: Generally a year-round resident

WATCHING BLUE JAYS FEED

We find that the best place to feed jays is at our large ground feeder. Generally, each Blue Jay defends its own personal distance of about a foot and will lunge at any other Blue Jay that comes too close.

Depending on where you live, there are other beautiful blue birds that may come to your ground feeders. *At right:* male Indigo Bunting in east, midwest, and some southwestern states; *at far right:* male Lazuli Bunting in western states; *below:* male Painted Bunting in Texas-Louisiana-Oklahoma areas.

Jays feed on a wide variety of foods in the wild and sometimes fly off with extra food and store it. One of their favorite foods in fall and winter is acorns. They peck off the cap and then store it in the ground or eat the rest of the nut.

BLUE JAY MYTHS

Blue Jays are blamed for a lot of things. One is giving "false alarms" when they arrive at the feeder to scare other birds away and get more feed. While it is true that Blue Jays often call as they land at a feeder, this is probably not intended to scare away other birds; they call even when no other birds are present.

Blue Jays are also blamed for being aggressive to other birds while at the feeder. This is not unique to Blue Jays; it is true of any bird that is larger than another. The best way to alleviate this is to have more space at the feeders. Our ground feeders are large, and Blue Jays can feed peacefully there with Dark-eyed Juncos and other ground-feeding birds.

It is also not true that Blue Jays keep other birds away from the feeder forever. If you watch, you will see that they feed only for a short time and then leave. Any smaller birds that they have scared off will most likely return when the Blue Jays leave.

JUNCO
A WINTER VISITOR

Each fall we try to guess on which day the first Dark-eyed Junco will arrive. These snowbirds, as some people call them, breed north of where we live in Massachusetts and come down into our area for the winter. Studies have shown that juncos usually return to the same winter area each year, so when they arrive we feel as if we are welcoming old friends.

WHO'S THE BOSS?

Junco flocks have an interesting and complex social arrangement. In a winter flock, males usually dominate females, and adults of both sexes tend to dominate first-year birds. Once the winter flock has arrived, the members form a social hierarchy that remains stable for the winter. This means there is one top bird that is

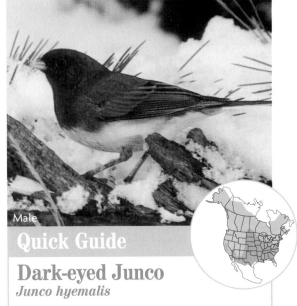

Male

Quick Guide

Dark-eyed Junco
Junco hyemalis

ID Clues: A small, 6-inch bird; the eastern variety (shown here) is all dark gray on its upper half and white below with a pale bill; varying plumage in other parts of country

Habitat: Woods, bogs, mountains above tree line, brush

Food: Seeds on ground and off trees; mixed seed at feeders

Breeding Period: April to August

Nests: Nest of moss and grass placed in depression in ground

Eggs: 3 to 6, gray or pale bluish with dark blotches

Incubation: 12 or 13 days

Nestling Phase: 9 to 13 days

Broods: 1 or 2

Migration: Year-round resident in some states; generally migrates north to breed in Canada

Bird Feeder Journal

March 31, 3:30 P.M. There are 6 Dark-eyed Juncos at the feeder. A chipmunk is feeding peaceably near them; 2 juncos come close and alternately raise and lower their heads to one another and make a "chip, chip, chip, kew, kew, kew" sound all strung together. Something frightens the flock, and they all fly into the brush pile, giving "tsip" sounds.

April 1, 5:00 P.M. Juncos have been singing more and more. At sundown, they went from our feeder to a nearby field, and there was much singing and chasing. They finally went to roost for the night in a very bushy spruce tree.

This female Dark-eyed Junco feeding her nestlings is similar to the male, but the dark parts of her body are browner.

when they leave. During dominance interactions, they often give "kew, kew, kew" calls.

The flock will remain in a defined foraging area all winter. You will not see all of the members of the flock at once because they do not travel together all the time. You are more likely to see them together in bad weather, when they frequent the feeder more often.

A CHANGE IN BEHAVIOR

In late winter, there is a change in junco behavior. There are more chases between birds in which they flash their white outer tail feathers. The males will start to sing more frequently. Their song is a musical trill, and many people confuse it with the song of a chipping sparrow.

This changed behavior is a sign that the breeding season is approaching, even though the Dark-eyed Juncos have not quite yet left your feeders. One day you will look out and realize they have gone—back to the north country until next year.

IDENTIFYING THE JUNCOS IN YOUR YARD

Juncos' plumage varies in different areas of the country, which originally led scientists to name four species of juncos. Now they are all considered one species, the Dark-eyed Junco.

In the East, juncos (formerly called Slate-colored Juncos) are dark gray above and white underneath. In general, adult males tend to have an all dark-gray body with no brown; fe-

dominant over all the others, then a second-ranked bird, and so on down the line. (Chickadees have a similar winter hierarchy.)

If you watch Dark-eyed Juncos at your feeder, you can often tell which birds are dominant just by their behavior. A dominant bird will fly or run at another bird as if it were going to peck it, making the other bird move away. Occasionally a subordinate bird will resist, and the two birds will face each other and raise and lower their heads. Fights are rare but do occur; two birds will fly vertically up to 10 feet and claw at each other.

Dark-eyed Juncos make a variety of sounds during interactions. At a feeder they usually give a "zeet" call when arriving and a "tsip"

males and immature birds have varying amounts of brown.

In the West (where they were formerly called Oregon Juncos), males have black hoods and reddish brown backs and sides; females are a more drab brown. There is a pink-sided form of this junco in the Rocky Mountains.

In the southern Rocky Mountains, juncos (formerly called Gray-headed Juncos) are pale gray with bright reddish brown backs.

In the Black Hills area in South Dakota and Wyoming, juncos (formerly called White-winged Juncos) are bluish gray above and white below, with two white wing bars.

KESTREL
A PRETTY LITTLE FALCON

The American Kestrel used to be called the sparrow hawk, but this was definitely a misnomer; it is a member of the falcon family. It is small like a sparrow (but not as small *as* a sparrow) and occasionally will catch and eat small birds. However, the American Kestrel feeds almost exclusively on larger insects, such as grasshoppers and crickets, and meadow voles—small mouselike animals.

CONTINUED SUCCESS WITH BIRDHOUSES

Many people have been successful in attracting American Kestrels to birdhouses. The American Kestrel cannot excavate its own hole and is to a great degree dependent on finding the larger nest holes of Northern Flickers or Pileated Woodpeckers in which to nest. These are often in short supply; therefore, birdhouses help increase the population and density of these important, pretty predators.

Still, considering their occasional taste for songbirds, you may not want to place a kestrel birdhouse near other birdhouses or in your yard. It is better to put it in a large open field or orchard where everyone can profit from the bird's eating of voles and insects that can damage crops.

Some people recommend that 2 to 3 inches of wood chips be placed in the bottom of the

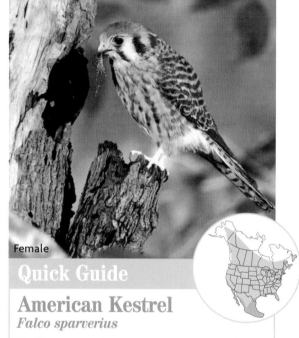

Female

Quick Guide

American Kestrel
Falco sparverius

ID Clues: A medium-size, 9-inch bird with rusty back and tail; two distinctive black "whiskers" on the side of the face; female has brown wings; male has steel blue wings

Habitat: Wide variety of open habitats, including urban areas

Food: Voles, mice, birds, insects; hovers and dives down to catch

Breeding Period: April through June

Nests: Needs large natural cavity in tree or birdhouse; no lining or additional materials

Eggs: 4 or 5, whitish with small brown dots

Incubation: 30 days

Nestling Phase: About 30 days

Broods: 1

Migration: Migrates to southern part of its range

box; others have found that the bird just pushes this away and lays its eggs on the bare wood.

BREEDING HABITS TO WATCH FOR

One of the most conspicuous behaviors seen around the nest site is the bringing of food by the male to the female. Once the two have paired and chosen a nest site, the female tends to remain near the nest, and the male brings most of her food to her. This continues through egg laying and incubation and into the nesting phase—a period of up to 11 weeks.

After the young leave the nest, they will perch together in trees, making short flights and waiting for either parent to bring them food. They flutter their wings and give a whining call when the adults approach. In the first days after leaving the nest, they may return to it at night.

Kestrel Birdhouse

Dimensions
Entrance-hole diameter: 3"
Height of hole above floor: 10" to 12"
Inside floor dimensions: 8" × 8" to 9" × 9"
Total height of box: 14" to 16"

Placement
Habitat: Open fields or the edge of woods
Height: 15' to 30' high on a tree or post

MOCKINGBIRD
THE BEST SONG MIMIC

The Northern Mockingbird has no distinct song of its own. It doesn't really need one—it can mimic the songs and calls of all other birds. Mockingbirds can even mimic other sounds; we had one that imitated the call of an American toad, and there was one well-known bird in California that imitated the fire sirens from a nearby station.

This mocking habit is shared by its close relatives the Gray Catbird and Brown Thrasher. Interestingly, each of these birds tends to repeat the songs of other birds a different number of times: The catbird sings them once, the Brown Thrasher repeats them twice, and the mockingbird imitates them three or more times.

Nobody has yet figured out why these birds act as mimics. Some people have suggested that when a mockingbird sings other birds' songs, those birds may be fooled into thinking the area is already occupied and move elsewhere, thus leaving the Northern Mockingbird with more resources for itself.

SONGS DAY OR NIGHT

In spring, Northern Mockingbirds are very conspicuous as they sit in the tops of trees, on chimneys, or on telephone poles and sing loudly. At this time of year, only the male sings; he is usually announcing his territory (1 to 2

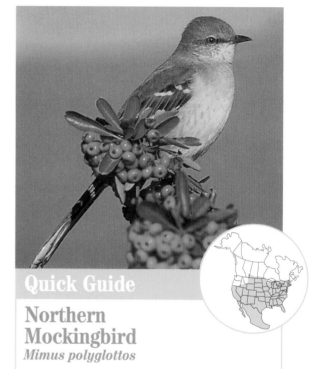

Quick Guide

Northern Mockingbird
Mimus polyglottos

ID Clues: Medium-size, 11-inch bird, grayish above and lighter below; white outer feathers on long tail and small white wing patch that, in flight, is a wide white bar; males and females look alike

Habitat: Open areas with shrubs, gardens, parks

Food: Berries, insects, snails, small snakes, lizards

Breeding Period: March to August

Nests: Nest of twigs, moss, leaves placed in dense shrub

Eggs: 2 to 6, blue-green with brown marks

Incubation: 12 or 13 days

Nestling Phase: 10 to 13 days

Broods: 1 to 3

Migration: Generally a year-round resident

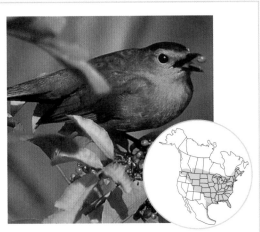

What's That Bird?

GRAY CATBIRD

ID Clues: About 9 inches, all-gray bird with black cap; males and females look alike

Habitat: Shrubs, tangled thickets, woods edges, suburbs

Food: Insects on ground, spiders, grapes, berries

Nests: Nest of twigs, grape bark placed in shrub

acres) to other males and trying to attract a female. As soon as he attracts a mate he stops singing, and the two begin building a nest and laying eggs.

In fall, both the males and the females start to sing. They are defending their territories, which center on a source of food, such as multiflora rose berries, that they will use throughout the winter.

Strangely, mockingbirds may sing at night in either the spring or the fall, often when there is a full moon—or even if the bird lives near a street lamp.

SEEDS ARE FINE BUT FRUITS ARE BEST

With the exception of hulled sunflower seed, mockingbirds are rarely attracted to the seed we put out for other birds. Instead, they are attracted to fruits, such as apples and raisins. They also will eat suet or peanut butter if it is in a spot they can reach.

In the wild, mockingbirds tend to live wherever berries and fruits grow, and they especially like the fruits of multiflora rose and red cedar. Mockingbirds also eat a lot of insects, catching them on the ground or even occasionally in the air.

FIGHTING FOR TERRITORY

Some people complain they have a mockingbird chasing all other birds away from their feeder. This may occur in fall and winter if your feeder is in the bird's fall and winter territory. It is usually defending not the feeder but a nearby bush or tree with berries; it may fear the other birds will pillage this store of winter food. The only solution is to move your feeder away from the berries and, hopefully, out of the bird's territory.

There are several unusual territorial actions mockingbirds perform. One that males do in spring is called loop flight. In between bouts of song delivered from a high perch, the bird flies up, makes a short loop, and then settles back

What's That Bird?
WESTERN KINGBIRD

ID Clues: About 9 inches, grayish bird with whitish breast, yellow belly, whiter outer tail feathers on black tail; males and females look alike

Habitat: Open areas with some trees or shrubs

Food: Insects caught in air, some berries

Nests: Nests in trees 8 to 40 feet high; needs open perches to fly out from for food

on the perch. The white markings on its wings and tail are conspicuously displayed, and the bird may even do a loop-the-loop.

A border dance occurs in the fall. Two birds face each other on the ground with heads and tails raised and hop back and forth and from side to side. This usually takes place at the common border of two neighboring birds and may help them settle on its boundaries.

Finally, there is wing flashing, a display often given when the bird is on the ground. In it, the bird slowly raises its wings in a jerky fashion and then lowers them. Wing flashing may occur while the bird is alone and feeding, or it may be given between dispersing immature birds and resident adults in fall. In the first case it may scare up insects as the bird feeds; in the second case it may be an aggressive display. Its real function is still a mystery. What's your theory?

NUTHATCH
THE ONLY UPSIDE-DOWN BIRD

If you see a bird going headfirst down a tree trunk, it's a nuthatch, the only common species with this ability. They do this in order to find bits of food (insect larvae, for example) that "right-side-up" birds, such as woodpeckers and Brown Creepers, may miss.

A nuthatch is able to move upside down because of the structure of its feet, which is different from that of many other birds. Most birds have three toes pointing forward and one pointing backward. The nuthatch has two toes pointing forward and two pointing backward, which enables them to hold on better as they go down or up a tree trunk.

WHICH BIRD DO YOU HAVE?

Of the four species of nuthatches in North America, the White-breasted Nuthatch and Red-breasted Nuthatch are the most common feeder birds throughout the United States. (Pygmy and Brown-headed nuthatches are the other species.) They share most behaviors, but have some differences.

The White-breasted Nuthatch is a year-round resident, but the Red-breasted species, generally found in northern and western regions, migrates to southern areas. The White-breasted Nuthatch almost always looks for a cavity already made either by another bird or naturally, so it will be attracted to a birdhouse. Although

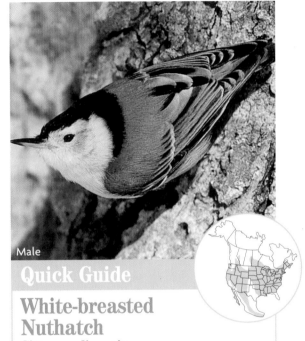

Male

Quick Guide

White-breasted Nuthatch
Sitta carolinensis

ID Clues: A small, 6-inch bird with blue-gray back, white face and breast, some reddish brown on rump and sides; black crown extends down nape of neck

Habitat: Deciduous and mixed woods

Food: Nuts, seeds, acorns, insects; suet and sunflower seed at feeders

Breeding Period: March to June

Nests: Bark, grasses, rootlets, and fur in existing cavity in tree or birdhouse

Eggs: 5 to 10, white with small brown speckles

Incubation: 12 days

Nestling Phase: About 14 days

Broods: 1

Migration: Generally a year-round resident

The female White-breasted Nuthatch has a blue-gray back, dark gray to silver cap, and white breast.

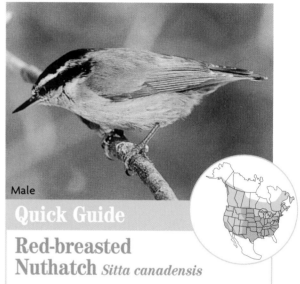

Male

Quick Guide

Red-breasted Nuthatch *Sitta canadensis*

ID Clues: 4½ inches long, blue-gray back, white eyebrow and black line through eye, black cap, rusty-colored breast and belly; female has silver cap and buff breast

Habitat: Coniferous woods

Food: Insects, seeds; suet and sunflower seed at feeders

Breeding Period: May through July

Nests: Bark shreds, roots, grasses in cavities or birdhouses

Eggs: 5 or 6, white or slightly pink with small brown speckles

Incubation: 12 days

Nestling Phase: 14 to 21 days

Broods: 1, possibly 2

Migration: Migrates to southern United States

it is more likely to excavate its own hole in soft, partially rotted wood, the Red-breasted Nuthatch will also use a birdhouse.

You can distinguish male and female nuthatches by the extent and darkness of the black on their heads. The male has a large, jet black marking; on the female, it is more limited and either all silver-gray or gray with blotches of black. Look for these differences to help recognize pairs. In the southeastern states, unfortunately, these differences on male and female White-breasted Nuthatches are less obvious or may not exist.

SONGS AND CALLS

Like all birds, nuthatches have their own special language.

"Ank ank": This loud call is given by male and female all year. When given as a simple

"ank ank," it is usually a contact note between the pair. When given as a long series of rapid "anks," it is probably a response to some disturbance.

"Ip ip": This is a very high, quiet sound given between the pair as they move about the woods, feeding close together. It is a close-distance contact call that helps them keep track of each other.

"Werwerwerwer": This rapid series of notes is the song of the male nuthatch. It is usually given from high in trees in late winter or spring when the birds are beginning their courtship.

The sounds of the Red-breasted Nuthatch are distinctive. Its most common sound is a nasal "meep meep."

EARLY COURTSHIP

Nuthatches begin their courtship as early as January. On a clear morning you often can hear the male giving his song. In response, the female may perch nearby and remain still. After a while, the two will go feed together for the day. At the end of the day, each goes to a separate hole to roost for the night.

Another engaging feature of nuthatch courtship is mate feeding. The male collects a

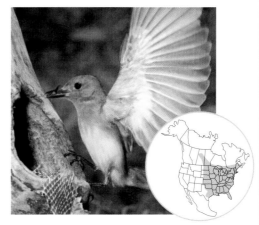

What's That Bird?
GREAT CRESTED FLYCATCHER

ID Clues: 8 inches with large, crested head; olive back and head with yellow belly and bright rusty tail; males and females look alike

Habitat: Woods and wooded urban areas

Food: Aerial insects caught while flying; some berries

Nests: Grass, pine needles, fur, feathers, bits of paper, bits of shed snake skins; uses natural cavities or birdhouses

Nuthatch Birdhouse

Dimensions
Entrance-hole diameter: $1\frac{1}{8}$" to $1\frac{1}{2}$"
Height of hole above floor: 6" to 7"
Inside floor dimensions: 4" × 4" to 5" × 5"
Total height of box: 9" to 12"

Placement
Habitat: Suburban or rural woods, or locations with a mixture of trees and open space
Height: 5' to 10' high on a tree or post

morsel of food, flies to the female, and places the food in her bill.

DOWN THE HATCH

The name nuthatch comes from the old English word "nuthack," which referred to the bird's eating habits: When nuthatches eat a sunflower seed or a nut, they often wedge it into a bark crevice and hack it open. The bird could also have been named "nutstore" because it often takes food from the feeder and stores it in bark crevices for later use, even covering the stored food with a piece of bark or lichen. You can watch them do this after they leave your feeder. (Of course, other birds see this habit as well and will often steal the stash.)

Not only do nuthatches store food in bark crevices in winter for later use, they do the same around the nest box when breeding. The male will subsequently retrieve the food and feed it to the female while she is incubating or to the developing nestlings.

MORE IS NOT MERRIER

If you hear excited, rapid "ank" calls, go outside and you will probably see two or more nuthatches moving about near each other on a tree trunk with their heads down and back feathers ruffled. They may also spread their tails and slightly open their wings or chase after each other in flight.

Male and female nuthatches remain together through winter in an area of 25 to 45 acres. In spring, during breeding, they more aggressively defend a smaller portion of this area as their territory. Aggressive behavior will break out between two males, two females, or a pair and an intruding third bird in a spot where their ranges overlap.

GUARDING THE HOME

One interesting nuthatch habit involves protecting the home with beetle juice. A nuthatch will hold a beetle in its bill and rub it around the entrance hole to its nest. It is believed that this leaves a chemical residue secreted defensively by the beetle, which may deter certain nest predators from entering the hole.

ORIOLE
STRIKING BEAUTY, AMAZING NEST

Orioles are stunning and fascinating birds. With their flame-colored plumage, melodic whistles, and incredible nests, it is little wonder that they have common names like firebird, golden oriole, and hammock bird. There are many species of orioles found in the United States. Several species are unique to particular regions, but Baltimore, Bullock's, and Orchard Orioles are probably the most commonly seen in backyards and gardens around the country.

ATTRACTING ORIOLES TO YOUR YARD

In the wild, orioles eat nectar and many kinds of insects. One account says that orioles will spend a lot of time probing into the blossoms of agaves, aloes, hibiscus, lilies, and other tubular flowers to sip the nectar. Sometimes they perch on the stem and puncture the base of the blossom to get at the nectar.

Orioles have been such constant visitors to hummingbird feeders that there are commercially made oriole feeders. These are like large-capacity hummingbird feeders with orange instead of red parts. Orioles take a more dilute sugar-water concentration than hummingbirds—a mixture of 1 part sugar to 6 parts water.

Besides nectar, orioles eat blackberries, mulberries, elderberries, serviceberries, and many other kinds of fruits. They also consume

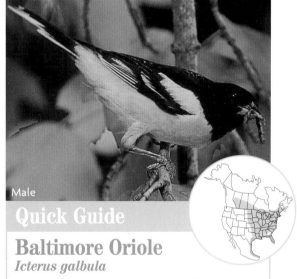

Male

Quick Guide

Baltimore Oriole
Icterus galbula

ID Clues: About 9 inches long, black head and back with orange breast and, in flight, orange corner tail feathers; female is paler with no black on head

Habitat: Deciduous trees near openings, such as parks, gardens, roads

Food: Insects, fruits, flower nectar; sugar-water and oranges at feeders

Breeding Period: April to June

Nests: Suspended nest of plant fibers, 4 to 8 inches long, hung from branch tips 6 to 60 feet above ground

Eggs: 4 to 6, bluish white or grayish with brown markings

Incubation: 12 to 14 days

Nestling Phase: 12 to 14 days

Broods: 1

Migration: Migrates to southern United States

Bullock's Oriole is so closely related to the Baltimore Oriole that they were once considered to be the same species. As shown here, the male Bullock's has a black eyeline, orange on his cheeks, and a wide white wing patch. Bullock's Orioles live in the western and mountain states; Baltimore Orioles inhabit the eastern and central states.

a large variety of caterpillars and insects, including many that harm crops. At bird-feeding stations they eat orange halves, suet, peanut-butter mixtures, grapes, watermelon pulp or rind, and other fruits.

SINGING FOR LOVE

Arriving on their northern breeding grounds when spring is well underway, orioles engage in only a brief courtship. Male orioles usually arrive ahead of females and stake out territories, which may be quite close to those of other orioles—so close that they sometimes nest together in colonies.

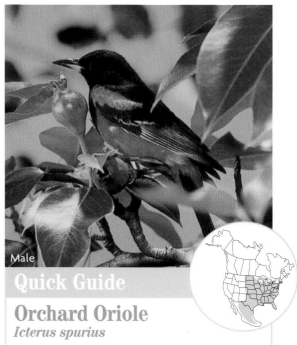

Male

Quick Guide

Orchard Oriole
Icterus spurius

ID Clues: 7 inches long, all-black head and upper parts with reddish brown breast and rump; female is yellowish green on head and breast with white wing bars

Habitat: Orchards, open woods, wetlands, parks, streamside trees

Food: Insects, fruit, tree blossoms, flower nectar; sugar-water at feeders

Breeding Period: April to July

Nests: Shallow, 3-inch pouchlike nest of plant fibers woven to a horizontal fork of a branch; nests singly or in loose colonies

Eggs: 3 to 5, bluish white with brown markings

Incubation: 12 days

Nestling Phase: 11 to 14 days

Broods: 1

Migration: Migrates to southern United States and Mexico

When the females arrive, the males court them with a rich, melodic, whistled song that has a bell-like quality. Unlike most songbirds,

These two southwestern orioles (*left:* male Hooded Oriole; *right:* male Scott's Oriole) may be found in Texas, New Mexico, Arizona, Nevada, Utah, and California.

females of most species of orioles also sing. Listen for a pair using their whistled notes to stay in contact as they hop about the trees, looking for food and building their nest.

THE HAMMOCK BIRD

Orioles have some of the most beautiful and fascinating nests of all birds: intricately woven affairs made of plant fibers. They are usually suspended from the tips of tree branches, not supported by the base like other nests. Some are longer and more pendulous than others, ranging from 4 to 25 inches long.

Even though the nest looks like it could be the work of a master weaver, there is actually no organized design in its weaving. First, foundation fibers are attached to supporting twigs to form hanging loops. As more and more fibers are added, the oriole randomly pokes and pulls at the fibers until the nest is completed. One ornithologist found that an Orchard Oriole had taken a 13-inch length of grass and hooked it in and out of the nest structure 34 times. Often an oriole will also add an inner lining of soft material.

Orioles will frequently accept nesting material laid out for them during their breeding season. Cut pieces of neutral-color string or twine into 4- to 8-inch lengths, and drape them in places where the birds can see them.

OWL
DENIZEN OF THE DARK

Activity for most owls starts when it begins to get dark. The birds stir, stretch, and, putting it as delicately as we can, often regurgitate pellets containing the indigestible fur and bones of animals they caught and ate the previous night. Then they usually go off to hunt, returning before dawn.

Their nighttime routine is one of the main reasons owls are seldom seen, but that does not mean they are not living close to your property. Owls will live in suburban, urban, and rural locations in deep woods and wood edges, farmland, or swampy habitats. If you put up an owl birdhouse, you will expand the variety of

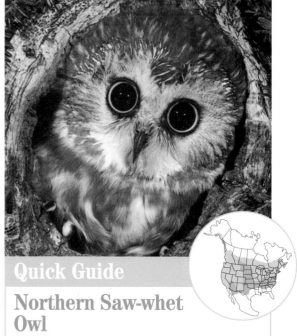

Owl Birdhouse

For Northern Saw-whet Owl, Eastern Screech-Owl, Western Screech-Owl

Dimensions
Entrance-hole diameter: 2 ½" to 4"
Height of hole above floor: 10" to 12"
Inside floor dimensions: 6" × 6" to 8" × 8"
Total height of box: 15" to 18"

Placement
Habitat: Screech-Owls, in or at the edge of woods, in urban or rural areas; Saw-whet Owls, in deep woods, preferably near swamps
Height: 5' to 20' high on a tree, post, or building

Quick Guide

Northern Saw-whet Owl
Aegolius acadicus

ID Clues: A small, 8-inch bird with dark bill, yellow eyes, no ear tufts, and reddish brown facial disk; males and females look alike
Habitat: Pine or mixed woods
Food: Mice, voles, shrews, chipmunks, bats, insects
Breeding period: March into July
Nests: Uses existing tree cavity or birdhouse; adds no lining
Eggs: 5 or 6, pure white
Incubation: 26 to 28 days, mostly by female
Nestling phase: 28 to 33 days
Broods: 1, occasionally 2
Migration: Some migrate from northern areas

birds living in your "neck of the woods" and help these birds prosper despite diminishing natural habitats.

NESTING HABITS

None of our North American owls builds nests. The five species featured here all nest in cavities and readily take to birdhouses. There are eight other North American species of owls that nest in cavities, but they do not normally use birdhouses. For a list of all cavity-nesting owls, see "Cavity Nesters of North America" on page 95.

The Eastern and Western screech-owls and Northern Saw-whet Owl are so small that they may compete for some of the natural cavities and birdhouses that can be used by other birds. For example, these owls commonly use old Northern Flicker nest holes, which are about 2½ inches in diameter. Other birds that might like to use these holes include the Great Crested and Ash-throated flycatchers, American Kestrel, Purple Martin, and Red-bellied and Red-headed woodpeckers. In fact, screech-owls have been reported to nest in Purple Martin birdhouses.

Our other owls, which do not live in cavities or use birdhouses, also do not build nests. Two of these, the Snowy Owl and Short-eared Owl, nest on the ground. One species, the Burrowing Owl, nests in old mammal burrows. And the other three, the Great Gray Owl, Great Horned Owl, and Long-eared Owl, use the

Quick Guide

Barred Owl
Strix varia

ID Clues: A large, 21-inch bird, with all-dark eyes, no ear tufts, barring on its upper breast, and streaks on its lower breast; males and females look alike

Habitat: Woods and wooded swamps

Food: Mice, amphibians, reptiles, rabbits, insects

Breeding period: March into August

Nests: Uses existing tree cavity, abandoned hawk or crow nest, or birdhouse; adds no lining

Eggs: 2 or 3, white

Incubation: 28 to 33 days, mostly by female

Nestling phase: 4 to 7 weeks or longer

Broods: 1

Migration: Generally a year-round resident

abandoned open-cup nests of other birds, such as those of crows and hawks, or the nests of squirrels.

OWL DIETS

The two largest owls mentioned here, the Barn and Barred owls, eat meadow voles and other rodents almost exclusively. The three smaller owls—Eastern and Western screech-owls and Northern Saw-whet Owl—have a more varied diet. Screech-Owls, for instance, may feed on night-flying insects. When nesting in the city, they may frequent the areas under streetlights to which moths and other insects are attracted.

The smaller owls also eat other small birds that may roost on branches at night. Because of this, **do not put owl birdhouses near those of your other birds.**

THE DAY SHIFT

If owls are having trouble finding enough food at night, their hunting may continue into the dawn hours, but the daytime program for owls is generally to sleep and stay still. Some owls, however, are more "day owls" than "night

Eastern

Quick Guide

Eastern Screech-Owl
Otus asio

Western Screech-Owl
Otus kennicottii

ID Clues: Adult Western and Eastern Screech-owls look similar; a small, 9-inch bird with yellow eyes and prominent ear tufts; males and females look alike

Habitat: Woods, swamps, parks, suburbs

Food: Mice, insects, amphibians, birds

Breeding period: March into July

Nests: Uses large natural cavity in tree or birdhouse; adds no lining

Eggs: 4 to 6, white

Incubation: 27 to 30 days, by female only

Nestling phase: About 4 weeks

Broods: 1

Migration: Generally a year-round resident

Barred Owl Birdhouse

Dimensions

Entrance-hole diameter: 6" to 8"
Height of hole above floor: 14" to 18"
Inside floor dimensions: 13" × 13" to 14" × 14"
Total height of box: 22" to 28"

Placement

Habitat: Woods or swamps in suburban or rural areas
Height: 10' to 20' high on a tree

owls." One of these is the Barred Owl, which you might hear hooting in the middle of a summer day. Barred Owls do most of their hunting at night, as do the other owls, but they also make short flights around the nesting area during the day.

SOUNDS OF THE NIGHT

Since owls are impossible to see as they move about at night, the best clues to their presence are their often harsh or bizarre sounds in the nighttime air. Although it is commonly believed that all owls hoot, the fact is that only a few do; all the others make a variety of screeches, caterwauls, and whistles.

Of the cavity-nesting owls mentioned here, only the Barred Owl hoots. Its familiar call is four hoots in a phrase that sounds like "Who cooks for you?" The Barred Owl also gives many other calls that range from something like maniacal laughter to the sound of howls of monkeys.

Barn Owl Birdhouse

Dimensions
Entrance-hole diameter: 6" to 8"
Height of hole above floor: 4"
Inside floor dimensions: 16" wide, 22" deep
Total height of box: 16"

Placement
Habitat: Open farmland
Height: 10' to 20' high on a tree, barn, or shed

Quick Guide

Barn Owl
Tyto alba

ID Clues: Slender, 18-inch bird with dark eyes and white, sparsely spotted breast; most easily recognized by its white, heart-shaped facial disk; males and females look alike

Habitat: Open farmlands, grasslands, deserts, suburbs

Food: Mice, rats, insects, bats, reptiles

Breeding period: March into July

Nests: Nests in barns and other buildings, tree cavities, holes in banks and cliffs, birdhouses; no added lining

Eggs: 4 or 5, white to pale buff

Incubation: 30 to 34 days, by male and female

Nestling phase: 52 to 56 days

Broods: 1 or 2

Migration: Migrates slightly south from northern areas

The Northern Saw-whet Owl is named for its call. To "whet" a saw, you grip it in a vise and run a small file over it. The resulting sound is similar to the Northern Saw-whet Owl's repeated short whistles. These whistles are often given too softly to be heard.

The Eastern and Western Screech-owls do not really screech. Rather, the two main vocalizations are a descending quavering whistle and a continuous series of notes on one pitch. The Barn Owl makes some of the most unusual of all bird sounds. One of its calls resembles the screech of metal scraping against metal. Another is similar to the sound of a tremendous rush of steam coming out of an engine. Hearing these calls in the dead of night can be either terribly frightening or terribly exciting, depending on your perspective.

PURPLE MARTIN
OUR MOST WANTED BIRD

After the book *America's Most Wanted Bird*, by J. L. Wade, was published in 1966, putting up Purple Martin houses became a national pastime. Thousands of Purple Martin houses have been placed in parks and backyards, which has undoubtedly increased the population of this much-loved, beautiful deep purple bird.

AN EASTERN THING?

For hundreds of years, people have been putting up houses to attract Purple Martins. They have usually been groups of gourds with entrance holes or large birdhouses with many compartments. In the eastern half of the United States, Purple Martins seem to like these colonial nesting situations. In the West, however, many Purple Martins nest singly in old woodpecker holes and other crevices.

HOUSING CONSIDERATIONS

You can contribute to the health and welfare of Purple Martins by putting up clusters of hollowed-out gourds or a birdhouse in an open area like a field, preferably near water. Interestingly, gourds are extremely popular in the Southeast, and Purple Martins seem to prefer them to the colony-type house. They seem to moderate the effects of cooler and hotter weather.

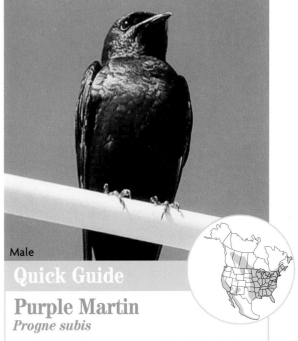

Male

Quick Guide
Purple Martin
Progne subis

ID Clues: Medium-size, 8-inch bird; dark, shiny purple body with black wings and tail; female has dull purple back and whitish gray breast and belly

Habitat: Open areas, often near water

Food: Insects caught in air

Breeding Period: May into August

Nests: Grass stems, twigs, paper, mud, green leaves

Eggs: 5 or 6, pure white

Incubation: 15 or 16 days, by female only

Nestling phase: 27 to 35 days

Broods: 1

Migration: Migrates to South America

Purple Martin Birdhouse

Dimensions
Entrance-hole diameter: 2" to 2 1/2", ideally
 2 1/8"
Height of hole above floor: 1"
Inside floor dimensions: 6" × 6"
Total height of box: 6"

Placement
Habitat: Open areas near human habitations,
 preferably with water nearby
Height: 8' to 20' high on a post

These Purple Martins are enjoying a colonial-type birdhouse. The House Sparrow on the left side of the roof may be looking for a place to stay, too.

Besides the dimensions provided on this page, keep these features in mind when buying or building a Purple Martin birdhouse. (Also see "Building Birdhouses" on page 122.)

- Paint nest-compartment interiors white to discourage starlings.
- Include easy-opening nest compartments for cleaning.
- Provide plugs for entrance holes in winter to keep out starlings and House Sparrows.
- Equip with a way to easily lower and raise the whole house for weekly inspection.

This last component is essential: House Sparrow nests must be removed each week or they will take over. This can be quite a chore unless the house is light. This is why most good Purple Martin houses are made of aluminum and placed on steel poles that have a winch or pulley attached for easy raising and lowering.

Here are some facts, based on a survey of people who had Purple Martin houses, that may also help you select, place, and enjoy your birdhouse.

- Houses less than 30 yards from buildings attract more birds than those farther away.
- The height of the house has little effect on occupancy; neither does aluminum or wood construction.
- Starlings are not a severe threat to Purple Martin colonies because starlings are territorial; one nesting pair keeps others away.
- House Sparrows use colonies made out of gourds less often.

SPARROWS
LITTLE BROWN JOBS

A lot of people refer to any type of sparrow as an LBJ: little brown job. That's because many people think that to tell one species of sparrow from another is a tough task only a dedicated birder or compulsive hairsplitter wants to handle. This is far from the truth. Many sparrows are easy to tell apart, and this includes the ones that regularly visit feeders.

EASY TO IDENTIFY

There are only six sparrows commonly seen at feeders. They are the American Tree Sparrow, Fox Sparrow, House Sparrow, Song Sparrow, White-crowned Sparrow, and White-throated Sparrow. (The House Sparrow is not a real sparrow; it's a weaver finch. Because they are similar in appearance to true native sparrows, they are described here.)

To identify sparrows, look past their brownish body to the patterns on their breast and head. Four of these sparrows have clear, *unstreaked breasts*—the American Tree Sparrow, White-throated Sparrow, White-crowned Sparrow, and House Sparrow. They are easily distinguished from each other if you know what to look for:

White-throated Sparrow: obvious white patch on its throat (also known as a bib), head is striped with black and white or tan and brown

What's That Bird?
HOUSE SPARROW

ID Clues: Small, 6-inch bird; rich brown back, grayish crown and cheek; black around eyes and down chin; unstreaked upper breast; female has grayish brown breast, brown crown; buff eyebrow

Habitat: Urban areas, parks, open farmland

Food: Insects, spiders, small fruit, weed seeds, waste grain, crumbs; mixed seeds from ground feeders

Nests: Grasses, leaves, twigs, cloth, feathers, in natural cavities or birdhouses

White-crowned Sparrow: all grayish except for black and white stripes on head

American Tree Sparrow: rusty cap and dark dot in the center of its clear breast

House Sparrow: black around eyes, on chin, and top of the breast

The two other sparrows have *breasts streaked with brown*. Both also have a darker spot on the center of their breast where some of the streaking is denser. The Song Sparrow is a fairly dull brown, while the Fox Sparrow has a rusty red tail (in the East, it's rusty red all over) and is clearly larger than other sparrows.

THE SPRING SONG IS REVEALING

Even though the Fox, American Tree, White-crowned, and White-throated sparrows do most of their singing on their breeding grounds—which are far to the North, and in the case of the White-crowned in the West—you may have a chance to hear each give its song at your feeder in late winter and spring before it starts to migrate.

The sparrow with the most easily recognized song is the White-throated Sparrow. Its song is one or two slow, clear whistles followed by three quavering whistles on a different pitch. Some people say it sounds like "pure, sweet Canada Canada Canada."

The songs of the other sparrows that nest to the north and west are not as readily described and not as easily distinguished by the beginner. The Song Sparrow breeds all across the continent, and after being attracted to your feeder it may even nest in your yard. Its song is one short note repeated several times, followed by a series of warblings. Listen for it singing from the top of a shrub or small tree; it loves to announce its territory in the open. It

Quick Guide

White-throated Sparrow *Zonotrichia albicollis*

ID Clues: 6½-inch bird with unstreaked breast, white bib on throat, white and black stripes on head, yellow marks just above bill at each eye; males and females look alike

Habitat: Coniferous and mixed woods, brushy areas

Food: Seeds, insects, fruit on or near ground; mixed seed at feeders

Breeding Period: May to August

Nests: Nest of grasses on ground near base of small tree or shrub

Eggs: 4 to 6, light blue-green with dark marks

Incubation: 11 to 14 days

Nestling Phase: 7 to 12 days

Broods: 1 or 2

Migration: Migrates north into a few northern states and all across Canada

generally nests in open habitats, such as suburban areas and farmland.

The song of the House Sparrow has less melodious charm than the other sparrows. It is a monotonous series of notes that sound like "chirup-chireep-chirup."

WATCHING SPARROWS FEED

It is fun to watch sparrows feed both at your feeders and in the wild. Most of our sparrows prefer to feed at ground or tray feeders, and they usually like some brushy cover nearby that they can dash into for protection. In the wild they love weed seeds and can be found in weedy fields or patches along roads and paths. This is particularly true of Song Sparrows and White-crowned Sparrows.

American Tree Sparrows often feed above the ground, taking seeds directly off weeds and trees, so they may visit one of your hanging feeders. You may see them with American Goldfinches eating seeds off birches and alders. They also occasionally perch atop a weed and flutter their wings, causing seeds to fall out, and then drop down to feed on them.

Fox Sparrows and White-throated Sparrows have a slightly different way of feeding. They take repeated short jumps forward and then backward, scraping away vegetation with their feet as they do so. This uncovers fallen seeds and possibly some insects under leaves and debris.

FLOCKS RULE IN WINTER

Most of the sparrows you see in winter are on their wintering grounds—their Florida vaca-

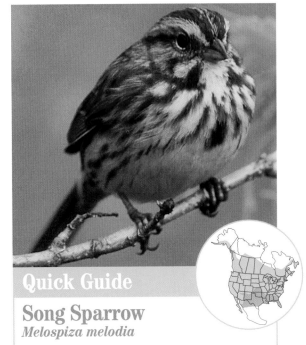

Quick Guide

Song Sparrow
Melospiza melodia

ID Clues: Small, 6-inch, reddish brown bird; whitish breast with brown streaks and central dark dot; long, rounded tail; males and females look alike

Habitat: Dense shrubs at edges of open areas such as fields, lawns, streams

Food: Seeds, insects, some berries on or near ground; mixed seed at feeders

Breeding Period: February to August

Nests: Nest of grasses on ground or in shrub or small tree

Eggs: 3 to 5, greenish white with dark marks

Incubation: 12 to 13 days

Nestling Phase: 10 days

Broods: 2 or 3

Migration: Generally a year-round resident; some may migrate farther north into Canada

tion, as it were. Just as your family might go to the same place for vacation several times,

What's That Bird?

CHIPPING SPARROW

ID Clues: 5½ inches, bright rusty-colored crown with whitish eyebrows and black eyestripes; males and females look alike

Habitat: Grassy areas, open woods, lawns, parks

Food: Insects and seeds on ground; mixed seed at feeders

Nests: Nest of grasses in dense shrub or evergreen

What's That Bird?

LARK SPARROW

ID Clues: 6½ inches, bright red-brown cheek patch and head stripes; unstreaked gray breast with central dot; males and females look alike

Habitat: Open woods, farmlands, roadsides, suburbs

Food: Mostly seeds on ground, some insects

Nests: Nest of grasses and rootlets on ground in tall grasses or other protection

sparrows tend to return to the same wintering spot each year. Thus, of the sparrows that you see at your feeders, many of the older ones may have been there before.

In winter, each species of sparrow has a slightly different social arrangement. The Song and Fox Sparrows tend to be alone or in small, loose flocks of several birds. These species generally stay in the same area all winter. Male Song Sparrows may even remain on their

breeding territories and leave only when there is a shortage of food.

American Tree Sparrows form large flocks of about 50 birds that seem to roam a large area, taking advantage of the local abundance of tree seeds. All of the American Tree Sparrows in a given area may be organized into a hierarchy.

White-throated Sparrows tend to feed in small flocks of 5 to 10 birds that stay in shrubbery and

Can You Distinguish These LBJs?

These sparrows are easy to identify at your feeders when you know what to look for (males and females look alike).

White-crowned (*left*): A 7-inch grayish bird with unstreaked breast and bold black and white stripes on head

Fox (*center*): A 7-inch red-brown bird with rufous streaking on gray head and back, heavy streaking on breast with central breast dot, wings and tail are quite reddish

American Tree (*right*): A 6-inch bird with unstreaked gray breast and central dot, gray face with rufous eyeline and crown

other dense cover. White-Crowned Sparrows stay in large flocks of 25 to 50 birds, which have a fairly fixed membership and remain in a defined area that does not overlap others.

Bird Feeder Journal

November 11, 9:00 A.M. Our first American Tree Sparrows and Dark-eyed Juncos arrived today. Will they fly farther south or will they be our winter residents? With their arrival at our ground feeder, winter has officially started.

March 12, 4:00 P.M. Three Fox Sparrows at the feeder! They are the first we have seen this winter. They look so big and red compared to other sparrows. They must be migrating north.

In fall and winter, you will see House Sparrows form tight little flocks two times each day. Around noon they gather in bushes or low shrubbery for about an hour, preening and chirping. These flocks are noisy and conspicuous, and why the birds gather like this is not known. It may be a resting and digesting period, during which the birds feel safer in a flock.

Again in late afternoon, various loudly chirping flocks join together. As it gets dark they gradually travel to a nearby roost: dense shrubbery, trees, ivy-covered walls, or a protected structure like a bridge. In the morning they all leave to go about their daily activities.

HOUSE SPARROWS WILL NEST ANYWHERE

The House Sparrow is sometimes referred to as the English Sparrow because in the 1850s it was imported to North America from England. The bird was originally introduced to reduce the number of certain insect pests. Although the birds did not help with those particular insects, they did multiply rapidly.

The House Sparrow population peaked around 1900, but this little bird is still a ubiquitous denizen of cities and suburbs. These birds will nest in any cavity that they can find, including air conditioners, street lamps, store awnings, and neon signs. (The nest, unlike the cuplike nests of grasses of native sparrows, is usually a woven sphere of plant fibers and other materials—string, leaves, paper, feathers—with an entrance on the side, which both male and female build together.) In these locations, it is not competing with any of our native birds and doesn't need to be disturbed.

Unfortunately, House Sparrows, like starlings, aggressively compete with native cavity-nesting species of birds for nest holes. Because of this they should be discouraged from nesting in your birdhouses. For details about how to do this, see "Protecting Your Birdhouses" on page 118.

STARLING
A BOLD AND BEAUTIFUL IMMIGRANT

Most of our common feeder birds are native to the continent, but humans have introduced a few from other parts of the world. The European Starling is one. In 1890, 60 pairs were released into Central Park in New York City, and they began to breed that same year in the crooks and crannies of buildings. The next year, 40 more pairs were released in the same area. A mere 50 years after that, the European Starling had spread to almost every part of the United States and southern Canada. They are one of nature's most remarkable success stories.

GOOD BIRD OR BAD BIRD?

One of the most amazing things about starlings is how much they change in appearance for winter, going from the familiar all-black coat to a lovely speckled bird. After the yearly molt of all their feathers in late summer, their bill is dark and their black plumage is speckled all over with small white Vs. By spring, the white tips of their feathers have worn off, leaving the birds totally dark and—if you look closely—iridescent, especially on the head and neck. Their bills also change from dark to light; the males' bills turn bright yellow.

People are often surprised by the starling's beauty; their reputation as raucous, dominating birds can make them a hard bird to love. While some consider starlings overly aggressive,

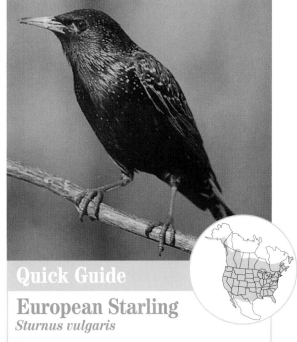

Quick Guide
European Starling
Sturnus vulgaris

ID Clues: 8-inch bird with iridescent purple-black all over and long, yellow bill; males and females look alike
Habitat: Urban and suburban areas
Food: Insects, spiders, earthworms, snails, weed seeds, berries, garbage; seeds and suet at feeders
Breeding Period: March into July
Nests: Dead leaves, moss, lichens, bark, grasses, tree flowers, in natural tree cavities or birdhouses, 2 to 60 feet high
Eggs: 4 or 5, pale bluish or greenish white
Incubation: 12 to 14 days, by male and female
Nestling phase: 18 to 21 days
Broods: 1 to 3
Migration: Generally a year-round resident

others see their success as having come from an opportunistic nature.

In one aspect, however, their aggressiveness presents a problem: The starling lives in cavities, so it competes with all of our other native cavity-nesting species. An aggressive bird, it can oust these other birds from their homes— even those a little larger than itself. Because of this, it is best to discourage them from nesting in your birdhouses. (See "Protecting Your Birdhouses" on page 118.)

WHAT STARLINGS EAT

Starlings often feed in flocks. In fall you may see a flock descend on a shrub in fruit, pick it clean in a few minutes, and then fly off.

Starlings also feed on insects in grassy areas and are important predators of insect pests such as cutworm and Japanese beetle larvae, grasshoppers, and other insects found in fields

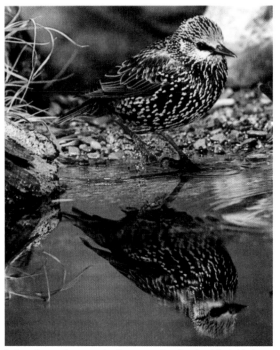

In its winter plumage, the European Starling is a black bird heavily speckled with white and has a dark bill.

or lawns. Because of this, starlings can be very beneficial.

At the feeder, starlings are attracted to suet, white millet, peanut hearts, and, to a lesser extent, striped sunflower seed. Many people find starlings objectionable at their feeders because their aggressiveness seems to scare off other birds. One way to counteract this is to lessen the competition by adding more feeders to other spots around your yard.

WATCHING STARLING BEHAVIOR

Starling behavior is particularly fascinating in spring when males defend their nest holes.

Bird Feeder Journal

May 5, 10:00 A.M. There are young starlings feeding in a flock on the short-grass area of our field. We can tell they are fledglings by their calls and brownish color. It is hard to believe that the adults have already completed one brood; many other species have not even arrived for the summer.

June 5, 8:00 A.M. There are starlings peering into the nest boxes in our field. Our swallow colony, which uses the boxes, is very upset and is swirling about the starlings. Luckily, the box openings are 1 1/2 inches in diameter and just a little too small for the starlings to enter. After about a half-hour of trying, the starlings give up.

Female

What's That Bird?
PHAINOPEPLA

ID Clues: A small, 6 ½-inch dark gray bird with tall crest, long tail, and pale gray wing bars; males have all-black body and tail
Habitat: Desert washes, oak woods, canyons
Food: Aerial insects and berries, especially mistletoe
Nests: Nest of twigs and grasses in fork of tree

They perch near the site and give a crowing call, a jumble of whistled and screeched sounds. When a female flies near, the male will display a behavior called rowing, in which it rotates its wings as if it were rowing and calls loudly, trying to attract the female's attention to himself and his nest hole.

If another male starling lands on the branch, the owner performs the comical action of sidling: It keeps stepping sideways toward the intruder, forcing it farther and farther out on the branch, until the competitor finally has to fly away or fall off. Male starlings try to defend nest sites in fall, hoping to retain ownership into the breeding season the next spring.

NIGHTTIME GATHERINGS

Most people do not know about starling roosting habits unless they live near a roost site. Roosts are places where starlings gather for the night, in numbers ranging from a few hundred to a few hundred thousand. They are located in protected spots, such as marshes or in groves of trees; in the city they are often located on the ledges beneath large bridges.

Every evening just before sundown, the birds start to fly into the roost from outlying areas, which are sometimes 10 or more miles away. Along their route they often stop in the tops of trees and gather with other flocks of starlings. At these stopovers the birds call noisily, periodically flying up into the air and then settling down again.

The final flight to the roost is fascinating—you will see large flocks circling above the spot and then diving with great speed into the roost. The roost is noisy, often long into the night.

No one knows exactly why the birds roost together, especially in such large numbers. Some theories propose that roosts provide some protection from predators and that they are close to alternative sources of food that the birds can exploit on their way to and from their daily centers of activity.

SWALLOW
A BUILT-IN BUG ZAPPER

Swallows are wonderful to have on your property: They constantly swoop about, catching insects in their wide mouths. Whether they catch insects that are actually bothering us, such as mosquitoes, is another matter. Chances are they do not: The mosquitoes are more active after the swallows have retired for the night.

YOUR OWN SWALLOW COLONY

Both the Violet-green and Tree swallows are very easy to attract. Simply place boxes out in the open in rural or suburban areas. The Violet-green Swallow is slightly more of a suburban bird than the Tree Swallow, but both are very comfortable near humans. The Tree Swallow is slightly larger than the Violet-green Swallow and will prefer a house with a 1½-inch entrance hole.

Swallow Birdhouse

Dimensions
Entrance-hole diameter: 1¼" to 1½"
Height of hole above floor: 6" to 7"
Inside floor dimensions: 4" × 4" to 5" × 5"
Total height of box: 9" to 12"

Placement
Habitat: Open fields or open woods near water
Height: 4' to 10' high on a tree or post

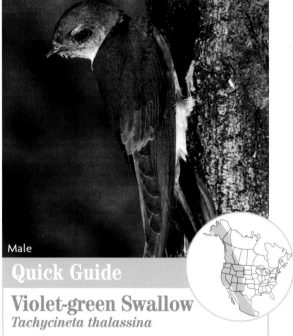

Male

Quick Guide
Violet-green Swallow
Tachycineta thalassina

ID Clues: About 5 inches long; dark, iridescent emerald-green bird with white breast and large white patches on rump; white on cheeks extends above eye; female is paler
Habitat: Open areas near woods and water
Food: Insects caught in air
Breeding period: April through July
Nests: Straw, grasses, string, hair, feathers in natural cavities or birdhouses
Eggs: 4 to 6, pure white
Incubation: 13 or 14 days, by female only
Nestling phase: About 21 days
Broods: 1 or 2
Migration: Migrates to Central America

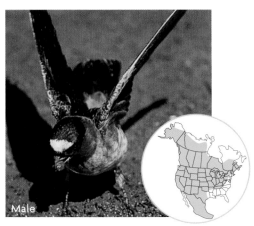

Male

What's That Bird?

CLIFF SWALLOW

ID Clues: 6-inch bird with dark back, white breast, rusty color at top of tail, white forehead, iridescent cap, reddish brown throat

Habitat: Open areas near cliffs, bridges, outbuildings

Food: Insects caught in air, sometimes berries

Nests: Nest of mud built on cliff, on bridge, in culvert; nests in colonies

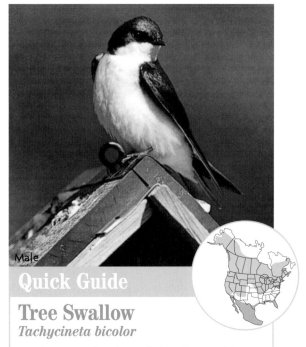

Male

Quick Guide

Tree Swallow
Tachycineta bicolor

ID Clues: 6 inches long; dark iridescent blue-green on head, back, and wings, bright white underparts; males and females similar but females may have brownish forehead

Habitat: Open areas near woods and water

Food: Insects caught in air, berries

Breeding period: April through July

Nests: Grasses lined with feathers in tree cavities or birdhouses

Eggs: 5 or 6, pure white

Incubation: 14 or 15 days, by female only

Nestling phase: About 21 days

Broods: 1

Migration: Migrates to southern United States and Central America

Once swallows successfully nest on your property, chances are that the adults and their young will return the next year to breed. If you put up additional boxes each year, you will find your swallow colony growing. We have had as many as 13 pairs nesting on our 2-acre field. It is wonderful to walk out among them and have them all flying about overhead. Because swallows like to line their nests with feathers, we have fun tossing them in the air to see our Tree

Swallows dive after them. (We also just leave them on the ground or in a string bag for the birds to use.) The only limit to the size of your colony may be the number of boxes you are willing to put up and the abundance of insects in the area.

VULNERABLE TO BAD WEATHER

When the weather gets rainy or cold for extended periods, swallows have trouble collecting enough insects to feed themselves or to support their growing nestlings. Then the adults may leave the colony for a day or two to find insects elsewhere. Their departure can result in the death of the young. This is always a sad event, but you will be glad to know that the adults will return and start a second nesting. This nesting is usually successful because it is well past the time of extended cold weather.

TITMOUSE
ONE OF THE LIVELIEST FEEDER BIRDS

The titmouse is one of the easiest birds to attract. If you live in a suburban or rural area and have bird feeders and birdhouses on your property, you have a good chance of having titmice nest in your yard. They are very comfortable around human habitations and are generally not afraid of people.

Interestingly, the titmouse's nearest relative at the feeder is another popular feeder bird, the chickadee. In fact, both birds are in the genus *Parus*, and their relatedness is apparent in their behavior. They have similar nesting and breeding habits and calls, and when they come to the feeder, both have the tendency to take one seed, fly away, peck at it under one claw, eat it, and then return for the next.

Titmice are always active and are real busybodies among the backyard birds, curious about everything that goes on in the area and seeming to scold forever—even long after the slightest disturbance, imagined or otherwise, has stopped or gone away.

NORTH, SOUTH, EAST, AND WEST

Before 1955 the Tufted Titmouse was common in the South but considered a rare bird in New England and most other northern states. Since then, it has become quite common from southeastern Minnesota to southern Ontario and southern New England. Some of this expansion

Quick Guide
Tufted Titmouse
Parus bicolor

ID Clues: Small, 5-inch crested bird; light gray on top, buff white breast, small rufous area along flanks, small black patch just above bill; males and females look alike

Habitat: Woods and suburbs

Food: Insects, berries, seeds; suet and sunflower seed at feeders

Breeding period: March through June

Nests: Mosses, hair, grasses, leaves, cotton, wool, bark strips in natural cavities or birdhouses

Eggs: 4 to 8, white with small brown speckles

Incubation: 13 or 14 days, by female only

Nestling phase: 17 or 18 days

Broods: 1 or 2

Migration: Generally a year-round resident

The Plain Titmouse—a small, all-gray, crested bird—is the western counterpart to the Tufted Titmouse, residing year-round in Colorado, New Mexico, Arizona, Utah, Nevada, and the coastal areas of California.

may be a result of the tremendous popularity of bird feeding, enabling the birds to survive through the winter.

In the West, the Plain Titmouse is the most common counterpart of the Titmouse. The behavior of the two species is quite similar, and the description that follows applies equally well to both.

WHAT'S IN A NAME?

Some people wonder if the name "titmouse" has anything to do with mice. Actually, "mouse" comes from the Anglo-Saxon word "mase," which meant a kind of bird, and "tit" is from the old Icelandic word for small. The "tuft," of course, refers to the crest on the head, which the bird can raise or lower to reflect its emotional state. When the crest is raised, the bird may be more competitive or combative; when it is lowered, the bird may be either more at ease or fearful.

SONGS AND CALLS

Titmice have a variety of sounds they like, for the most part, to give loudly from their tree perches.

"Peer peer peer" or "peter peter peter": This series of clear, down-slurred whistles constitutes titmouse song. It is given mostly by males from late winter into early summer, although occasionally it is given softly by the female as she approaches the nest with food. If you imitate this call, a male will often come close to investigate.

Titmouse Birdhouse

Dimensions
Entrance-hole diameter: 1 $\frac{3}{8}$" to 1 $\frac{1}{2}$"
Height of hole above floor: 6" to 7"
Inside floor dimensions: 4" × 4" to 5" × 5"
Total height of box: 9" to 12"

Placement
Habitat: Suburban or rural locations with a
    mixture of trees and open areas
Height: 5' to 10' high on a tree or post

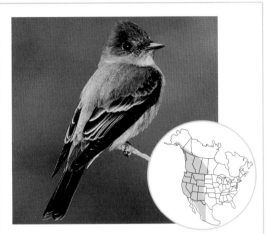

What's That Bird?
WESTERN WOOD-PEWEE

ID Clues: About 6 inches; grayish olive upper body, whitish throat, grayish chest and belly; prominent peak at back of head; males and females look alike

Habitat: Open woods, streamside trees

Food: Insects caught in the air

Nests: Nest of plant down and fibers in tree 8 to 40 feet high

"Tseep": This is a high, short sound given between a pair or members of a flock as a contact call to keep in touch while they look for food.

"Jway jway jway": This is a scolding call given during any disturbance, including your presence near the feeder.

"Seee": This is an extremely high-pitched, rapidly repeated call given during mate feeding or aggressive encounters between two or more males.

WINTER SOCIETY

Every species of bird has some kind of social arrangement during winter. Some remain as lone individuals; some form pairs; some are loose, roaming flocks; and others are stable flocks that stay in open areas. Generally, titmice fall into this last category, remaining through winter as a family group of three to six birds (parents and young) on a fixed range of about 15 to 20 acres.

Throughout winter you can see this flock visit your feeder. When you see one bird, there will be several others nearby or on their way. If you can determine the number of birds in the flock, you can tell whether you have more than one flock at your feeder.

SIGNS OF BREEDING

The behavior of titmouse flocks undergoes a change in late winter: Members of the flock will chase each other and give lots of scolding calls. This signals the beginning of the breeding period. The flocks are breaking up, and individual birds are starting to defend smaller territories. In most cases it is probably the younger birds that are forced to leave and find their own areas in which to breed.

At the same time you may hear male titmice give their clear, down-slurred whistle that sounds like "peer peer peer" as they define their territory to other males and advertise their presence to females in the area.

What's That Bird?
EASTERN PHOEBE

ID Clues: 7 inches long; gray-brown body and head, whitish throat and breast; males and females look alike
Habitat: Woods, farmlands, suburbs
Food: Insects in air or on ground
Nests: Nest of mud and moss, under bridge or eaves of house

Fairly soon you will see mated pairs flying about together. Part of their courtship is mate feeding, when the male gets food (possibly from your feeder) and presents it to the female, beak to beak. She usually gives the soft, high-pitched call "seee seee seee," a little like a whistling teapot, and quivers her wings when receiving it.

NESTING TIME

Starting around late March, you may see the birds inspecting nest boxes. If you leave a string bag full of hair or fur, such as that combed from a dog or cat, hanging near your bird feeders, the titmice will find it irresistible. They will carry large wads of these materials back to their nest. This is a good way to locate the nest—just follow the birds.

When the female is incubating the eggs, you may see the male approach with food and give a soft "peer, peer, peer" song. The female will come out of the nest at this signal, take the food from the male, and then continue incubating her eggs.

After the young have hatched and fledged, you may see the whole family group flying about together. The young are very noisy at this time and give a variety of calls.

TOWHEE
THE RED-EYED CHIRPER

The scientific name of the Eastern Towhee is *Pipilo erythrophthalmus*, which is practically impossible to pronounce but interesting in translation. It means "red-eyed chirper" and refers to the red eye of the bird and its most common call, a short sound variously described as "chewink," "towhee," or "joreee." "Chewink" is, in fact, another common name for towhees.

MALE/FEMALE, WESTERN/EASTERN

The appearance of the towhee varies in different parts of the country. Towhees in the East have a dark head and back, rufous sides, a white belly, and a red eye. Towhees in the West are similar but add white spots on their dark wings and back.

The differences between males and females also vary from East to West. They are more pronounced in the East, where the head, back, wings, and tail of the female are rich brown, while those of the male are black. In the West the female plumage is brown-black or gray-black and closer to the pure black of the male.

At one time, the eastern and western towhees were so close in appearance and traits that they were considered one species, the Rufous-sided Towhee. Scientists have now separated this most widespread form of towhee into two separate species: Eastern Towhee and Spotted

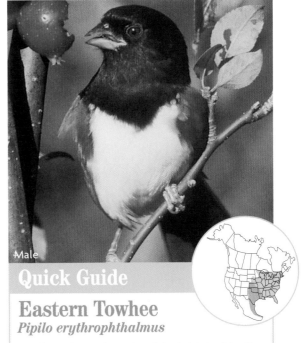

Male

Quick Guide

Eastern Towhee
Pipilo erythrophthalmus

ID Clues: A medium-size, 8-inch bird with all-black head and throat; black wings, back, and tail; rufous coloring on sides of white belly; red eyes
Habitat: Open woods with shrub understory
Food: Insects, spiders, lizards, seeds, berries on or near ground; mixed seed at feeders
Breeding Period: April to August
Nests: Nest of leaves and bark strips in shallow depression in ground
Eggs: 2 to 6, creamy with brown spots
Incubation: 12 or 13 days
Nestling Phase: 10 to 12 days
Broods: 1 to 3
Migration: Migrates to southern part of its range and Mexico

The female Eastern Towhee is rich brown everywhere the male is black.

This male Spotted Towhee inhabits the entire western half of the United States. This bird is identical to the Eastern Towhee except for the white spots on its black wings and back.

Towhee. Because their behaviors are so similar, our discussion below applies to both species.

SONGS AND CALLS

The "chewink" call is slightly different in the West, where the Spotted Towhee—the Eastern Towhee's counterpart—makes it sound more like the meow of a cat. East or West, the call seems to be used to help a mated pair keep in contact as they move about the dense underbrush, where they nest.

The song of the towhee is aptly described as "drink your tea" and is given only by the male. The last part of the song is a long, trilling "eee" sound and in some cases is the only part of the song that is given. It can be heard throughout the year, but is given most often in spring and summer as the male is defining a territory and attracting a mate. The "chewink" call and song may be your only indication that towhees are in your area, for the birds often stay in dense brush and shrubbery, making them hard to see.

EATING WITH THEIR FEET

Towhees feed almost exclusively on the ground in a distinctive manner. They hop forward and then quickly jump backward, dragging their feet as they do so; this method is similar to that of the White-throated Sparrow. This backward scraping pulls away leaves and debris from the soil to reveal insects and seeds. A towhee on a platform feeder will still scrape in this manner even though seeds are visible; this usually scatters all of the seed off the platform.

Towhees eat primarily seeds and berries, but in spring and summer insects found on the ground compose about half their diet. Of all feeders they will be most attracted to your ground feeder, and then only if there is underbrush and other cover very close by. They are usually shy at feeders and dive into cover at the slightest disturbance.

HIDDEN BREEDING BEHAVIOR

On their wintering grounds, towhees often form loose flocks containing as many as 25 birds. They range over an area of 20 to 30 acres, and they may join with flocks of other species, such as cardinals. Following spring migration and their arrival in breeding areas, the flocks stay together for a few days before individual males leave for their own territories.

If you hear towhees in your yard in spring and summer, chances are they are nesting there. Male towhees usually arrive first and start singing to defend a territory of about 1½ to 2 acres. Two changes in behavior will alert you to the arrival of a female and its pairing with the male: The male will stop singing, and you will hear the "chewink" call given back and forth between the pair.

The female does all building of the nest, which is placed on the ground, usually under the bough of a tree or shrub. It is hard to locate the nest because the female rarely flies directly to it; instead, she lands on a perch a few feet away and then walks to it along the ground and under cover.

WOODPECKER
DRUMMER OF THE ALL-BIRD BAND

Although there are about 20 species of woodpeckers in North America, only a few of them are widespread and regularly come to feeders or use a birdhouse.

WOODPECKERS THAT COME TO BACKYARDS

The Downy and Hairy woodpeckers and Northern Flicker all live throughout the continent and will come to suet feeders (and occasionally feeders with hulled sunflowers). The Red-bellied and Red-headed woodpeckers live mainly in the eastern half of North America and also enjoy suet and seed feeders.

WHO'S WHO

Their names give few or no clues on how to tell these species of woodpeckers apart. Here are some things to look for through your binoculars or when they're close by.

DOWNY OR HAIRY

These black-and-white woodpeckers look almost identical, but neither seems downy or hairy. There are, however, several ways to distinguish between them. The first is size. The Downy is the smaller bird, about 6 inches long, while the Hairy is a little over 9 inches long.

A better way to tell them apart is by the size of their bill in proportion to their head. The

Male

Quick Guide

Downy Woodpecker
Picoides pubescens

ID Clues: 6 inches long; white back and breast; black, white-spotted wings; black-and-white streaked head; bill is about half the length of the head; males have red spot on back of head

Habitat: Woods, farmlands, suburbs

Food: Insects under tree bark; suet and sunflower seed at feeders

Breeding period: April into July

Nests: Excavates nest in standing, dead wood; sometimes uses birdhouse

Eggs: 4 or 5, pure white

Incubation: 12 days, by male and female

Nestling phase: 20 to 22 days

Broods: 1, occasionally 2 in the South

Migration: Generally a year-round resident

These females clearly show the difference in the length of the bills of the Hairy Woodpecker (*left*) and Downy Woodpecker (*right*). The Hairy's bill looks as long as the head is wide, while the Downy's bill is much shorter.

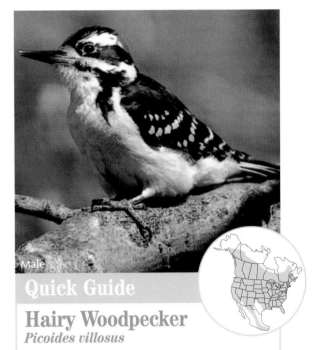

Male

Quick Guide

Hairy Woodpecker
Picoides villosus

ID Clues: About 9 inches; white back and breast, white spots on black wings, black-and-white streaked head; bill is almost as long as the head; males have red spot on back of head

Habitat: Woods, farmlands, suburbs

Food: Insects under tree bark; suet and sunflower seed at feeders

Breeding Period: April through June

Nests: Excavates nest in live wood; sometimes uses birdhouse

Eggs: 4 to 6, pure white

Incubation: 11 or 12 days, by male and female

Nestling phase: 28 to 30 days

Broods: 1

Migration: Generally a year-round resident

Downy bill is short, less than half the length of the bird's head, while the Hairy bill is long and more than half the length of its head; it often can seem as wide as the head.

One other subtle difference that you may be able to see is that the outer white tail feathers of the Downy are often barred with black; those of the Hairy are all white.

In both species, the male has a red spot at the back of his head; the female has no red on her head.

RED-BELLIED OR RED-HEADED
The Red-headed Woodpecker is the only woodpecker with a name that actually tells it like it

is; red covers the head of this bird completely. Its all-black back, pure white breast, and white wing patches make this bird hard to mistake for one of the other species. Males and females look alike.

The name of the Red-bellied Woodpecker, however, seems to make little sense; it often appears to have red only on its head. It is usually hard to see the small amount of red far down the belly of this bird. This woodpecker looks very different from the Downy and Hairy, though; it has less of a black-and-white ladder on its back than they do and no black-and-white markings on its head.

Both male and female Red-bellied Woodpeckers have red on their heads, but to different degrees. The red on the female is limited to the back of her head, whereas the red on the male extends from the back of his head all the way over the top to the base of his bill.

NORTHERN FLICKER

Neither its name nor appearance suggests the Northern Flicker will peck wood with the best of the woodpeckers. It is the only brownish gray woodpecker with a spotted breast that is likely to visit your feeders. Both genders look alike, except males have a black or red "whisker" at the side of the bill below the eye; females do not.

HOW MANY WOODPECKERS LIVE NEAR YOU?

Hairy and Downy woodpeckers live all year in the same area and do not migrate. They also tend to stay with or near their mate through the

Male

Quick Guide

Red-bellied Woodpecker
Melanerpes carolinus

ID Clues: Medium-size, 9-inch bird; black-and-white bars on back and wings, grayish underparts; male has red across head from base of bill to neck; female has red only on back of head

Habitat: Woodlands, parks, suburbs

Food: Insects under tree bark; suet, seeds, fruit at feeders

Breeding Period: April into July

Nests: Excavates hole in live wood, may use existing hole or birdhouse

Eggs: 4 or 5, pure white

Incubation: 12 to 14 days, by male and female

Nestling phase: 25 to 30 days

Broods: 2, possibly 3

Migration: May migrate south from northern parts of its range

year, although in winter they are more loosely associated. Therefore, if your feeder is in the middle of a Hairy or Downy home range, you will probably have only one pair of each showing up at your feeder. You may, however, be at the edge of two or more ranges and thus have two (or rarely, three) pairs around.

It's possible to identify individual Hairy or Downy woodpeckers, so you may be able to tell how many pairs you have. The patterns of red, black, and white on the back of their heads vary greatly among individuals. We like to keep a little notebook where we roughly sketch the pattern on the back of the head for individuals that come to our feeder. This lets us keep track of how many pairs use our feeders and live on our property.

Downy and Hairy woodpeckers coexist peacefully in the same area, occasionally even nesting in the same tree. Neither of these is tolerant of others of the same species in its home range, however.

Red-bellied and Red-headed woodpeckers and Northern Flickers may migrate south of where they breed, especially those breeding at the northern limit of their range. This may cause a greater concentration of these species in the southern regions of the United States during winter.

WHAT WOODPECKERS EAT

At your feeder, woodpeckers are especially attracted to suet, but they will also come to

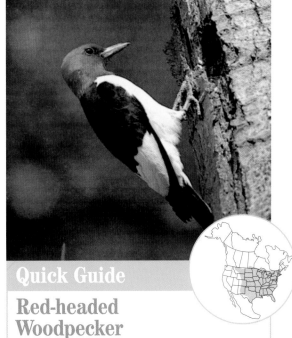

Quick Guide

Red-headed Woodpecker
Melanerpes erythrocephalus

ID Clues: 8 inches long; all-red head and neck, white belly, black wings with large white patches; males and females look alike

Habitat: Farmlands, open woodlands, suburbs, orchards

Food: Acorns, other nuts, insects under bark, tree sap, berries; suet at feeders

Breeding Period: April into August

Nests: Excavates hole in dead or live trees; sometimes uses birdhouse

Eggs: 4 or 5, pure white

Incubation: 12 or 13 days, by male and female

Nestling phase: About 30 days

Fledgling phase: 2 to 3 weeks

Broods: 1 or 2

Migration: Migrates from northern areas to southern United States

feeders that have sunflower seed. Downy Woodpeckers seem less shy than others and come more readily to feeders near our house.

In the wild, woodpeckers eat primarily insects, such as ants and the larvae of wood-boring beetles, which they uncover by pecking away bits of wood and bark. The Hairy and Downy woodpeckers probably are able to live peacefully in the same areas because their size difference allows them to take advantage of different food sources.

The Downy eats smaller insects that it finds just under the bark surface, and after it has pecked at a tree you can hardly see the marks left behind. The Hairy, with its larger bill, digs deeper into the wood for a different set of insects, and you can always see gouges in the wood where it has fed.

Red-bellied Woodpeckers and Northern Flickers also easily coexist with the Downy and Hairy, probably because their eating preferences are slightly different: They feed on ground insects—and fruit as well. In fact, the Red-bellied is known in the South for pecking on oranges. Occasionally, the Red-bellied and Red-headed woodpeckers will drink at sap from sapsucker holes made in trees, and they may store bits of food—such as nuts or insects—in bark crevices or other crannies.

PECKING VERSUS DRUMMING

Woodpeckers make two different kinds of sounds with their bills. One is a soft, irregular

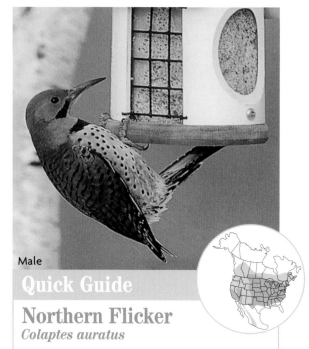

Male

Quick Guide

Northern Flicker
Colaptes auratus

ID Clues: 13-inch bird with brown and black barring on back and wings; buff breast with black spots; black across throat and black or red "whiskers" across cheeks; females do not have color on cheeks; yellow-shafted race (shown) has red spot at nape of neck; red-shafted race has no red spot and, in males, red "whiskers"

Habitat: Parks, suburbs, farmlands, woodlands

Food: Ants on ground, insects in air, fruit; suet and seed at feeders

Breeding Period: April into July

Nests: Excavates, usually in dead tree; may use existing hole or birdhouse

Eggs: 7 to 9, pure white

Incubation: 11 or 12 days, by male and female

Nestling phase: About 26 days

Broods: 1 or 2

Migration: Migrates from northern areas to southern United States

Male

What's That Bird?

GOLDEN-FRONTED WOODPECKER

ID Clues: 9 inches long; tan head and underparts; wings, back, and tail barred with black and white; golden-orange patch on forehead and back of neck; males have small red patch on crown
Habitat: Woodlands, parks, gardens
Food: Insects, berries, fruit; suet and seed at feeders
Nests: Excavates in live or dead wood; may use birdhouse

Northern Flicker Birdhouse

Dimensions
Entrance-hole diameter: 2" to 3"
Height of hole above floor: 10" to 20"
Inside floor dimensions: 6" × 6" to 8" × 8"
Total height of box: 14" to 24"

Placement
Habitat: In or at the edge of open woods
Height: 10' to 20' high on a tree or post

pecking; the other is a loud, rapid drumming occurring in bursts of 1 to 2 seconds.

The irregular pecking is the sound the bill makes when the woodpecker is searching for food or excavating a nest hole. During this pecking, wood is actually chipped away. The pecking is a quiet sound and not often heard.

The loud, rapid drumming is done by male or female woodpeckers on resonant surfaces.

It is really a signal, like song in other birds, that announces the bird's presence on its territory to its mate or competitors. When the bird does this, no wood is chipped away. The birds pick any resonant spot; it may be some part of your house, such as a drainpipe or gutter.

If a woodpecker drums on your house, it does not mean that you have termites, and generally it will not damage your house. Drumming is heard only during the breeding season (late winter to midsummer), and the first drumming is a good sign that the breeding cycle for woodpeckers has begun.

If a woodpecker is pecking on your house and chipping away wood, it is likely that there are insects at the spot. If you get rid of the insects, the woodpeckers will stop.

NEST HOLES

Woodpeckers are among the few birds that can create their own nest holes. They are primary cavity nesters with extra-strong bones in their sculls to take all the pounding from excavation (and feeding). Most other hole-nesting species—secondary cavity-nesters—depend on holes previously made by the hard head of the woodpecker.

You can distinguish between the holes of woodpeckers by the size of the entrance. Downy entrance holes are about 1¼ inches in diameter; Red-bellied and Red-headed entrances are about 1¾ to 2¼ inches in diameter; and Hairy entrance holes tend to be slightly oval, about 2 inches wide and 2½ inches high. The Northern Flicker drills holes about 2 to 3 inches wide.

SNAGGING A WOODPECKER

One of the best things that you can do to attract woodpeckers actually involves less rather than more work. Instead of trimming all the

Woodpecker Birdhouse

For Hairy Woodpecker, Red-bellied Woodpecker, Red-headed Woodpecker
Dimensions
Entrance-hole diameter: 1 ¾" to 2 ¾"
Height of hole above floor: 10" to 14"
Inside floor dimensions: 5" × 5" to 6" × 6"
Total height of box: 14" to 16"

Placement
Habitat: In or at the edge of woods
Height: 6' to 20' high on tree, fence post, or
    building

Downy Woodpecker Birdhouse
Dimensions
Entrance-hole diameter: 1 ¼" to 1 ½"
Height of hole above floor: 8" to 12"
Inside floor dimensions: 3" × 3" to 4" × 4"
Total height of box: 10" to 14"

Placement
Habitat: In or at the edge of woods
Height: 6' to 20' high in tree

dead wood from your trees, leave it there (as long as it does not endanger anyone).

Dead branches on trees are called snags, and they serve two purposes for woodpeckers. First, they attract the kinds of insects that the woodpeckers eat. Second, they provide soft wood in which the woodpeckers can excavate their nest holes. This is especially important for Downy Woodpeckers; their small bills are able to excavate only soft wood.

Once the woodpeckers leave their nests, other species of cavity-nesting birds—chickadees, titmice, or nuthatches—can use the empty holes. Thus, preserving snags and dead trees that are still standing is one of the most important conservation efforts you can make on your own property.

TRY A BIRDHOUSE

All of these woodpeckers will use a birdhouse, although the Hairy and Downy Woodpeckers are less likely to do so. (The Downy is more likely to use a box as a roosting spot than a nesting site.) With the declining availability of suitable nesting sites, you can help these birds thrive by adding a birdhouse or two just for them on your property.

There is one adjustment to a normal bird-house that may make it more attractive to woodpeckers: Add 1 to 2 inches of wood chips in the bottom of the box. Woodpeckers do not add any nesting material to their natural homes, but they do leave an inch or two of wood chips in the bottom of the cavity. It is better to use wood chips rather than sawdust because sawdust has a tendency to absorb and retain moisture.

WREN
DELIGHTFUL SONG, DELIGHTFUL BIRD

Wrens are primarily bug eaters that love to forage on the ground and under leaves for insects and spiders. While they occasionally will take sunflower seeds or fruit from feeders, you will attract them to your property with good nesting sites, especially birdhouses.

BUBBLY, BEAUTIFUL LYRICS

Wrens have wonderful songs that are a delightful addition to any backyard. The song of the House Wren is like a bubbly waterfall, while the Bewick's is surprisingly similar to that of the Song Sparrow: a beautiful trail of notes that is impossible to describe.

The song of the Carolina Wren is more easily described. Many catchy phrases have been used to imitate it, such as "teakettle, teakettle, teakettle," "sweetheart, sweetheart, sweetheart," or "sweet William, sweet William, sweet William."

Only the males give these songs, and this can help you to determine which member of a pair you are watching (the sexes look alike). Both male and female give the common, dry rattle sound—a scolding call that seems to be shared by all wrens.

Most singing occurs in late winter and spring, when the birds are actively courting and setting up territories. However, the Carolina Wren can be heard singing to some extent in any month of the year.

Quick Guide
House Wren
Troglodytes aedon

ID Clues: A small, compact, 5-inch bird; brown back and grayish white underparts with faint barring on flanks; short tail; males and females look alike

Habitat: Woods edges, mountain forests, aspen groves, suburbs

Food: Insects gathered in bushes and on ground

Breeding Period: April into August

Nests: Base of straight twigs, lined with grasses and spider egg cases, in existing natural cavities or birdhouses

Eggs: 5 or 6, white background densely speckled with light brown

Incubation: 12 to 15 days

Nestling phase: 16 or 17 days

Broods: 1 or 2

Migration: Migrates to southern North America

ANY PLACE CAN BE A HOME

The Carolina and Bewick's wrens are very flexible in their criteria for a nest site. Both may build nests in cavities or dense shrubbery. In choosing cavities they may use a woodpecker home, a rotted-out knothole, or a variety of other crevices, such as holes in fence posts.

Both of these wrens are also well known for choosing unusual nesting spots. For example, Carolina Wrens have been found nesting in discarded tin cans and coffeepots; in baskets, pitchers, cardboard boxes, and mailboxes; and even in an abandoned hornets' nest.

The Bewick's Wren has used these same places, as well as oil wells, deserted cars, and clothing hung on lines to dry. Bewick's will use broken bottles, old hats, the skulls of cows in old fields (a little creepy), and the abandoned nests of mockingbirds and orioles.

House Wrens are different in their nesting habits. They tend to prefer cavities and rarely build in the open. They also are more likely to look for a cavity in a tree or building and less likely to nest in odd spots, as the Carolina and Bewick's wrens do.

WHAT GIVES?
MALES BUILDING NESTS?

A fascinating habit of the House Wren and Bewick's Wren is that the male starts building the nest before the female arrives. He stuffs the bird box full of twigs, sometimes to the point where he can barely get in. If he finds other

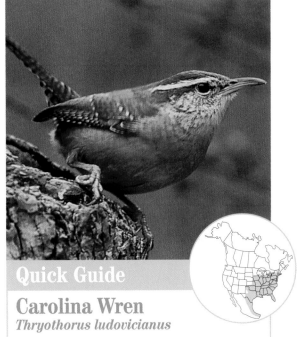

Quick Guide
Carolina Wren
Thryothorus ludovicianus

ID Clues: Small, 6-inch bird; rich brown back and buff belly; distinctive bold white eyebrow; males and females look alike

Habitat: Forest understory, vines, woodlands in suburbs

Food: Insects and tree frogs on or above ground; sunflower seed at feeders

Breeding Period: March through July

Nests: Weeds, leaves, grasses, bark strips; lined with feathers, moss, hair, fine grasses, wool; placed in natural cavities, birdhouses, or brush piles

Eggs: 5 or 6, white heavily speckled with light brown

Incubation: 12 to 14 days

Nestling phase: 12 to 14 days

Broods: 2 or 3

Migration: Generally a year-round resident

nest cavities or birdhouses on his territory, he may start to build nests in these as well. These

The Cactus Wren is a common year-round resident in southwest deserts and semideserts with cactus. It builds a large, globular nest in cacti or other thorny plants.

are sometimes referred to as "dummy" nests. When the female arrives, she chooses one of the nests and adds the final lining.

Why the male goes to all of this extra trouble is not known for sure, but there are several theories. One is that the abundance of nests may help to attract the female; she may believe that the male is particularly industrious or appreciate that his territory is abundant in nest cavities. Another theory suggests the male may be trying to monopolize all available nest cavities. In this way he keeps out competitors for food, cavities, and mates.

Because of this habit, a single wren can monopolize two or three of your birdhouses, leaving fewer available for other cavity-nesting birds. You can solve this problem in two ways. One is to put up more boxes; the other is to

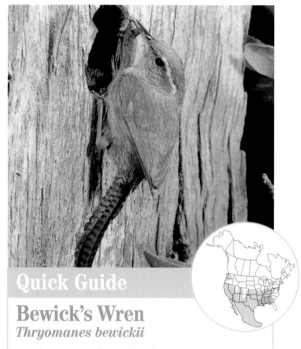

Quick Guide

Bewick's Wren
Thryomanes bewickii

ID Clues: Just 5½ inches long; sleek, dark brown body and grayish white belly; distinctive long tail and thin, white eyebrow; males and females look alike

Habitat: Thickets, brush, open woodlands, suburbs

Food: Insects and spiders on or above ground

Breeding Period: March into August

Nest materials: Twigs and grass, lined with grass and feathers, in existing natural cavities or birdhouses

Eggs: 5 to 7, white heavily speckled with light brown

Incubation: 14 days

Nestling phase: 14 days

Broods: 1, possibly 2

Migration: Generally a year-round resident, but some winter movement beyond its range

watch the wren and get an idea of the boundaries of its territory—only about a half-acre. Once you know his territory, move one or more of your boxes outside of that area.

PROTECTIVE NESTER

Wrens are quick to give scolding calls at the slightest sign of danger. The scolding call is a drawn-out rattling sound. If you are anywhere near the nest, the male or female will come out and scold. Sometimes this is a good way to locate a nest—if a wren is scolding you, chances are that either you are close to a nest or fledglings are in nearby bushes.

Many field guides show wrens with their tails up in the air or even suggest that this may be a field clue to their identification. However, most of the time wrens have their tails down, in

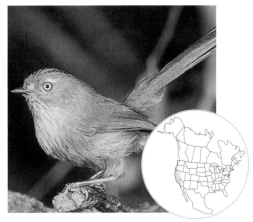

What's That Bird?
WRENTIT

ID Clues: 6½ inches long; plain brownish gray color with pinkish breast and long tail; males and females look alike
Habitat: Chaparral, tangled brush, dense shrubs
Food: Insects, caterpillars, small fruits, berries
Nests: Nest of spiderwebs, bark strips, grasses; lined with fine fibers and hair in bush or tall shrub 1 to 15 feet high

Wren Birdhouse

Dimensions
Entrance-hole diameter:
For House Wren: 1" to 1½"
For Bewick's Wren: 1¼" to 1½"
For Carolina Wren: 1½"
Height of hole above floor: 6" to 7"
Inside floor dimensions: 4" × 4" to 5" × 5"
Total height of box: 9" to 12"

Placement
Habitat: Suburban yards or open areas with a mixture of trees and dense shrubbery; brush piles
Height: 4' to 10' high on a tree, post, or building

the same position as most other birds. It is only when they are disturbed that their tails point up. In fact, tail-up is part of wren language for expressing disturbance or alarm.

WINTER MOVES

The House Wren migrates south for the winter, but the Carolina Wren—and, in some parts of its range, the Bewick's Wren—stay on their territories throughout the winter. They both habitually roost in protected spots during these cold months, probably because they are not entirely winter-hardy. They have been known to roost in hornets' nests and in enclosed porches where there is an accessible opening. They will also roost in birdhouses, which gives you a good excuse to leave them up in all seasons.

Both of these species tend to expand their range slightly during mild winters, which is probably a result of young birds' dispersing to new areas. Cold winters, however, take a toll on these birds. They are not usually found breeding in the same areas when spring arrives.

Resources

This is a list of what we think are some of the best resources for furthering your knowledge of attracting, identifying, and understanding birds. We also have provided contact information for bird supply companies and various bird societies. This list is by no means complete and we encourage you to explore on your own to find the resources, supplies, and groups that will meet your personal needs and tastes.

BIRD SUPPLY COMPANIES

FEEDERS, SEEDS, AND BIRDHOUSES

Aspects, Inc.
245 Child Street, P.O. Box 408
Warren, RI 02885
Phone: 888-ASPECTS (888-277-3287)
Web site: www.aspectsinc.com
Feeders

C&S Products Company, Inc.
Box 848
Fort Dodge, IA 50501
Phone: 800-373-2425
Web site: www.wildbirdssuets.com
Feeders, suet

Droll Yankees, Inc.
27 Mill Road
Foster, RI 02825
Phone: 800-352-9164
Web site: www.drollyankees.com
Feeders

Duncraft
102 Fisherville Road
Concord, NH 03303
Phone: 800-593-5656
Web site: www.duncraft.com
Feeders, seeds, birdhouses

North States Industries, Inc.
1200 Mendelssohn Avenue
Golden Valley, MN 55427
Birdhouses

Opus
P.O. Box 525
Bellingham, MA 02019
Web site: www.opususa.com
Feeders

Perky-Pet Products, Inc.
2201 South Wabash Street
Denver, CO 80231
Web site: www.perky-pet.com
Feeders, suet, birdhouses

SPECIAL SUPPLIES

Nelson Manufacturing Company
3049 12th Street, SW
Cedar Rapids, IA 52404
Phone: 888-844-6606
Web site: www.nelsonmfg.com
Birdbath heaters

Purple Martin Conservation Association
Edinboro University of Pennsylvania
Edinboro, PA 16444
Web site: www.purplemartin.org
Sparrow traps

BOOKS

ATTRACTING, IDENTIFYING, AND UNDERSTANDING BIRDS

National Geographic Society, *Field Guide to the Birds of North America*, 4th ed. (Washington, DC: National Geographic Society, 2002).

Roth, Sally, *Attracting Birds to Your Backyard* (Emmaus, PA: Rodale, 1998).

————, *Attracting Butterflies and Hummingbirds to Your Backyard* (Emmaus, PA: Rodale, 2001).

————, *The Backyard Bird Feeder's Bible* (Emmaus, PA: Rodale, 2000).

Schultz, Walter E., *How to Attract, House, and Feed Birds: 48 Plans for Bird Feeders and Houses You Can Make* (Indianapolis: Wiley Publishing, Inc., 1974).

Stokes, Donald W. *A Guide to Bird Behavior*, vol. I (New York: Little, Brown, 1979).

Stokes, Donald W., and Lillian Q. Stokes, *A Guide to Bird Behavior*, vol. II (New York: Little, Brown, 1983).

————, *A Guide to Bird Behavior*, vol. III (New York: Little, Brown, 1989).

Tyrrell, Esther Q., and Robert A. Tyrrell, *Hummingbirds* (New York: Crown, 1985).

GARDENING

Grant, K.A., and V. Grant, *Hummingbirds and Their Flowers* (New York: Columbia University Press, 1968).

McKenny, Margaret, and Roger Tory Peterson, *Field Guide to Wildflowers, Northeastern and North-Central North America*, rev. ed. (Boston: Houghton Mifflin, 1998).

Niehaus, Theodore, and Charles Ripper, *A Field Guide to Pacific States Wildflowers*, 2nd ed. (Boston: Houghton Mifflin, 1998).

Niehaus, Theodore, Charles Ripper, and Virginia Savage, *A Field Guide to Southwestern and Texas Wildflowers*, rev. ed. (Boston: Houghton Mifflin, 1998).

Roth, Sally, *Natural Landscaping* (Emmaus, PA: Rodale, 1997).

Schultz, Warren, *The Chemical-Free Lawn* (Emmaus, PA: Rodale, 1989) .

MAGAZINES

Birder's World
P. O. Box 1612
Waukesha, WI 53187
Phone: 800-533-6644
Web site: www.birdersworld.com

Bird Watchers Digest
P. O. Box 110
Marietta, OH 45750
Phone: 800-879-2473
Web site: www.birdwatchersdigest.com

WildBird
P.O. Box 52898
Boulder, CO 80322-2898
Web site: www.animalnetwork.com/wildbird/

SOCIETIES

National Audubon Society
700 Broadway
New York, NY 10003
Go to www.audubon.org for list of local Audubon chapters.

National Bird-Feeding Society
P.O. Box 23
Northbrook, IL 60065
Web site: www.birdfeeding.org

North American Bluebird Society
P. O. Box 244
Wilmot, OH 44689
Web site: www.nabluebirdsociety.org

Purple Martin Conservation Association
Edinboro University of Pennsylvania
Edinboro, PA 16444
Web site: www.purplemartin.org

SPECIAL PROJECT

ProjectFeeder Watch
Cornell Lab of Ornithology
159 Sapsucker Woods Road
Ithaca, NY 14850
Phone: 800-843-2473
Web site: www.birds.cornell.edu/PFW/
*Joint backyard bird feeder project with
Audubon Society*

Books by
Donald and Lillian Stokes

STOKES FIELD GUIDES

Stokes Field Guide to Birds: Eastern Region: ISBN 0–316–81809–7

Stokes Field Guide to Birds: Western Region: ISBN 0–316–81810–0

Stokes Field Guide to Bird Songs: Eastern Region:
  CD: ISBN 1–570–42483–7/cassette: ISBN 1–570–42482–9

Stokes Field Guide to Bird Songs: Western Region:
  CD: ISBN 1–570–42588–4/cassette: ISBN 1–570–42589–2

STOKES BEGINNER'S GUIDES

Stokes Beginner's Guide to Bats: ISBN 0–316–81658–2

Stokes Beginner's Guide to Bird Feeding: ISBN 0–316–81659–0

Stokes Beginner's Guide to Birds: Eastern Region: ISBN 0–316–81811–9

Stokes Beginner's Guide to Birds: Western Region: ISBN 0–316–81812–7

Stokes Beginner's Guide to Butterflies: ISBN 0–316–81692–2

Stokes Beginner's Guide to Dragonflies: ISBN 0–316–81679–5

Stokes Beginner's Guide to Hummingbirds: ISBN 0–316–81695–7

Stokes Beginner's Guide to Shorebirds: ISBN 0–316–81696–5

STOKES NATURE GUIDES

Stokes Guide to Amphibians and Reptiles: ISBN 0–316–81713–9

Stokes Guide to Animal Tracking and Behavior: ISBN 0–316–81734–1

Stokes Guide to Bird Behavior, Volume 1: ISBN 0–316–81725–2

Stokes Guide to Bird Behavior, Volume 2: ISBN 0–316–81729–5

Stokes Guide to Bird Behavior, Volume 3: ISBN 0–316–81717–1

Stokes Guide to Enjoying Wildflowers: ISBN 0–316–81731–7

Stokes Guide to Nature in Winter: ISBN 0–316–81723–6

Stokes Guide to Observing Insect Lives: ISBN 0–316–81727–9

STOKES BACKYARD NATURE BOOKS

Stokes Bird Feeder Book: ISBN 0–316–81733–3

Stokes Bird Gardening Book: ISBN 0–316–81836–4

Stokes Birdhouse Book: ISBN 0–316–81714–7

Stokes Bluebird Book: ISBN 0–316–81745–7

Stokes Butterfly Book: ISBN 0–316–81780–5

Stokes Hummingbird Book: ISBN 0–316–81715–5

Stokes Oriole Book: ISBN 0–316–81694–9

Stokes Purple Martin Book: ISBN 0–316–81702–3

Stokes Wildflower Book: East of the Rockies: ISBN 0–316–81786–4

Stokes Wildflower Book: From the Rockies West: ISBN 0–316–81801–1

OTHER STOKES BOOKS

The Natural History of Wild Shrubs and Vines: ISBN 0–060–14163–8

Photo Credits

Animals/Animals Marcia Griffen: 55; Breck P. Kent: 255; Z. Leszczynski: 252; R. Richardson: 141; L.L. Rue III: 286; Fred Whitehead: 120 right

Aspects, Inc. title, 7, 9 left

Steve Bentsen 23 top left, 24, 27, 46, 186 right, 205

Willard Colburn 98

Bruce Coleman, Inc. Bob and Clara Calhoun: 19 left, 23 bottom, 85 right, 146 top, 158, 166 right, 216, 218, 222, 233 left, 224, 227, 268, 283; Kenneth Fink: 231; Wayne Lankinen: 85 left; Laura Riley: 281; L.L. Rue III: 279 left; Joseph Van Wormer: 99; L. West: 172

David Collister 151

Cornell Laboratory of Ornithology L. B. Chapman: 178; Brian Daw: 226; L. Elliot: 186 left; Warren Greene: 193 right; J. R. Harris: 235; M. Hopiak: 60, 144 left, 156, 191, 200, 206, 238, 246 left and right; I. Jenkin: 230; H. Mayfield: 148 right; Patricia Meacham: 217; J. Sanford: 20 left; W. A. Paff: 228; Laurence Wales: 194; D. P. H. Watson: 265; T. Willcox: 78, 195, 196 left; J. R. Woodward: 13 right, 145, 169, 171, 201, 207, 237, 263 left and middle, 276 right

Mike Danzenbaker 3, 31 top right, 51 right, 68 right, 210, 244, 269 left, 273, 276 left

Larry R. Ditto 262 right

Irene Hinke-Sacilotto 167

Kevin T. Karlson 61, 197 right, 236 bottom left, 243

Frank Lane Picture Agency/CORBIS front cover

Denny Mallory 97

Maslowski Photo 9 right, 22, 23 top right, 29 left, 30 left and right, 31 top left, 45 bottom, 50, 51 left, 58, 59, 70, 71, 74, 79, 84 top, 87 bottom, 103, 105, 120 left, 138, 146 bottom, 153 right, 157, 159, 164, 165, 170 right, 173, 175 left, 179, 183, 190, 196 right, 197 left, 203, 204, 209, 234, 236 top left, 240, 247, 249, 250 right, 253, 254, 258, 260, 261, 262 left, 266, 271, 274, 278, 282, 287

Theron McCuen 19 right

Anthony Mercieca 18, 25, 87 top right, 110, 151 left, 220, 229, 236 right, 267, 272

A. Morgan 175 right

Opus 14

Myrna D. Pearman 192

Photo Researchers K. and D. Dannen: 182; C. Larsen: 148 left; Anthony Mercieca: 87 top left, 288 right; William H. Mullins: 113; L. L. Rue III: 263 right, 269 left

Sid Rucker 16, 17 left, 32 bottom, 84 bottom, 88 left, 223 right

Bryan Schantz 119, 154, 155

John Shaw 176

Brian E. Small 43, 170 left, 289

Hugh Smith, Jr. 13 left, 17 right, 20 right, 29 right, 65, 66, 100, 142, 144 right, 199, 242, 250 left, 288 left

George Stewart 26, 28

Stokes Nature Company Don and Lillian Stokes/ Dianne McCorry: 31 bottom, 83, 92, 108, 112, 115, 126, 127, 128, 129, 130, 131, 132, 133, 134

Lillian Stokes 8, 32 top, 34, 37, 38, 39, 40, 44, 45 top, 47, 49, 55 left, 57, 67, 68 left, 76, 80, 81, 88 right, 102, 109, 111, 257

Tom Vezo 153 left, 166 left, 245, 275, 280

VIREO Herbert Clarke: 174; A. Cruikshank: 185, 188, 259; H. Cruikshank: 251 right; Warren Greene: 193 left; C. H. Greenwalt: 219; F. K. Schleicher: 11; Barth Schorre: 160; J. Stasz: 279 left; D. and M. Zimmerman: 251 left

INDEX

Boldface page references indicate illustrations and photographs.